MARVEL GRAPHIC NOVEL SUPERI... L #1

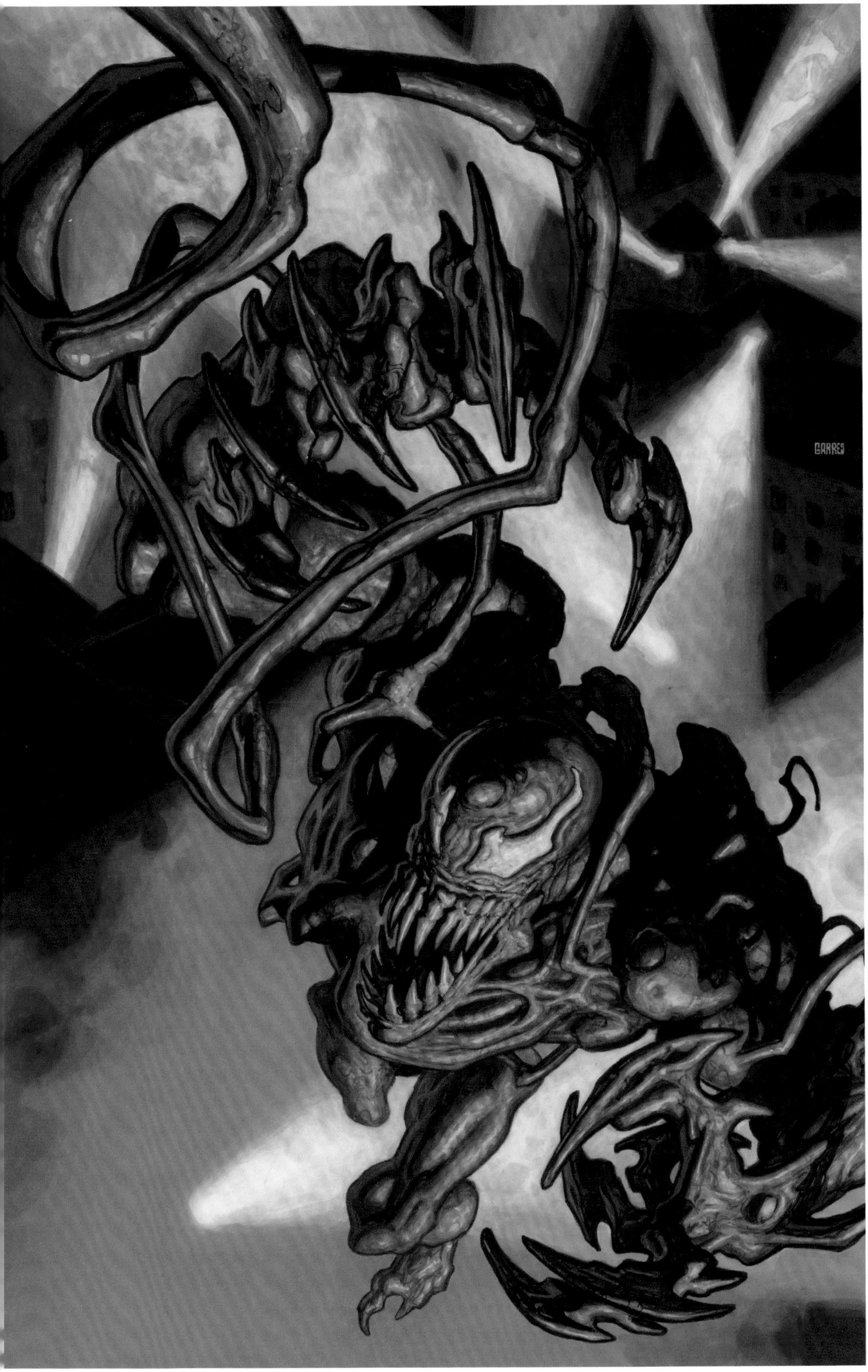
GARRES

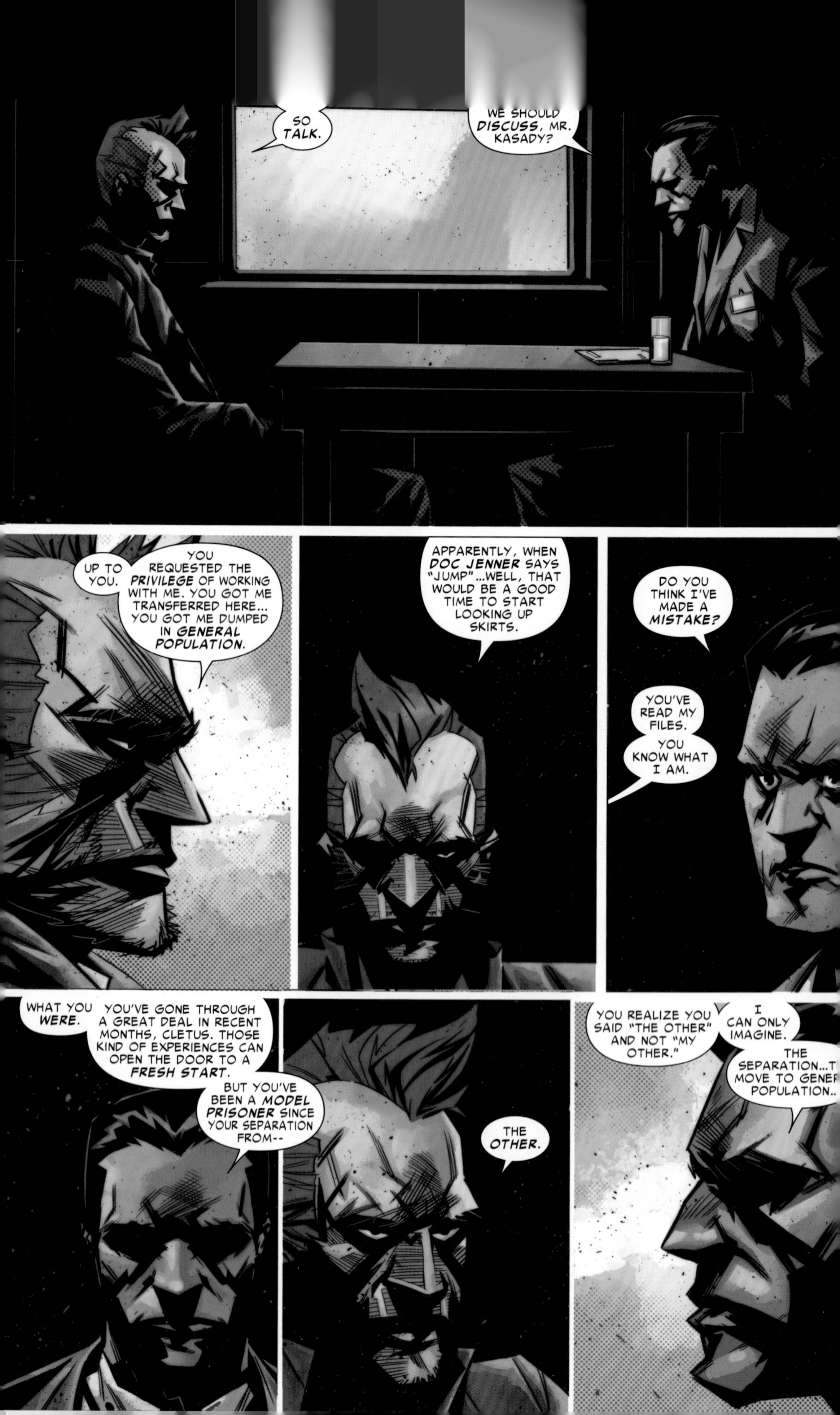
SO TALK.
WE SHOULD DISCUSS, MR. KASADY?
UP TO YOU.
YOU REQUESTED THE PRIVILEGE OF WORKING WITH ME. YOU GOT ME TRANSFERRED HERE... YOU GOT ME DUMPED IN GENERAL POPULATION.
APPARENTLY, WHEN DOC JENNER SAYS "JUMP"...WELL, THAT WOULD BE A GOOD TIME TO START LOOKING UP SKIRTS.
DO YOU THINK I'VE MADE A MISTAKE?
YOU'VE READ MY FILES.
YOU KNOW WHAT I AM.
WHAT YOU WERE.
YOU'VE GONE THROUGH A GREAT DEAL IN RECENT MONTHS, CLETUS. THOSE KIND OF EXPERIENCES CAN OPEN THE DOOR TO A FRESH START.
BUT YOU'VE BEEN A MODEL PRISONER SINCE YOUR SEPARATION FROM--
THE OTHER.
YOU REALIZE YOU SAID "THE OTHER" AND NOT "MY OTHER."
I CAN ONLY IMAGINE.
THE SEPARATION...T MOVE TO GENEF POPULATION..

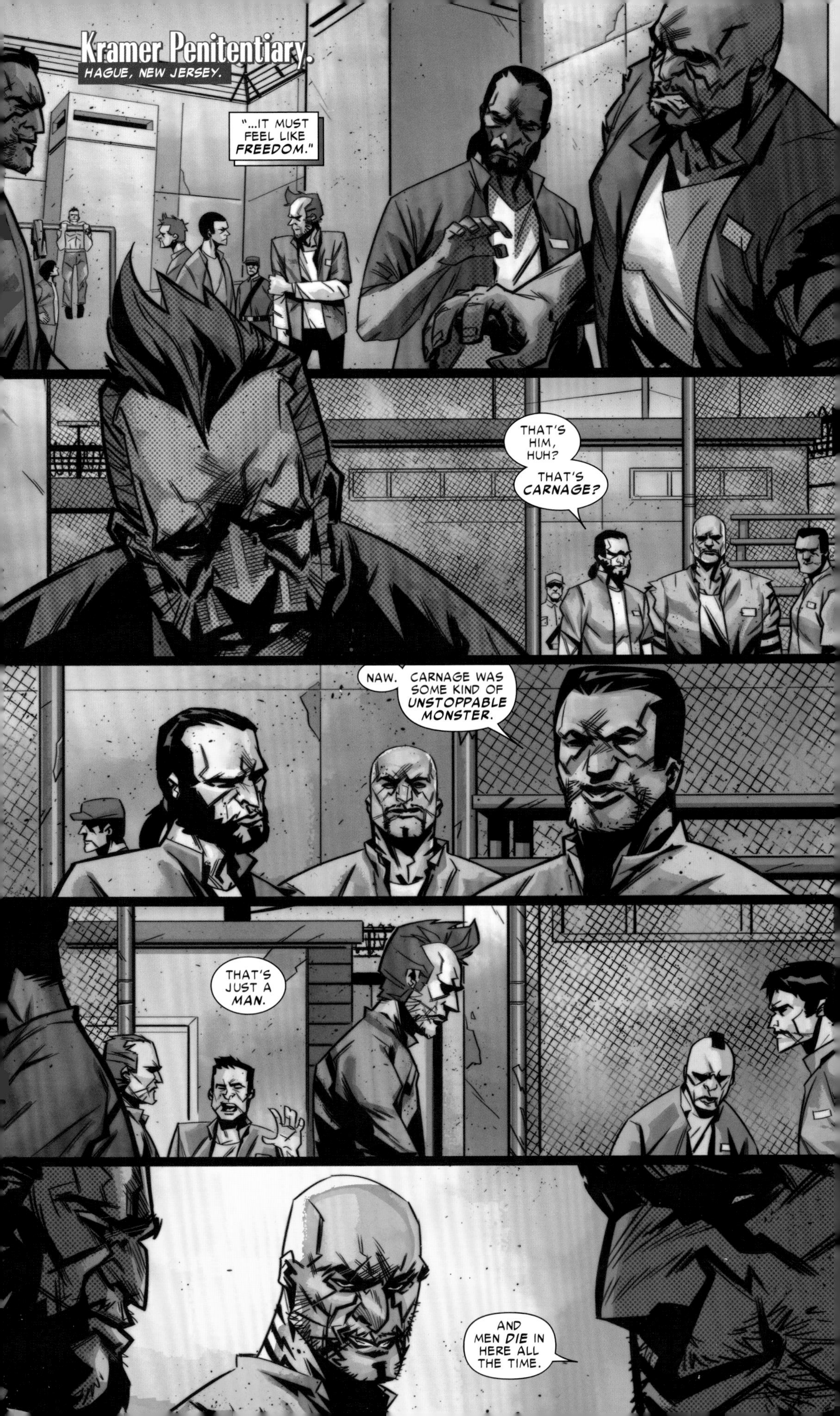
Kramer Penitentiary.
HAGUE, NEW JERSEY.
"...IT MUST FEEL LIKE FREEDOM."
THAT'S HIM, HUH?
THAT'S CARNAGE?
NAW.
CARNAGE WAS SOME KIND OF UNSTOPPABLE MONSTER.
THAT'S JUST A MAN.
AND MEN DIE IN HERE ALL THE TIME.

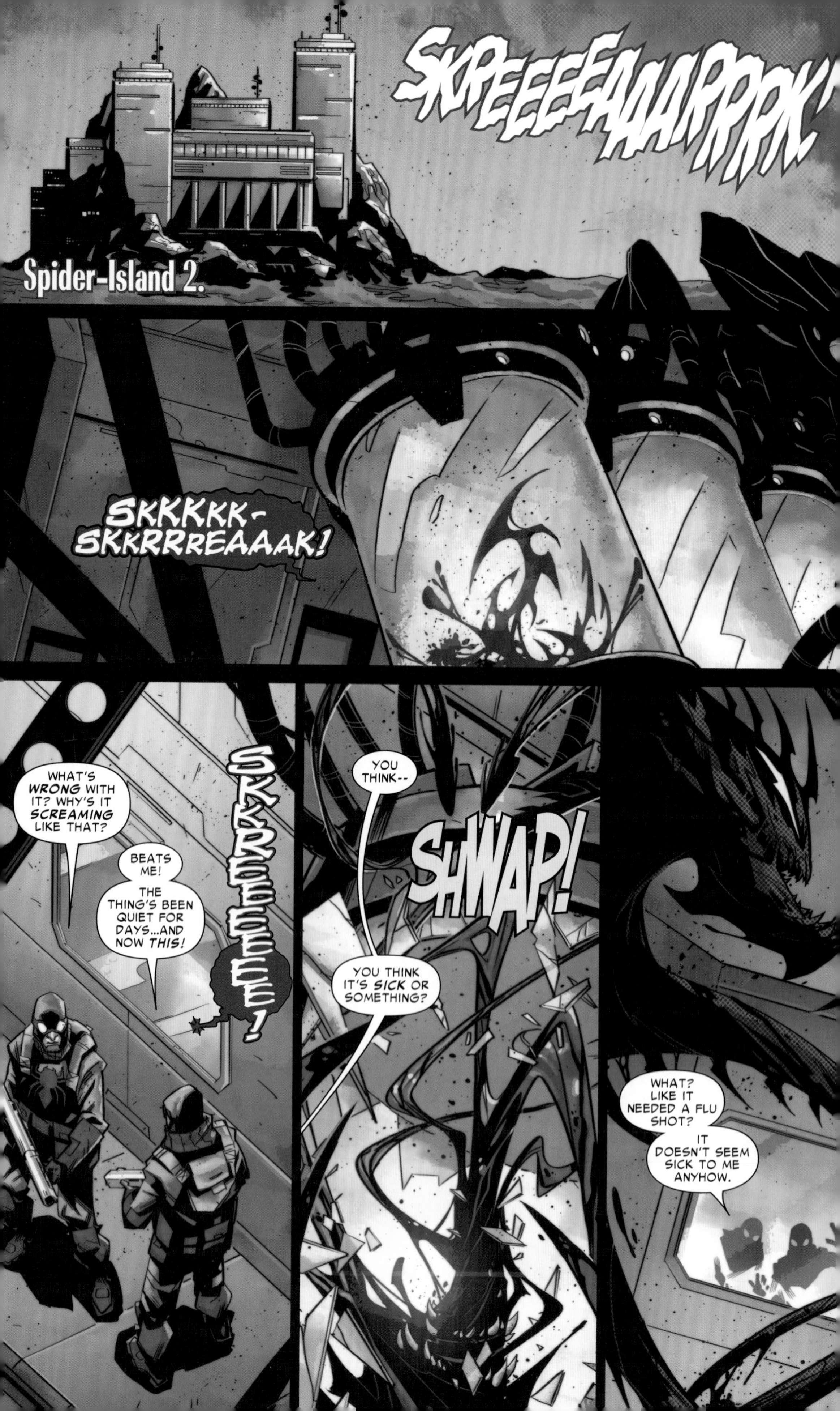
SKREEEEEAAARRRK!
Spider-Island 2.
SKKKKK-SKKRRREAAAK!
WHAT'S WRONG WITH IT? WHY'S IT SCREAMING LIKE THAT?
BEATS ME!
THE THING'S BEEN QUIET FOR DAYS...AND NOW THIS!
SKKRREEEEEE!
YOU THINK--
SHWAP!
YOU THINK IT'S SICK OR SOMETHING?
WHAT? LIKE IT NEEDED A FLU SHOT?
IT DOESN'T SEEM SICK TO ME ANYHOW.

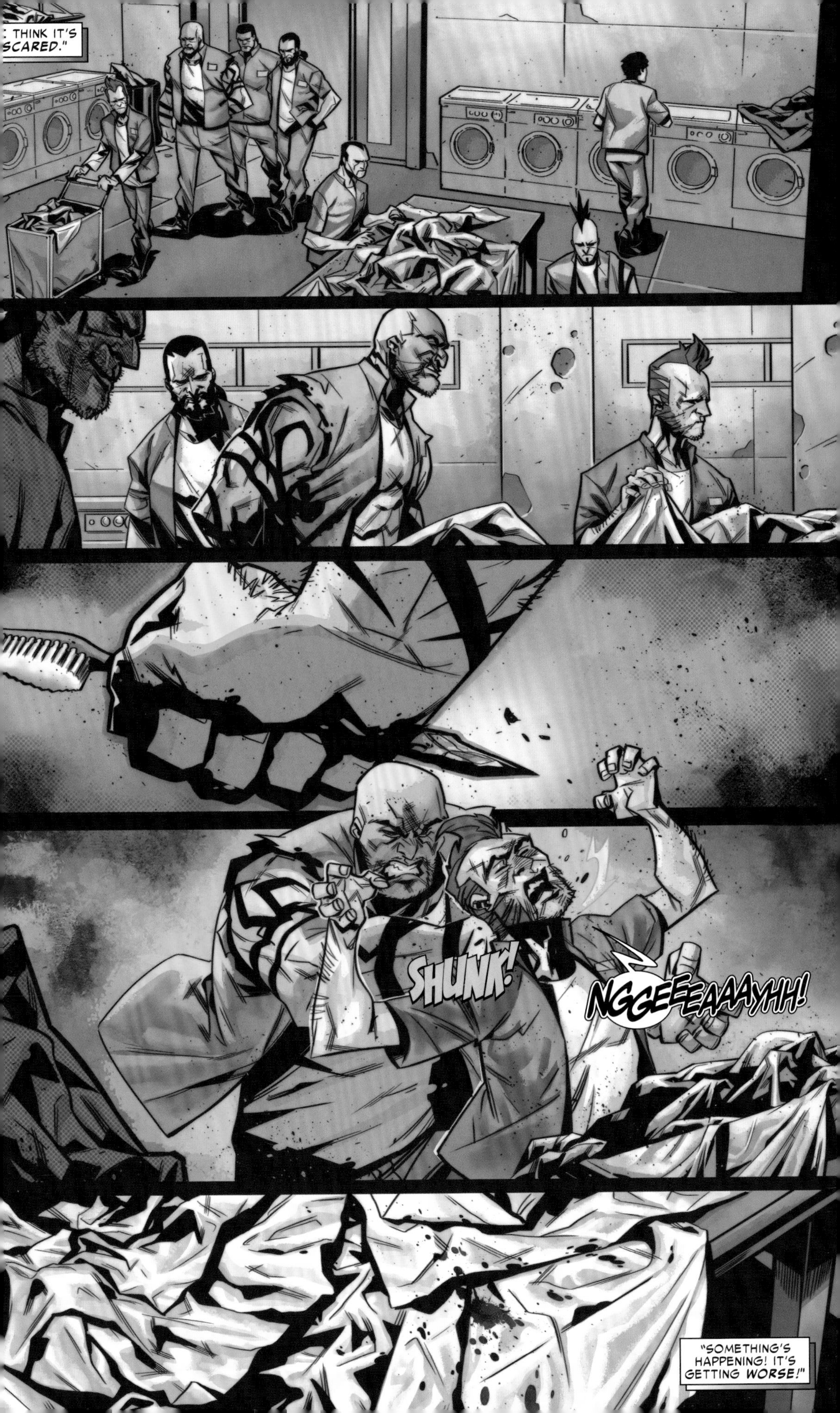

THINK IT'S SCARED."
SHUNK!
NGGEEEAAAYHH!
"SOMETHING'S HAPPENING! IT'S GETTING WORSE!"

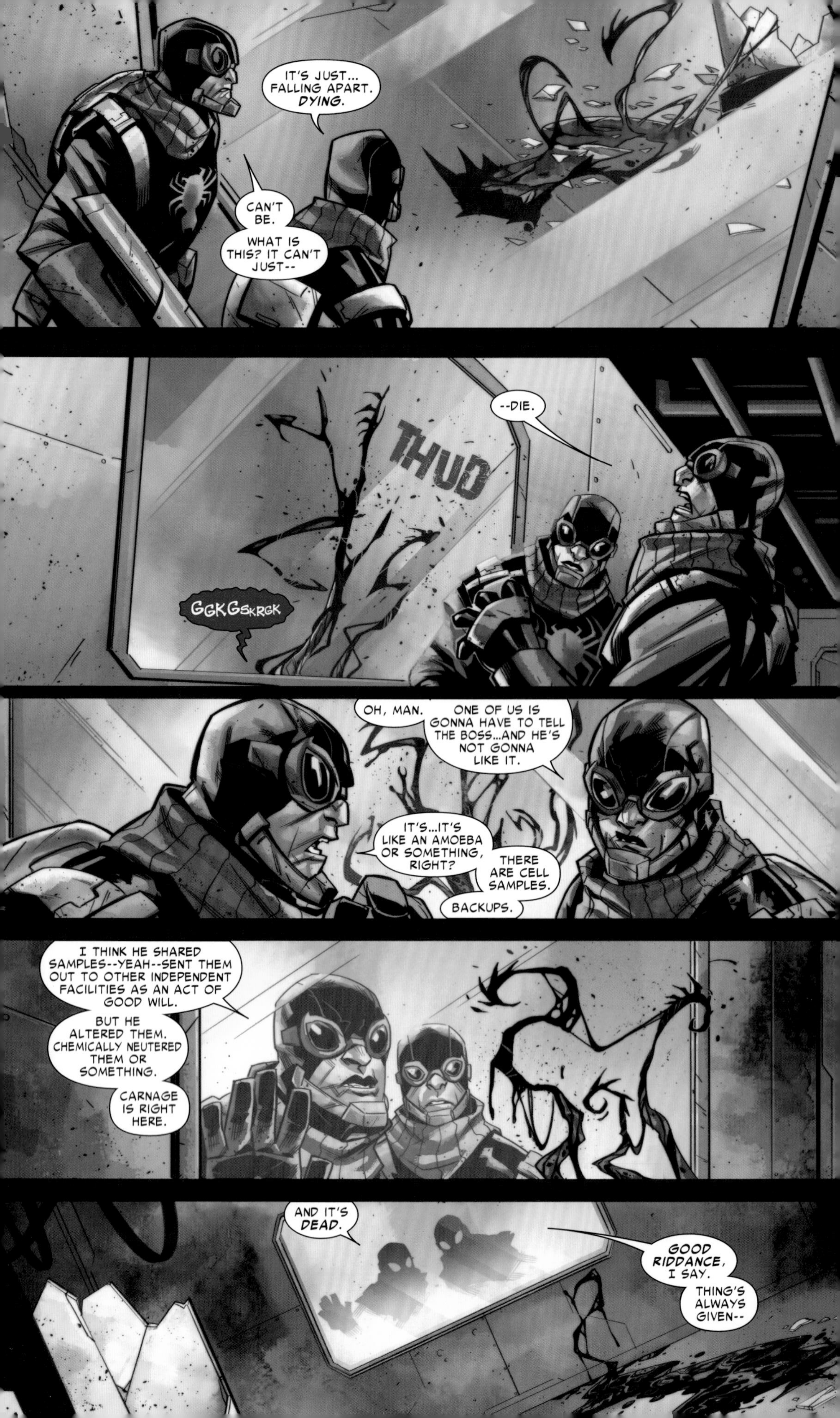
IT'S JUST... FALLING APART. DYING.
CAN'T BE.
WHAT IS THIS? IT CAN'T JUST--
--DIE.
THUD
GGKGSKRGK
OH, MAN.
ONE OF US IS GONNA HAVE TO TELL THE BOSS...AND HE'S NOT GONNA LIKE IT.
IT'S...IT'S LIKE AN AMOEBA OR SOMETHING, RIGHT?
THERE ARE CELL SAMPLES.
BACKUPS.
I THINK HE SHARED SAMPLES--YEAH--SENT THEM OUT TO OTHER INDEPENDENT FACILITIES AS AN ACT OF GOOD WILL.
BUT HE ALTERED THEM. CHEMICALLY NEUTERED THEM OR SOMETHING.
CARNAGE IS RIGHT HERE.
AND IT'S DEAD.
GOOD RIDDANCE, I SAY.
THING'S ALWAYS GIVEN--

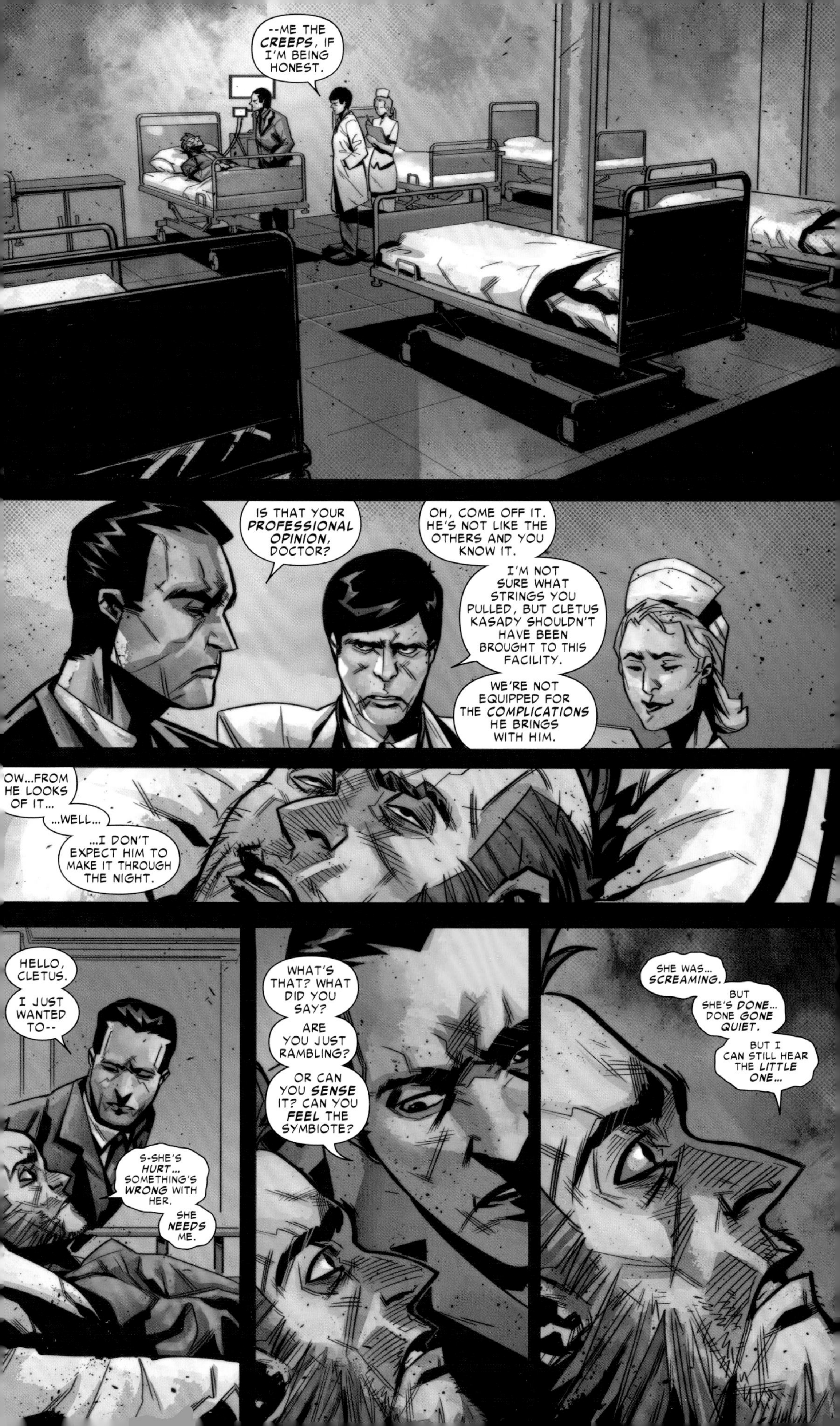
--ME THE CREEPS, IF I'M BEING HONEST.
IS THAT YOUR PROFESSIONAL OPINION, DOCTOR?
OH, COME OFF IT. HE'S NOT LIKE THE OTHERS AND YOU KNOW IT.
I'M NOT SURE WHAT STRINGS YOU PULLED, BUT CLETUS KASADY SHOULDN'T HAVE BEEN BROUGHT TO THIS FACILITY.
WE'RE NOT EQUIPPED FOR THE COMPLICATIONS HE BRINGS WITH HIM.
OW...FROM HE LOOKS OF IT...
...WELL...
...I DON'T EXPECT HIM TO MAKE IT THROUGH THE NIGHT.
HELLO, CLETUS.
I JUST WANTED TO--
S-SHE'S HURT... SOMETHING'S WRONG WITH HER.
SHE NEEDS ME.
WHAT'S THAT? WHAT DID YOU SAY?
ARE YOU JUST RAMBLING?
OR CAN YOU SENSE IT? CAN YOU FEEL THE SYMBIOTE?
SHE WAS... SCREAMING.
BUT SHE'S DONE... DONE GONE QUIET.
BUT I CAN STILL HEAR THE LITTLE ONE...

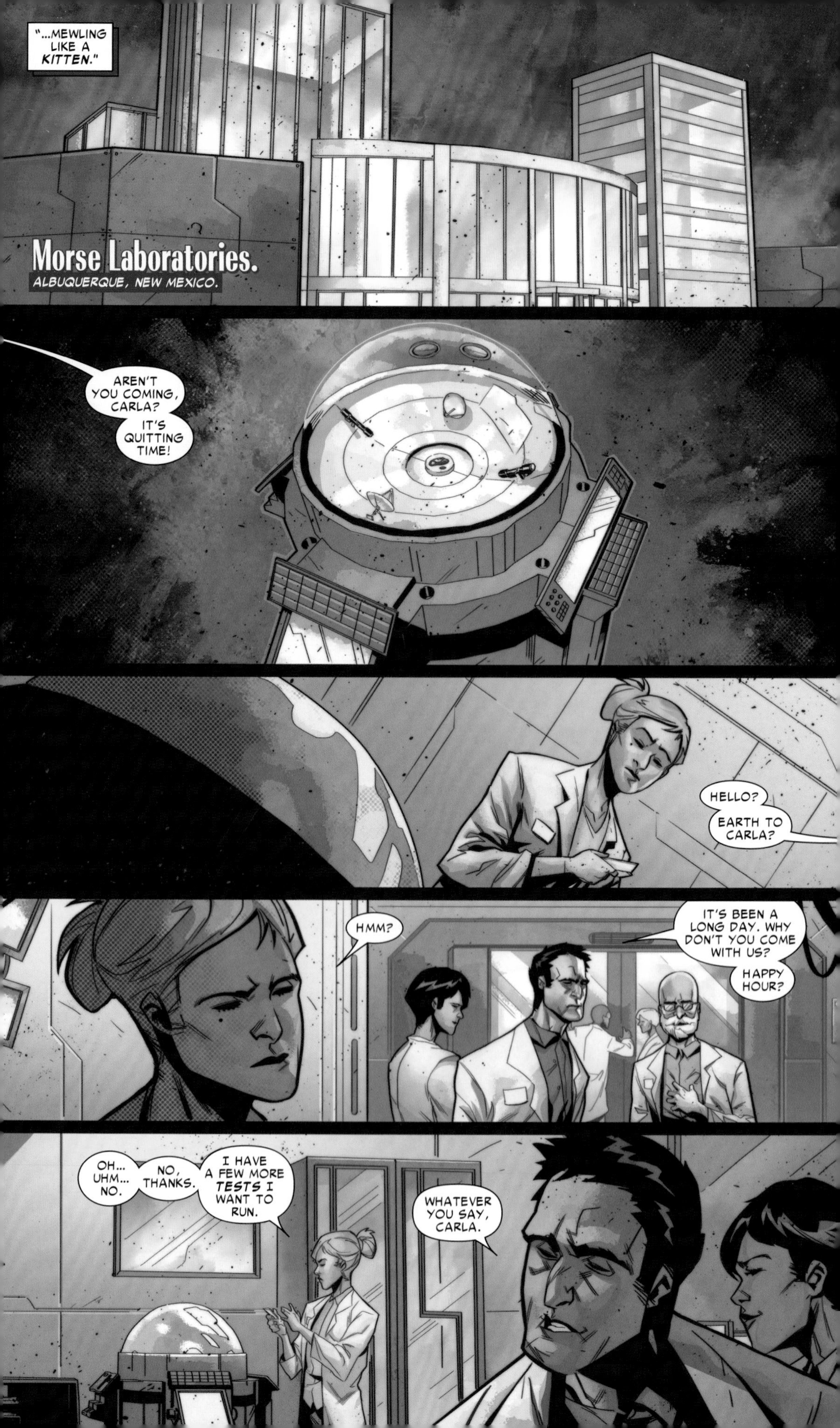
"...MEWLING LIKE A KITTEN."
Morse Laboratories.
ALBUQUERQUE, NEW MEXICO.
AREN'T YOU COMING, CARLA?
IT'S QUITTING TIME!
HELLO?
EARTH TO CARLA?
HMM?
IT'S BEEN A LONG DAY. WHY DON'T YOU COME WITH US?
HAPPY HOUR?
OH... UHM... NO.
NO, THANKS.
I HAVE A FEW MORE TESTS I WANT TO RUN.
WHATEVER YOU SAY, CARLA.

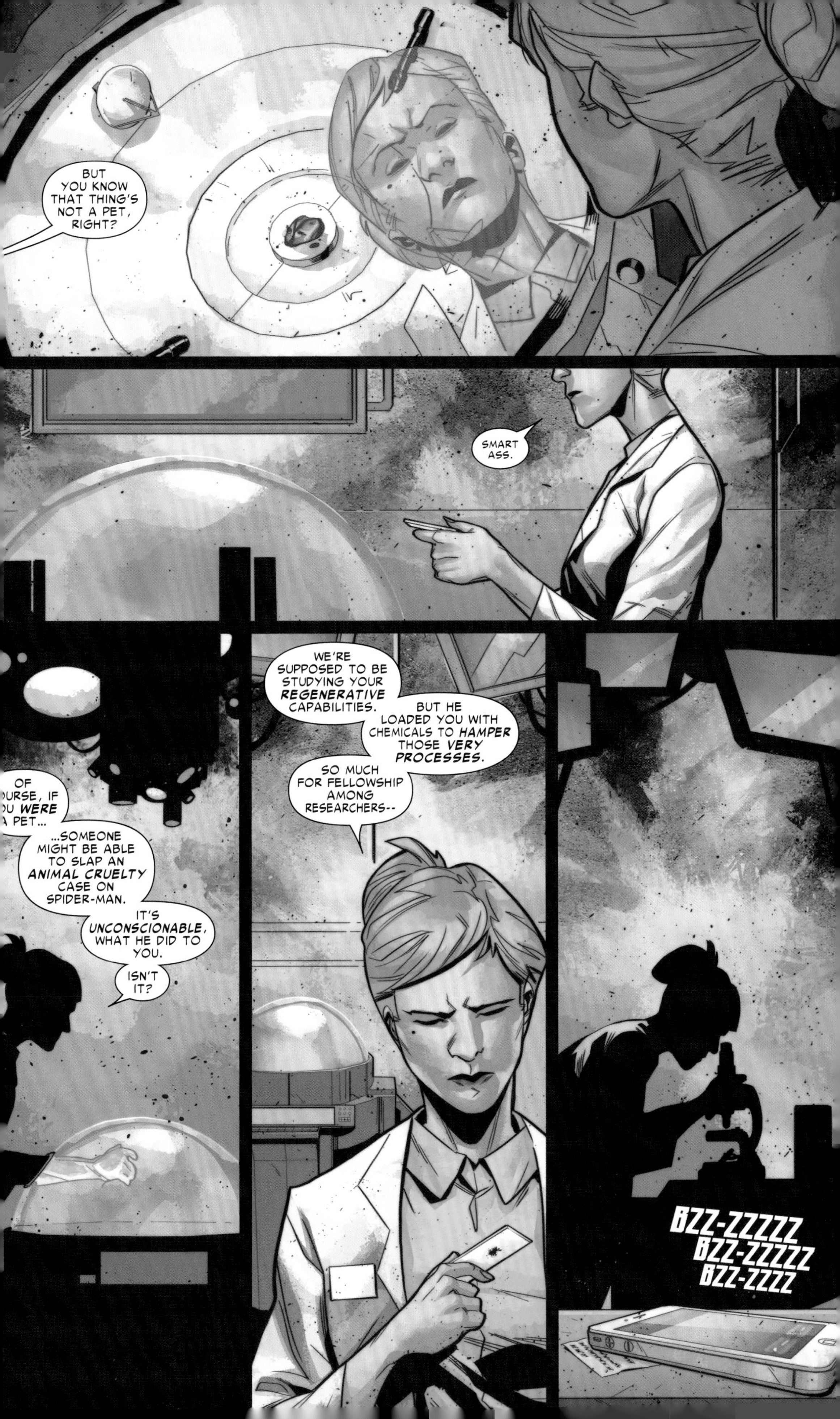
BUT YOU KNOW THAT THING'S NOT A PET, RIGHT?
SMART ASS.
OF OURSE, IF OU *WERE* A PET...
...SOMEONE MIGHT BE ABLE TO SLAP AN *ANIMAL CRUELTY* CASE ON SPIDER-MAN.
IT'S *UNCONSCIONABLE*, WHAT HE DID TO YOU.
ISN'T IT?
WE'RE SUPPOSED TO BE STUDYING YOUR *REGENERATIVE* CAPABILITIES.
BUT HE LOADED YOU WITH CHEMICALS TO *HAMPER* THOSE *VERY PROCESSES*.
SO MUCH FOR FELLOWSHIP AMONG RESEARCHERS--
BZZ-ZZZZZ
BZZ-ZZZZZ
BZZ-ZZZZ

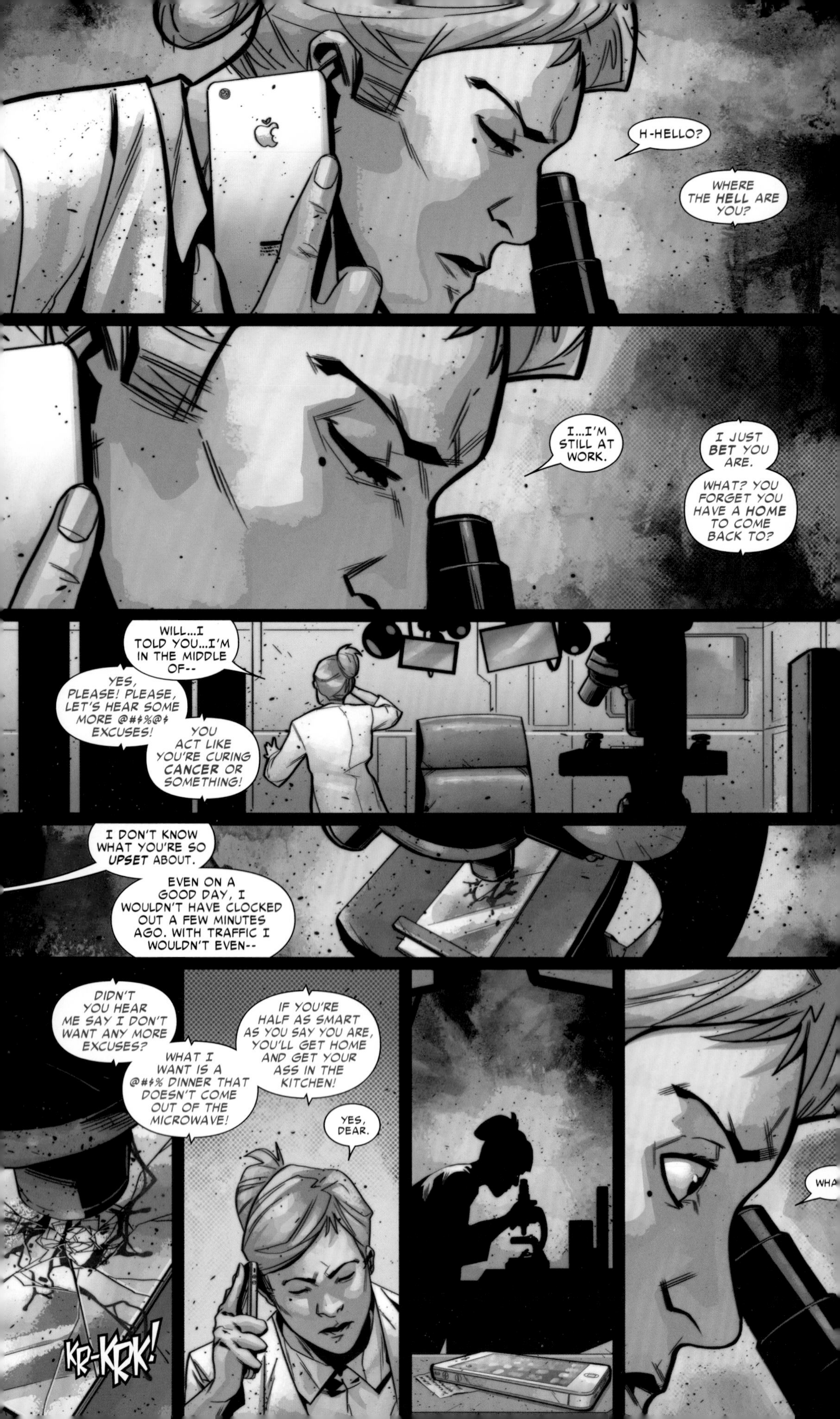

H-HELLO?
WHERE THE HELL ARE YOU?
I...I'M STILL AT WORK.
I JUST BET YOU ARE.
WHAT? YOU FORGET YOU HAVE A HOME TO COME BACK TO?
WILL...I TOLD YOU...I'M IN THE MIDDLE OF--
YES, PLEASE! PLEASE, LET'S HEAR SOME MORE @#$%@$ EXCUSES!
YOU ACT LIKE YOU'RE CURING CANCER OR SOMETHING!
I DON'T KNOW WHAT YOU'RE SO UPSET ABOUT.
EVEN ON A GOOD DAY, I WOULDN'T HAVE CLOCKED OUT A FEW MINUTES AGO. WITH TRAFFIC I WOULDN'T EVEN--
DIDN'T YOU HEAR ME SAY I DON'T WANT ANY MORE EXCUSES?
WHAT I WANT IS A @#$% DINNER THAT DOESN'T COME OUT OF THE MICROWAVE!
IF YOU'RE HALF AS SMART AS YOU SAY YOU ARE, YOU'LL GET HOME AND GET YOUR ASS IN THE KITCHEN!
YES, DEAR.
KR-KRK!
WHA

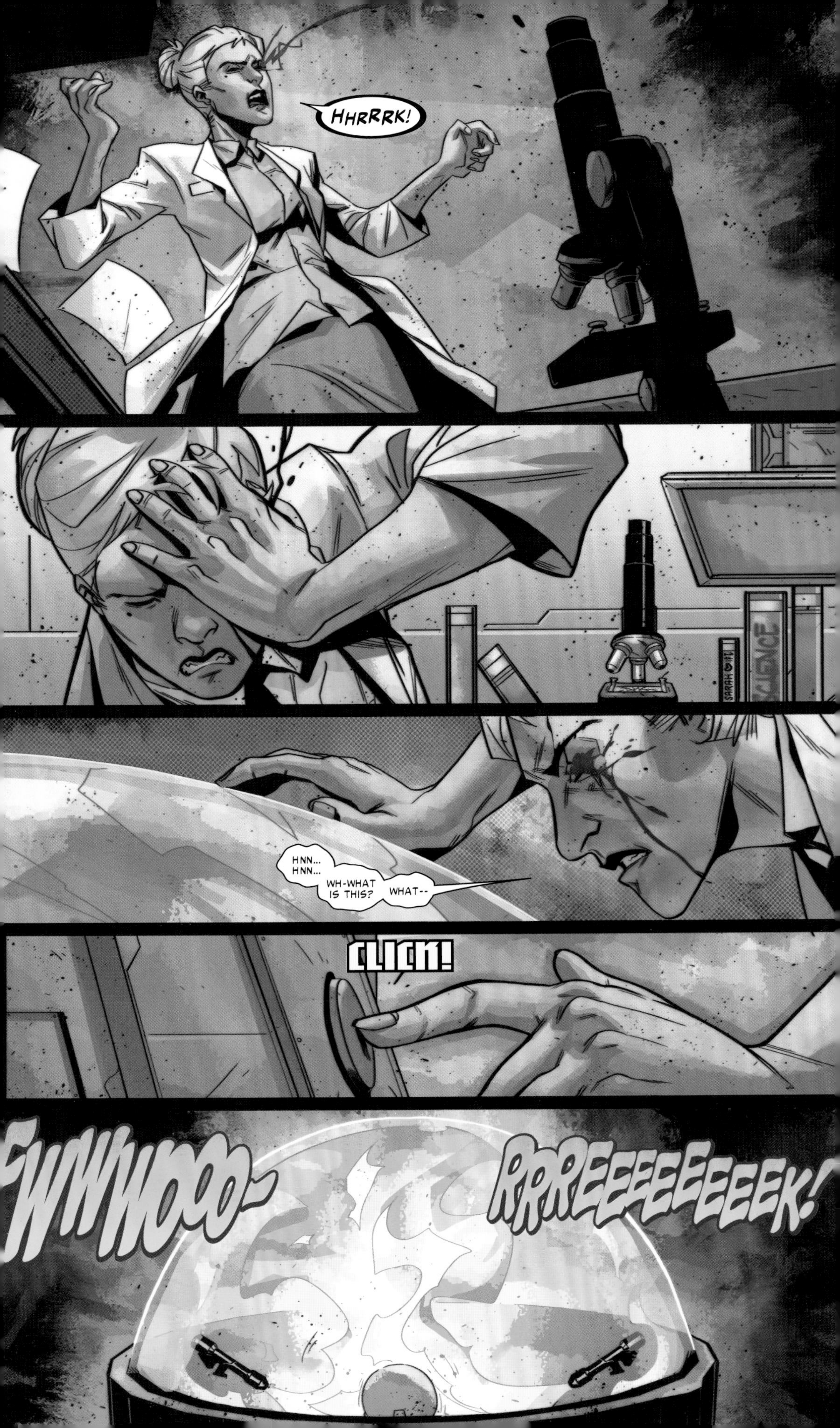
HHRRRK!
SARAH
SCIENCE
HNN... HNN...
WH-WHAT IS THIS?
WHAT--
CLICK!
FWWHOOO-
RRRREEEEEEEEEK!

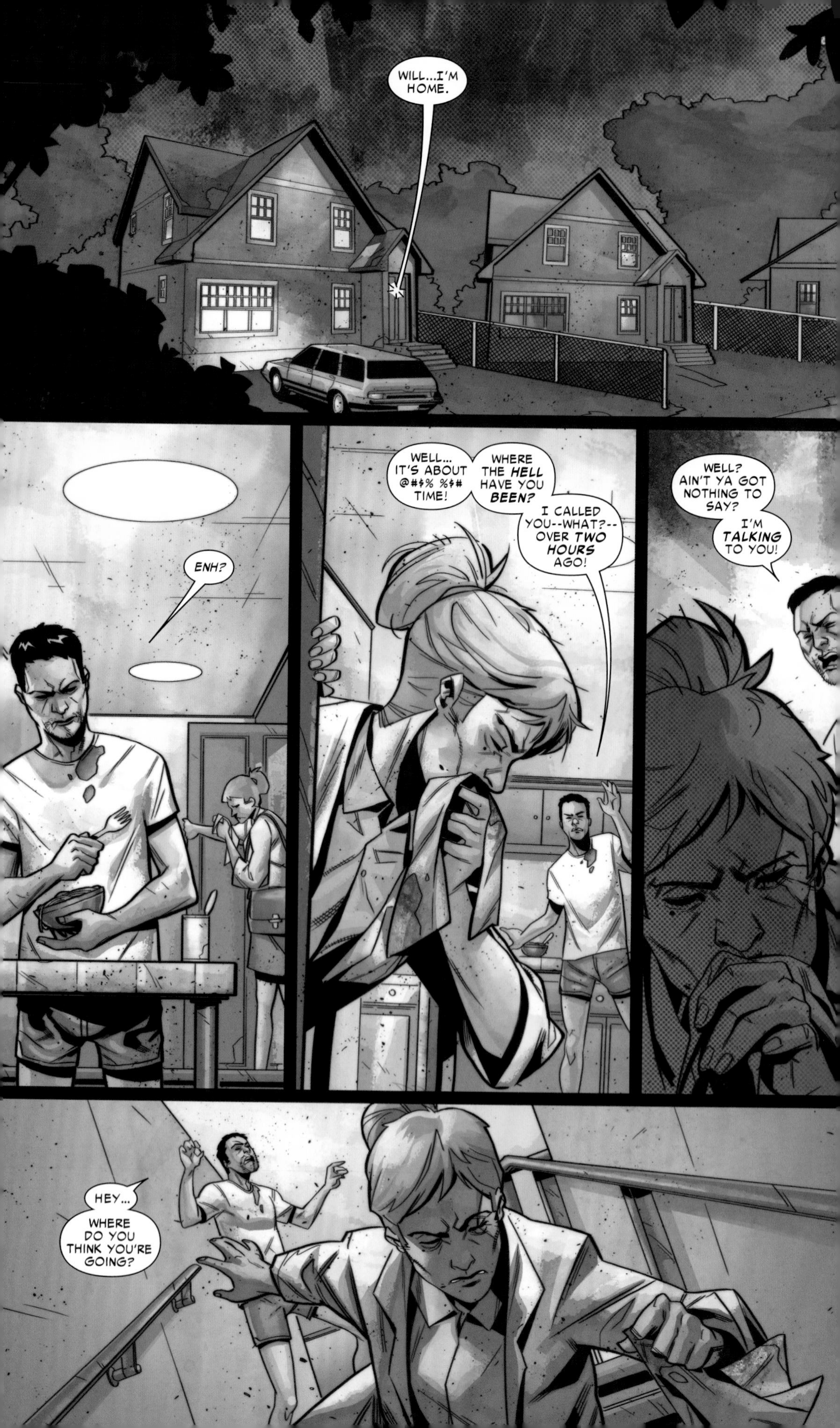
WILL...I'M HOME.
ENH?
WELL... IT'S ABOUT @#$% %$# TIME!
WHERE THE *HELL* HAVE YOU *BEEN?*
I CALLED YOU--WHAT?--OVER *TWO HOURS* AGO!
WELL? AIN'T YA GOT NOTHING TO SAY?
I'M *TALKING* TO YOU!
HEY... WHERE DO YOU THINK YOU'RE GOING?

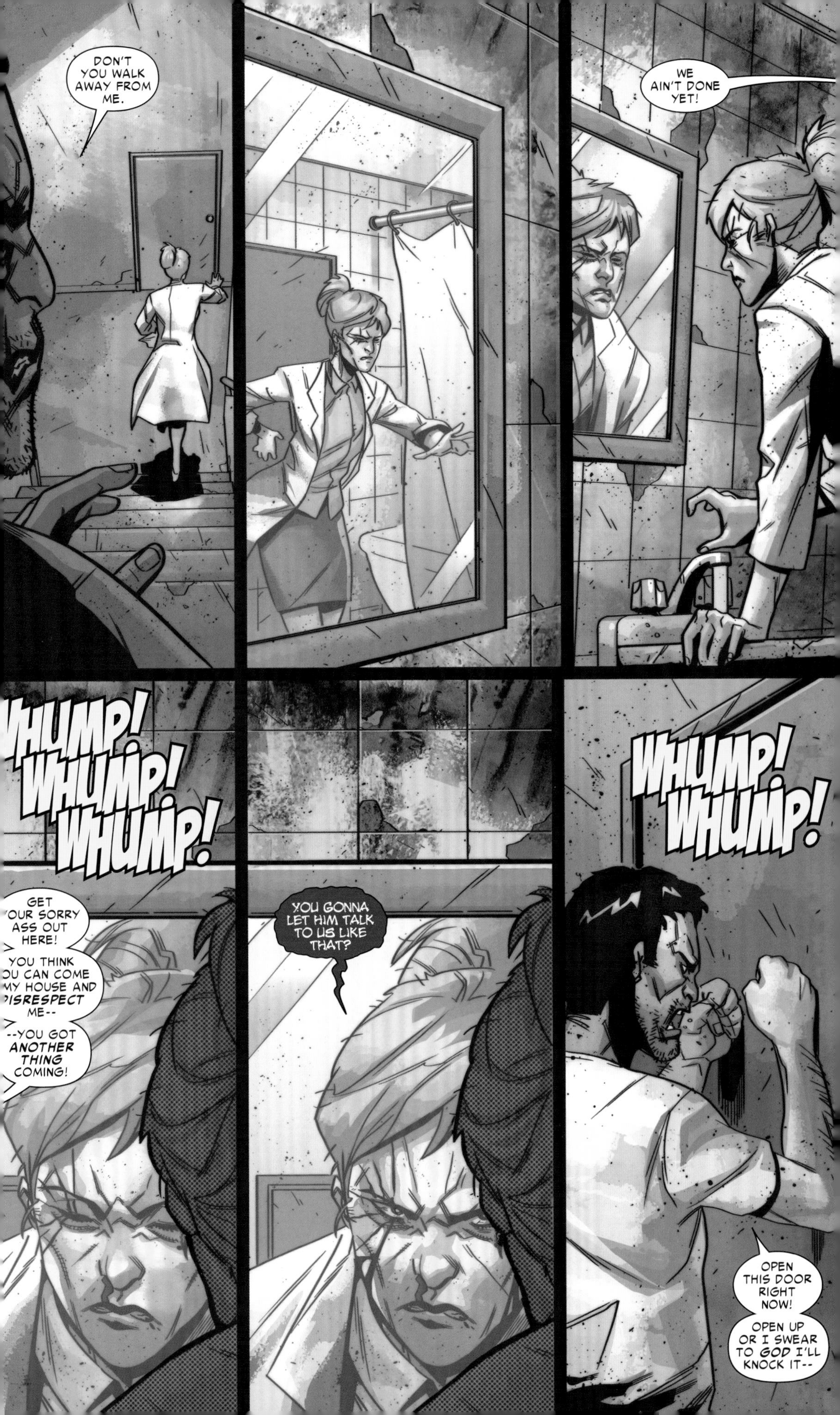
DON'T YOU WALK AWAY FROM ME.
WE AIN'T DONE YET!
WHUMP! WHUMP! WHUMP!
GET YOUR SORRY ASS OUT HERE!
YOU THINK YOU CAN COME MY HOUSE AND DISRESPECT ME--
--YOU GOT ANOTHER THING COMING!
YOU GONNA LET HIM TALK TO US LIKE THAT?
WHUMP! WHUMP!
OPEN THIS DOOR RIGHT NOW!
OPEN UP OR I SWEAR TO GOD I'LL KNOCK IT--

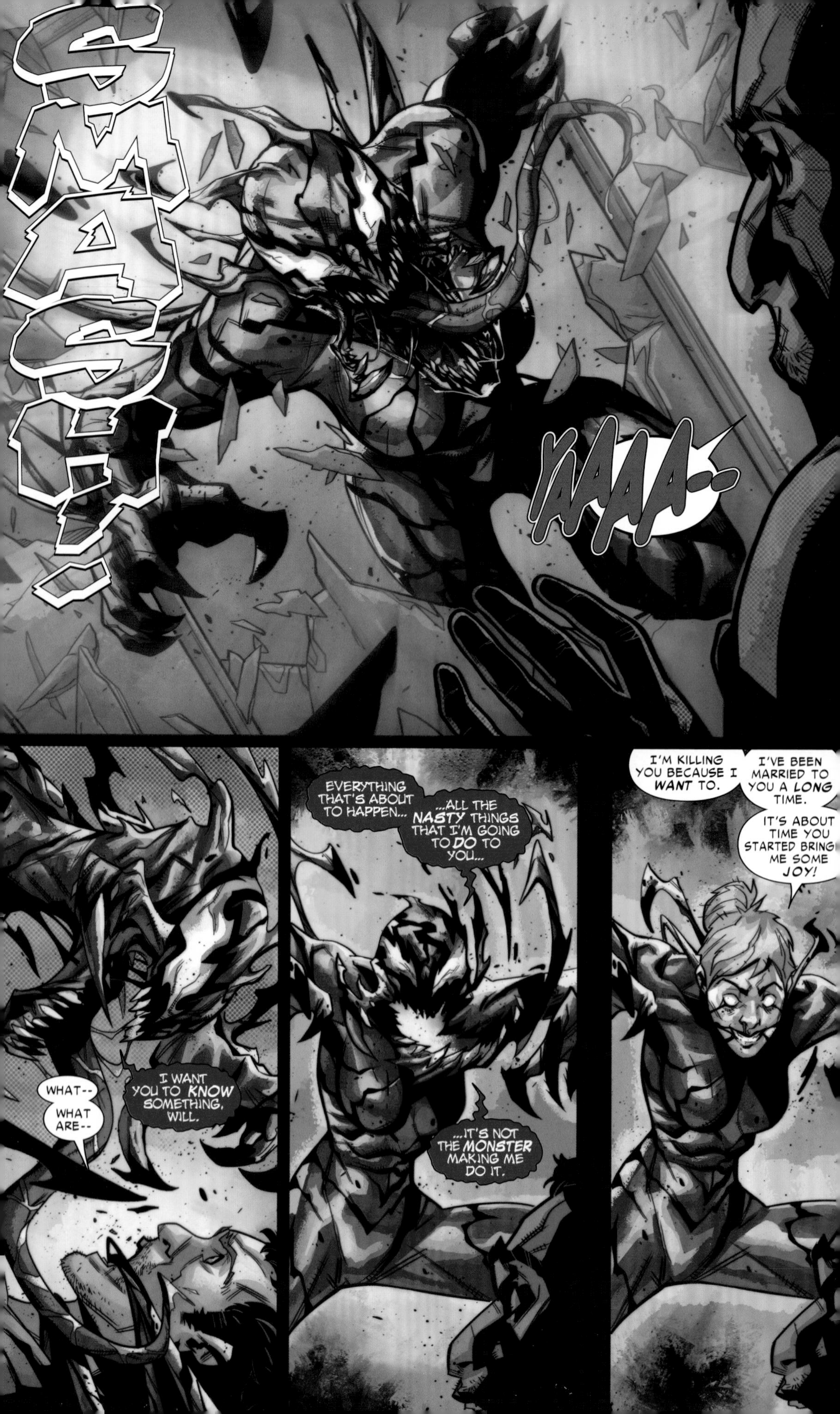
SMASH!
YAAAA--
WHAT-- WHAT ARE--
I WANT YOU TO KNOW SOMETHING, WILL.
EVERYTHING THAT'S ABOUT TO HAPPEN...
...ALL THE NASTY THINGS THAT I'M GOING TO DO TO YOU...
...IT'S NOT THE MONSTER MAKING ME DO IT.
I'M KILLING YOU BECAUSE I WANT TO.
I'VE BEEN MARRIED TO YOU A LONG TIME.
IT'S ABOUT TIME YOU STARTED BRING ME SOME JOY!

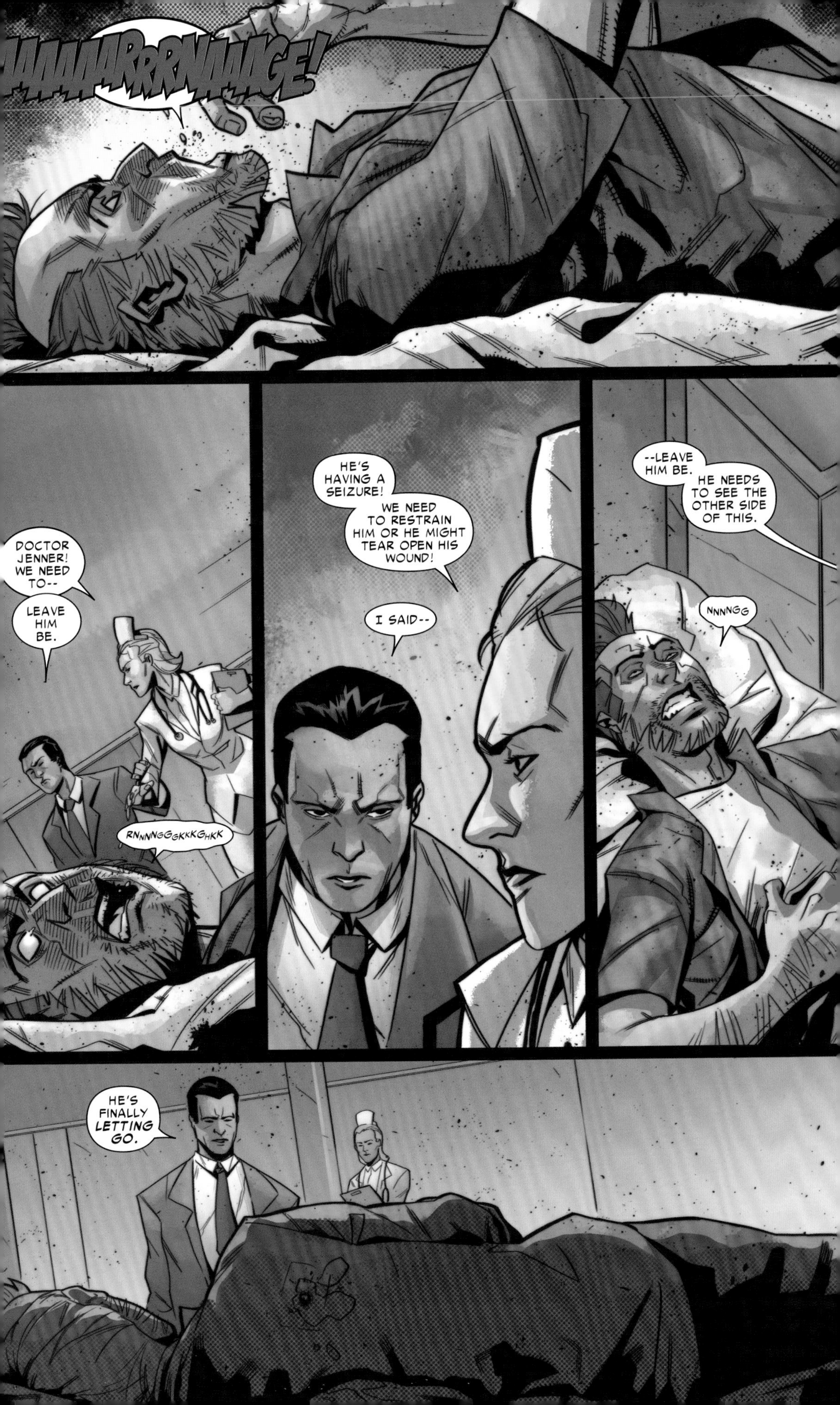
AAAAAARRRNAAAAGE!
DOCTOR JENNER! WE NEED TO--
LEAVE HIM BE.
RNNNNGGGKKKGHKK
HE'S HAVING A SEIZURE!
WE NEED TO RESTRAIN HIM OR HE MIGHT TEAR OPEN HIS WOUND!
I SAID--
--LEAVE HIM BE.
HE NEEDS TO SEE THE OTHER SIDE OF THIS.
NNNNGG
HE'S FINALLY LETTING GO.

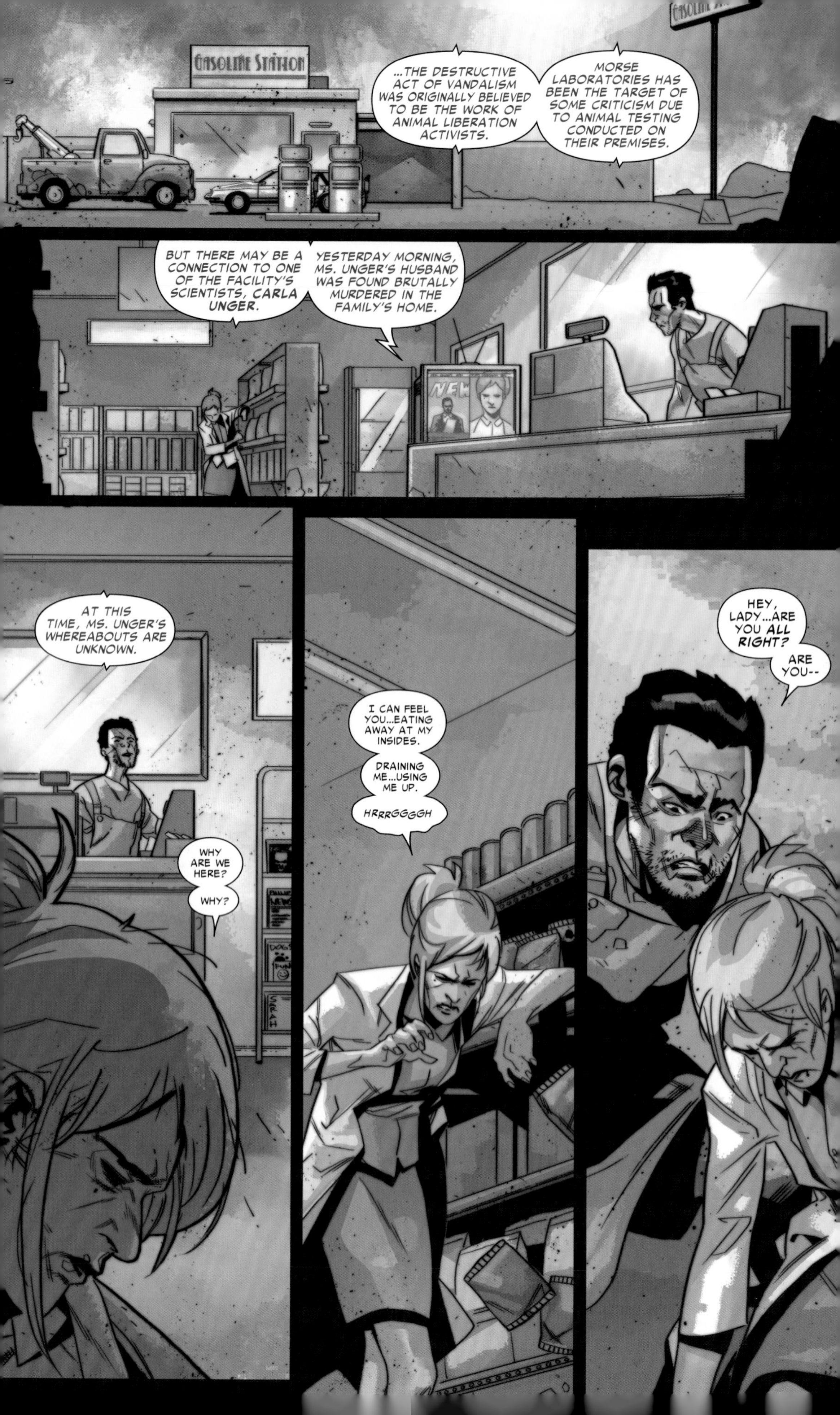
GASOLINE STATION
...THE DESTRUCTIVE ACT OF VANDALISM WAS ORIGINALLY BELIEVED TO BE THE WORK OF ANIMAL LIBERATION ACTIVISTS.
MORSE LABORATORIES HAS BEEN THE TARGET OF SOME CRITICISM DUE TO ANIMAL TESTING CONDUCTED ON THEIR PREMISES.
BUT THERE MAY BE A CONNECTION TO ONE OF THE FACILITY'S SCIENTISTS, CARLA UNGER.
YESTERDAY MORNING, MS. UNGER'S HUSBAND WAS FOUND BRUTALLY MURDERED IN THE FAMILY'S HOME.
AT THIS TIME, MS. UNGER'S WHEREABOUTS ARE UNKNOWN.
WHY ARE WE HERE?
WHY?
I CAN FEEL YOU...EATING AWAY AT MY INSIDES.
DRAINING ME...USING ME UP.
HRRRGGGGH
HEY, LADY...ARE YOU ALL RIGHT?
ARE YOU--

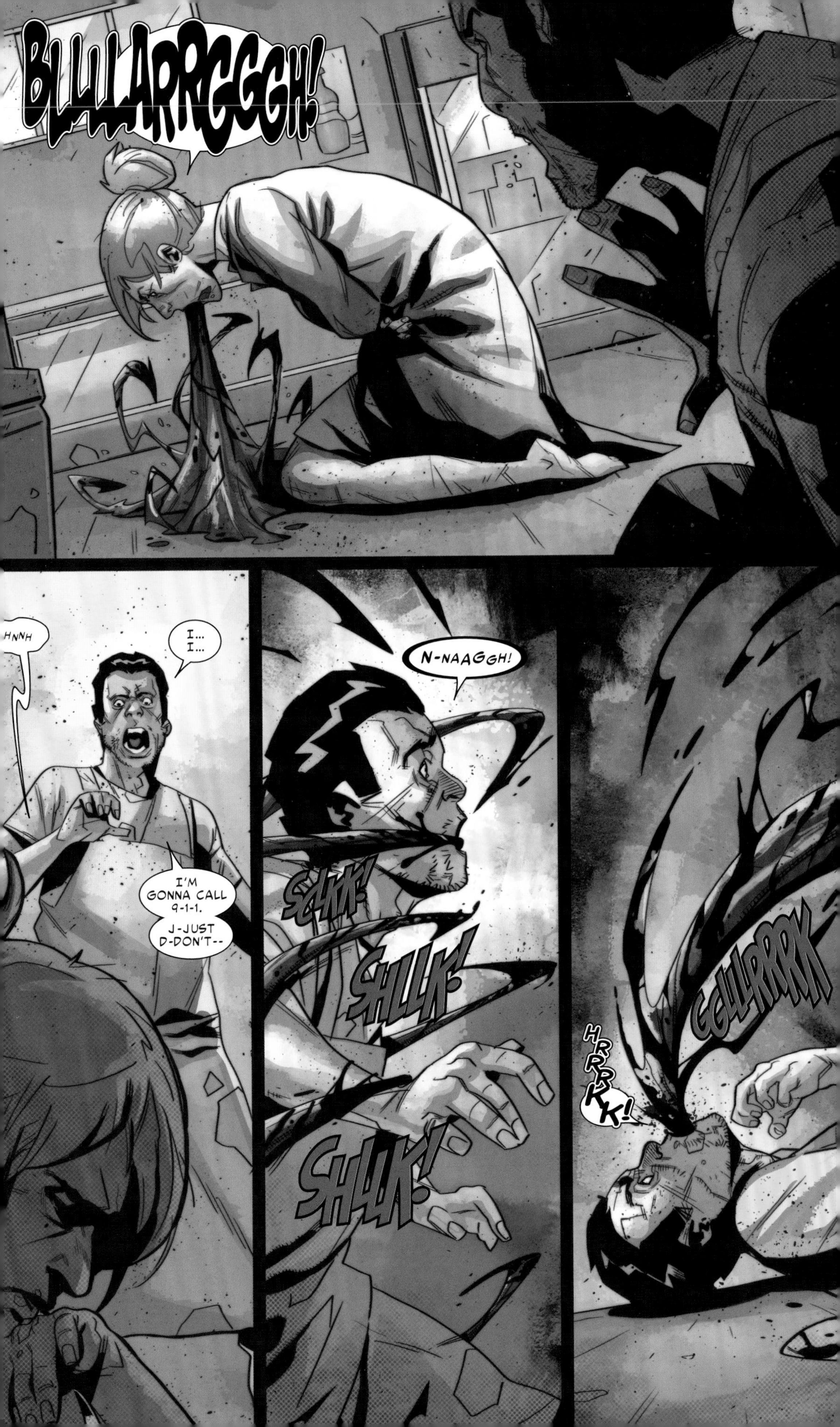
BLLLLARRGGGH!
HNNH
I...
I...
I'M GONNA CALL 9-1-1.
J-JUST D-DON'T--
N-NAAGGH!
SCLLK!
SHLLK!
SHLUK!
GGLLRRRK
HRRRKK!

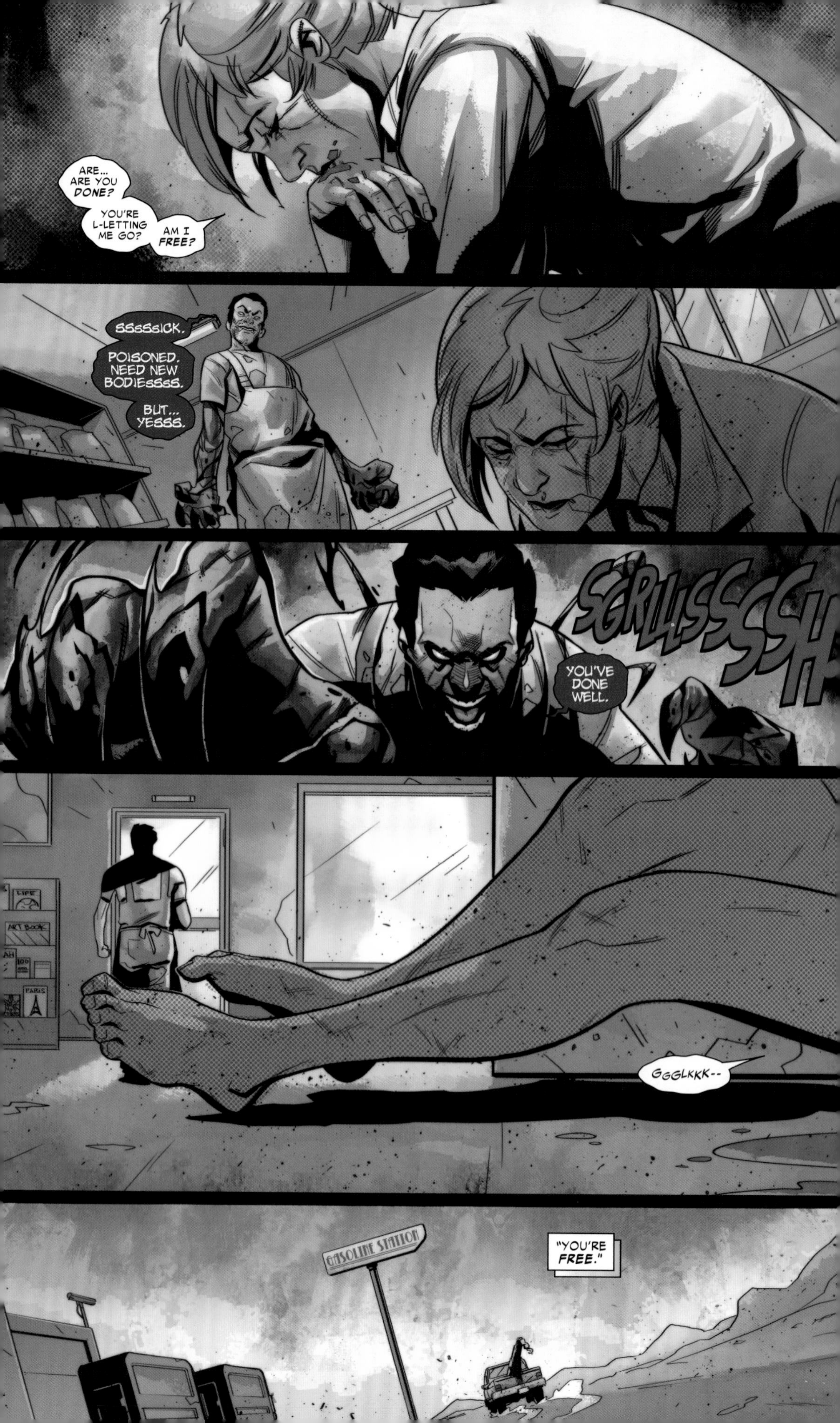
ARE... ARE YOU DONE?
YOU'RE L-LETTING ME GO?
AM I FREE?
SSSSSICK.
POISONED. NEED NEW BODIESSSS.
BUT... YESSS.
SGRLLLSSSSSH
YOU'VE DONE WELL.
LIFE
ART BOOK
PARIS
GGGLKKK--
GASOLINE STATION
"YOU'RE FREE."

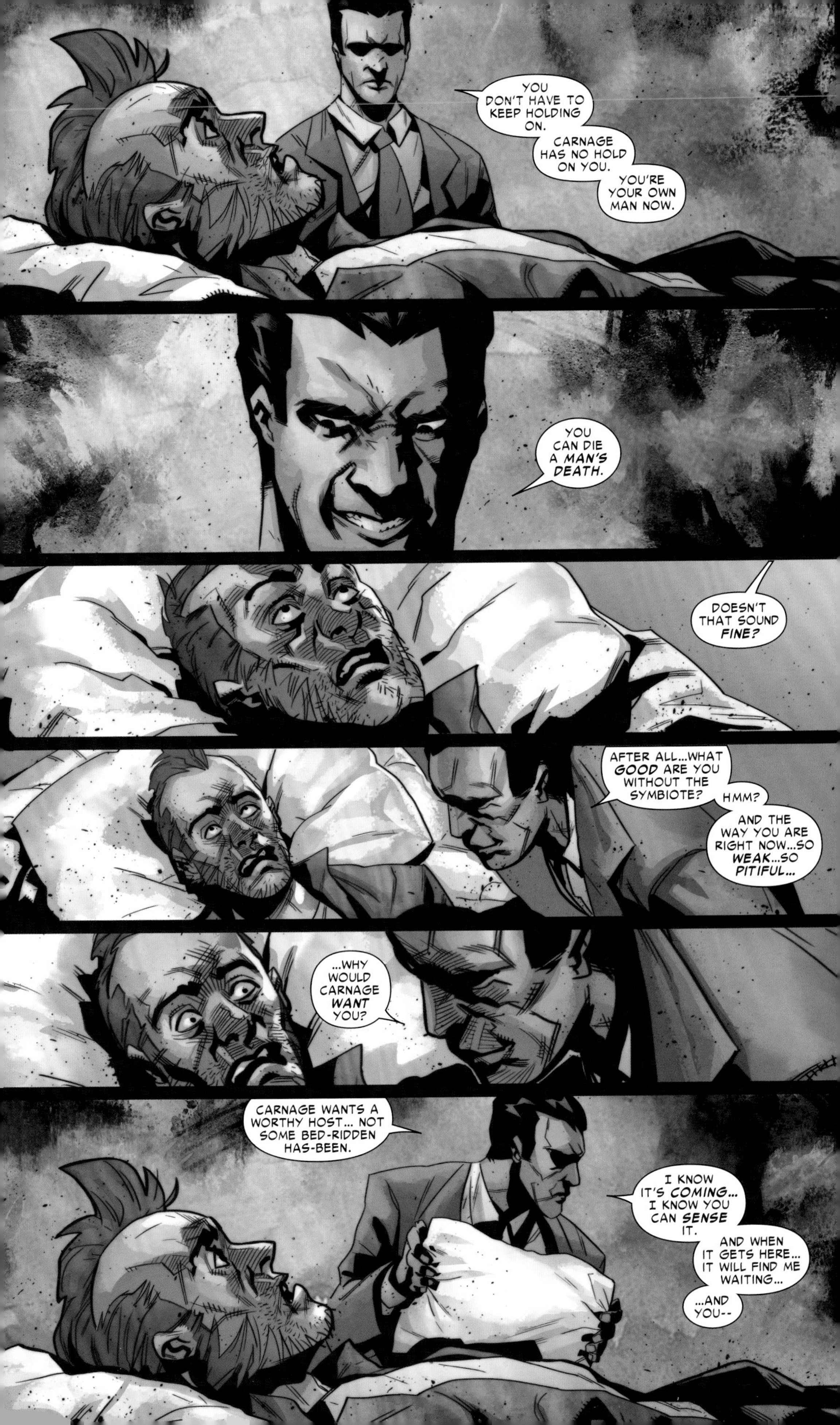
YOU DON'T HAVE TO KEEP HOLDING ON.
CARNAGE HAS NO HOLD ON YOU.
YOU'RE YOUR OWN MAN NOW.
YOU CAN DIE A MAN'S DEATH.
DOESN'T THAT SOUND FINE?
AFTER ALL...WHAT GOOD ARE YOU WITHOUT THE SYMBIOTE?
HMM?
AND THE WAY YOU ARE RIGHT NOW...SO WEAK...SO PITIFUL...
...WHY WOULD CARNAGE WANT YOU?
CARNAGE WANTS A WORTHY HOST... NOT SOME BED-RIDDEN HAS-BEEN.
I KNOW IT'S COMING... I KNOW YOU CAN SENSE IT.
AND WHEN IT GETS HERE... IT WILL FIND ME WAITING...
...AND YOU--

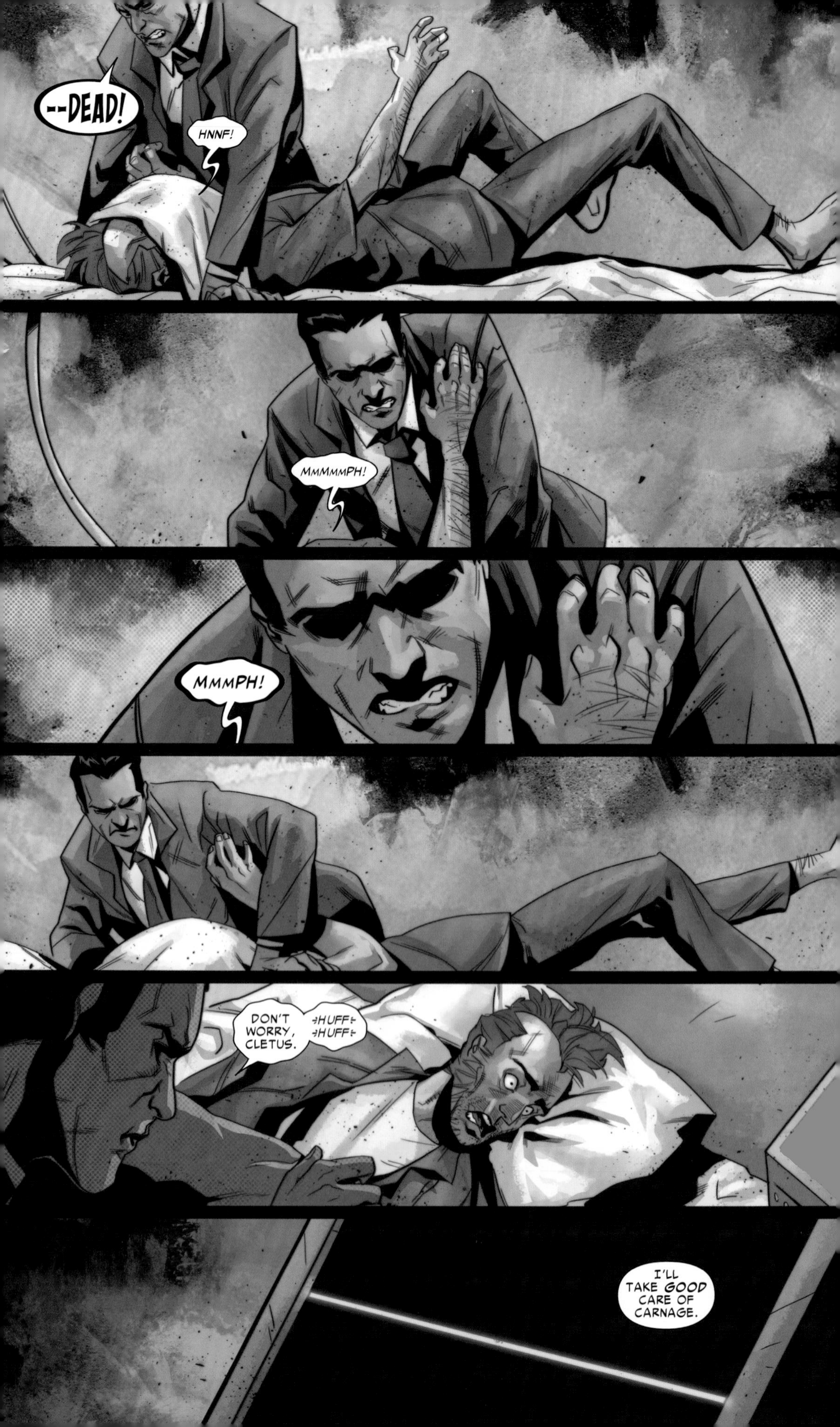
--DEAD!
HNNF!
MMMMMPH!
MMMPH!
DON'T WORRY, CLETUS.
HUFF HUFF
I'LL TAKE GOOD CARE OF CARNAGE.

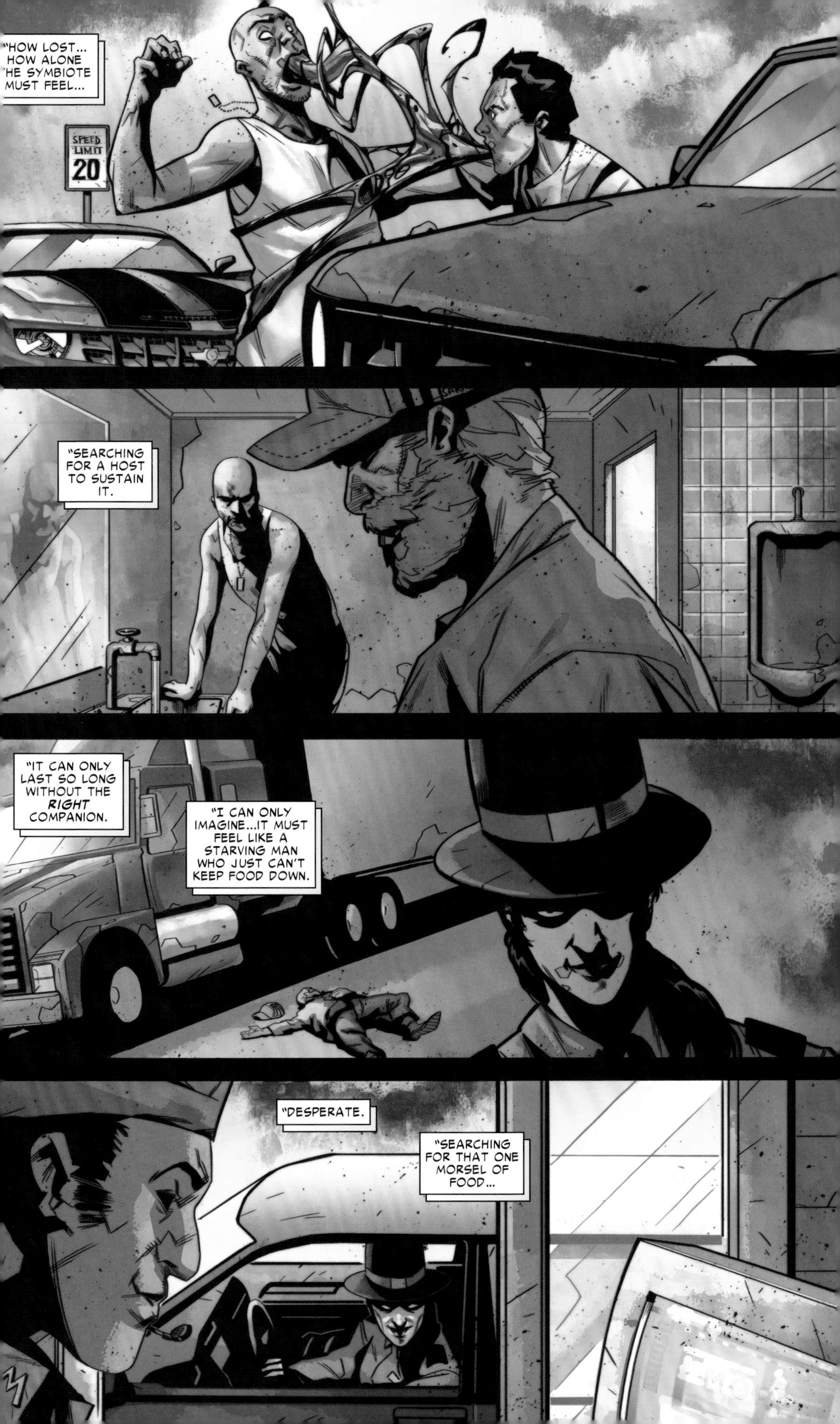

"HOW LOST... HOW ALONE HE SYMBIOTE MUST FEEL...
SPEED LIMIT 20
"SEARCHING FOR A HOST TO SUSTAIN IT.
"IT CAN ONLY LAST SO LONG WITHOUT THE *RIGHT* COMPANION.
"I CAN ONLY IMAGINE...IT MUST FEEL LIKE A STARVING MAN WHO JUST CAN'T KEEP FOOD DOWN.
"DESPERATE.
"SEARCHING FOR THAT ONE MORSEL OF FOOD...

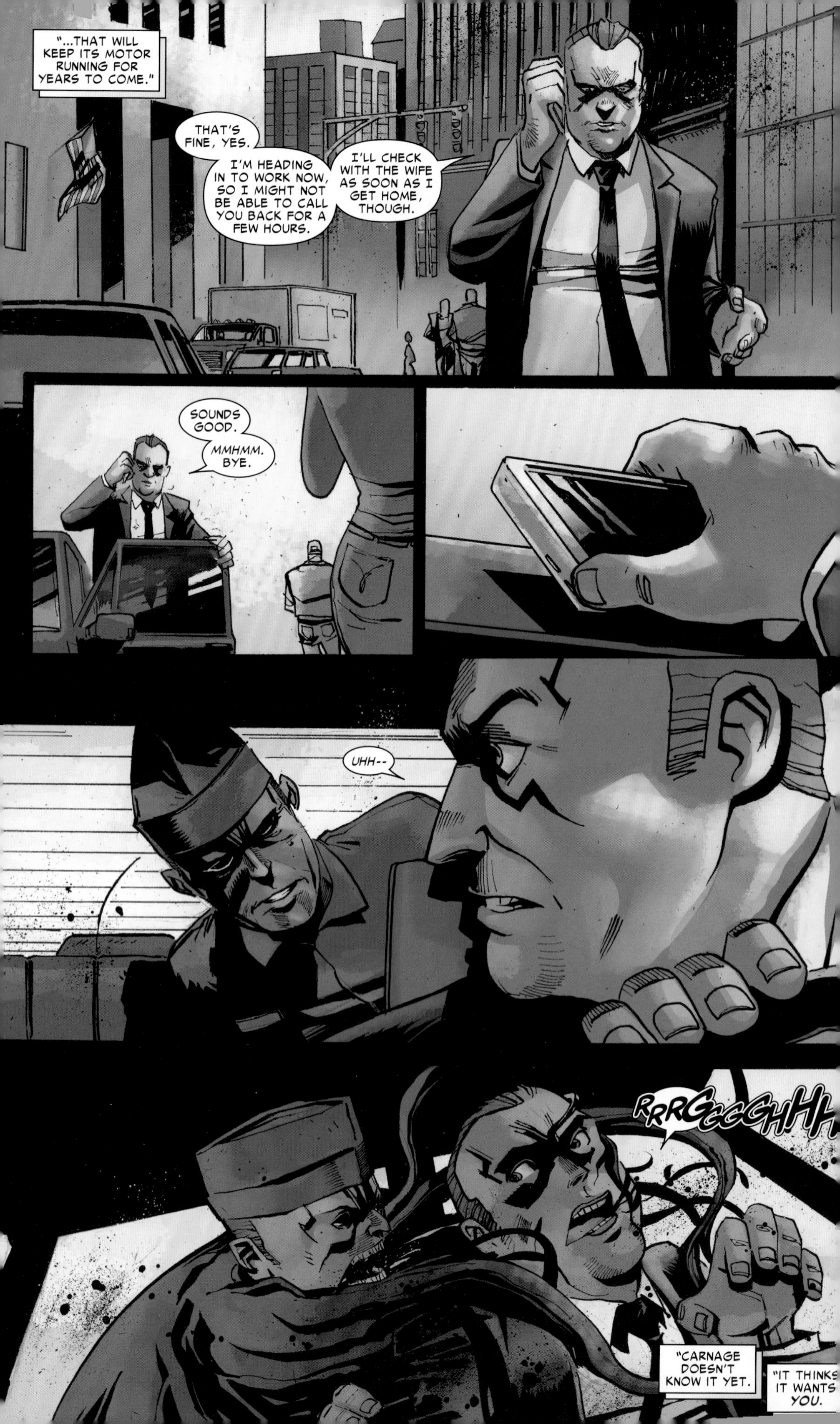
"...THAT WILL KEEP ITS MOTOR RUNNING FOR YEARS TO COME."
THAT'S FINE, YES.
I'M HEADING IN TO WORK NOW, SO I MIGHT NOT BE ABLE TO CALL YOU BACK FOR A FEW HOURS.
I'LL CHECK WITH THE WIFE AS SOON AS I GET HOME, THOUGH.
SOUNDS GOOD.
MMHMM. BYE.
UHH--
RRRGGGGHHH
"CARNAGE DOESN'T KNOW IT YET.
"IT THINKS IT WANTS YOU.

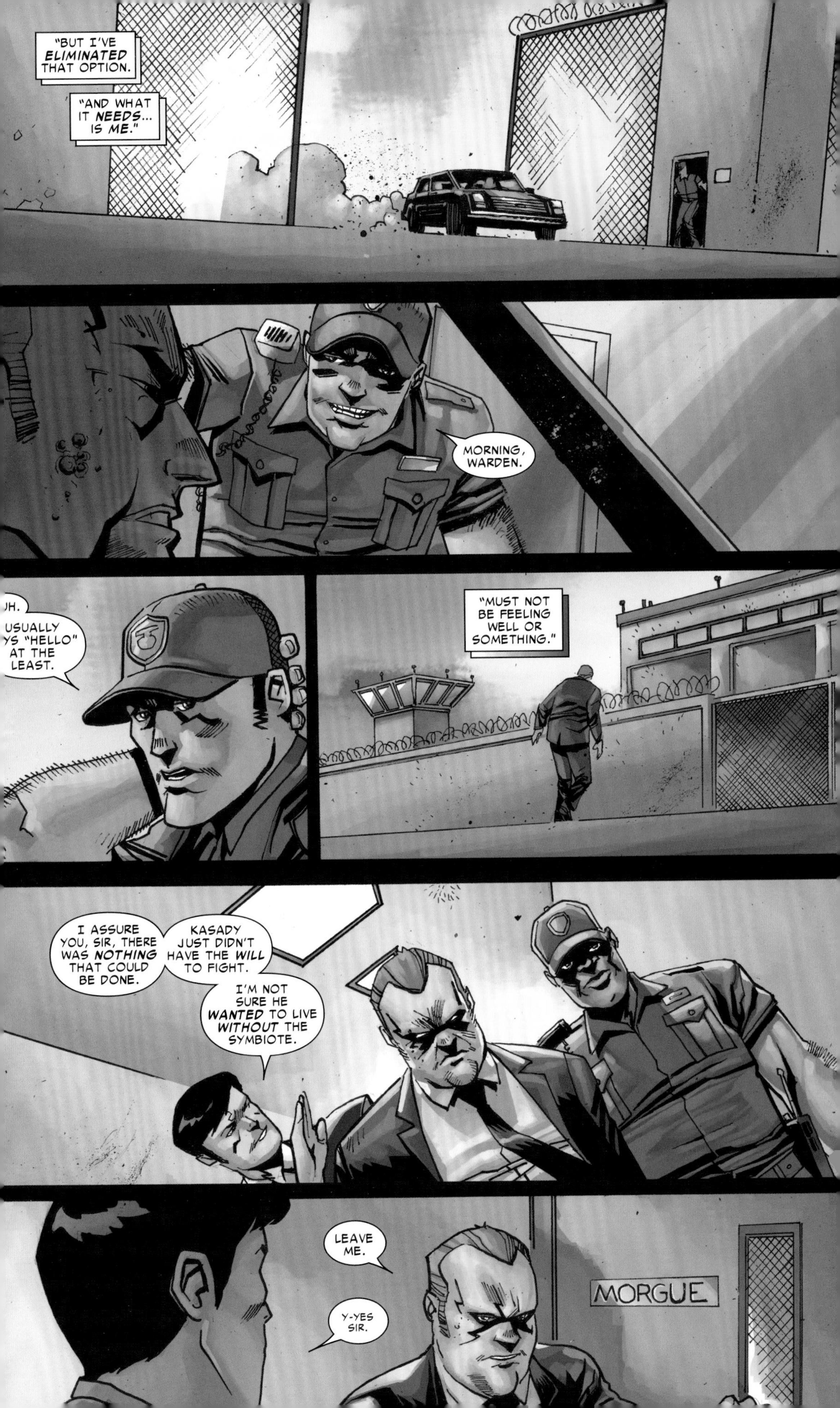
"BUT I'VE ELIMINATED THAT OPTION.
"AND WHAT IT NEEDS... IS ME."
MORNING, WARDEN.
UH.
USUALLY YS "HELLO" AT THE LEAST.
"MUST NOT BE FEELING WELL OR SOMETHING."
I ASSURE YOU, SIR, THERE WAS NOTHING THAT COULD BE DONE.
KASADY JUST DIDN'T HAVE THE WILL TO FIGHT.
I'M NOT SURE HE WANTED TO LIVE WITHOUT THE SYMBIOTE.
LEAVE ME.
Y-YES SIR.
MORGUE

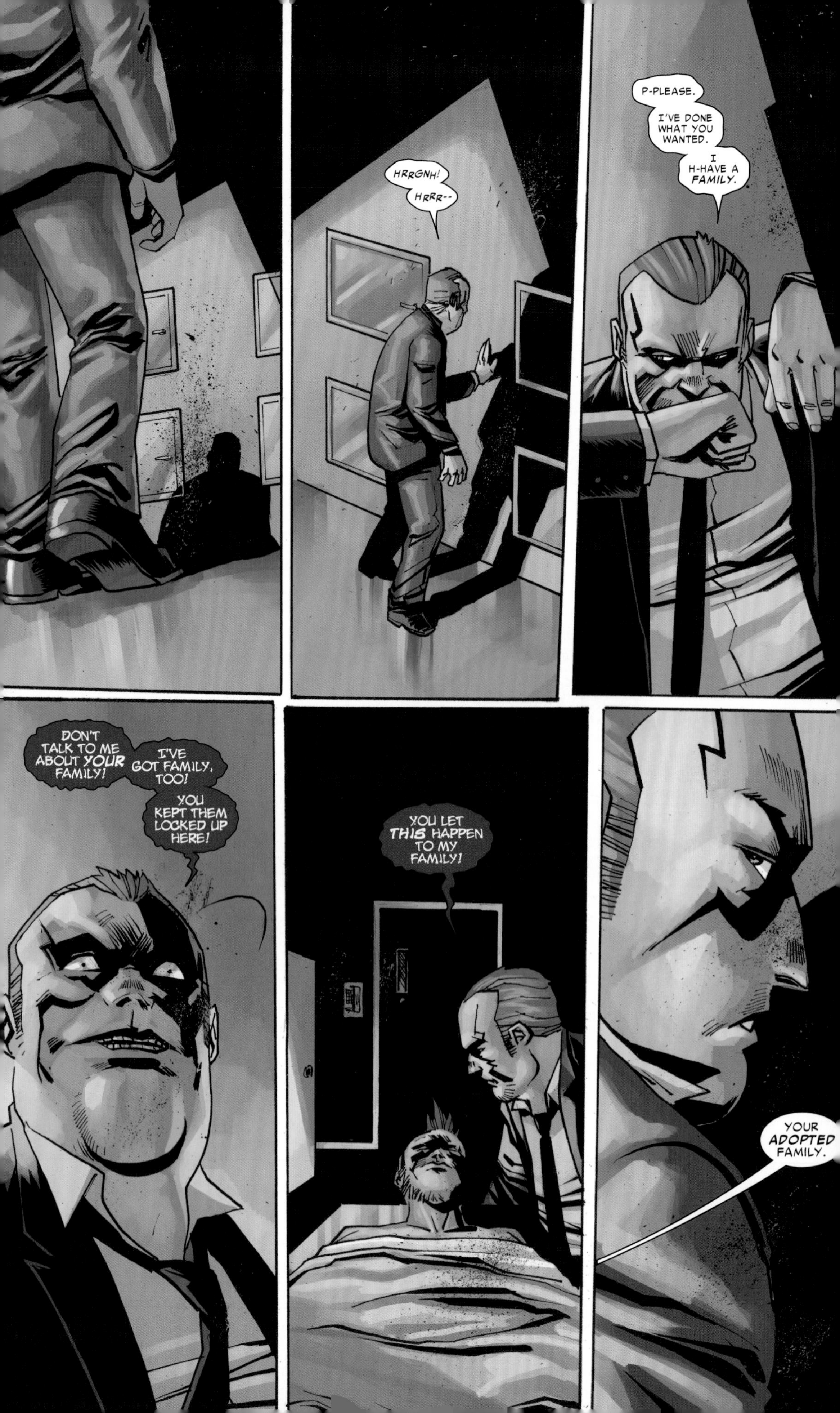

HRRGNH!
HRRR--
P-PLEASE.
I'VE DONE WHAT YOU WANTED.
I H-HAVE A FAMILY.
DON'T TALK TO ME ABOUT YOUR FAMILY!
I'VE GOT FAMILY, TOO!
YOU KEPT THEM LOCKED UP HERE!
YOU LET THIS HAPPEN TO MY FAMILY!
YOUR ADOPTED FAMILY.

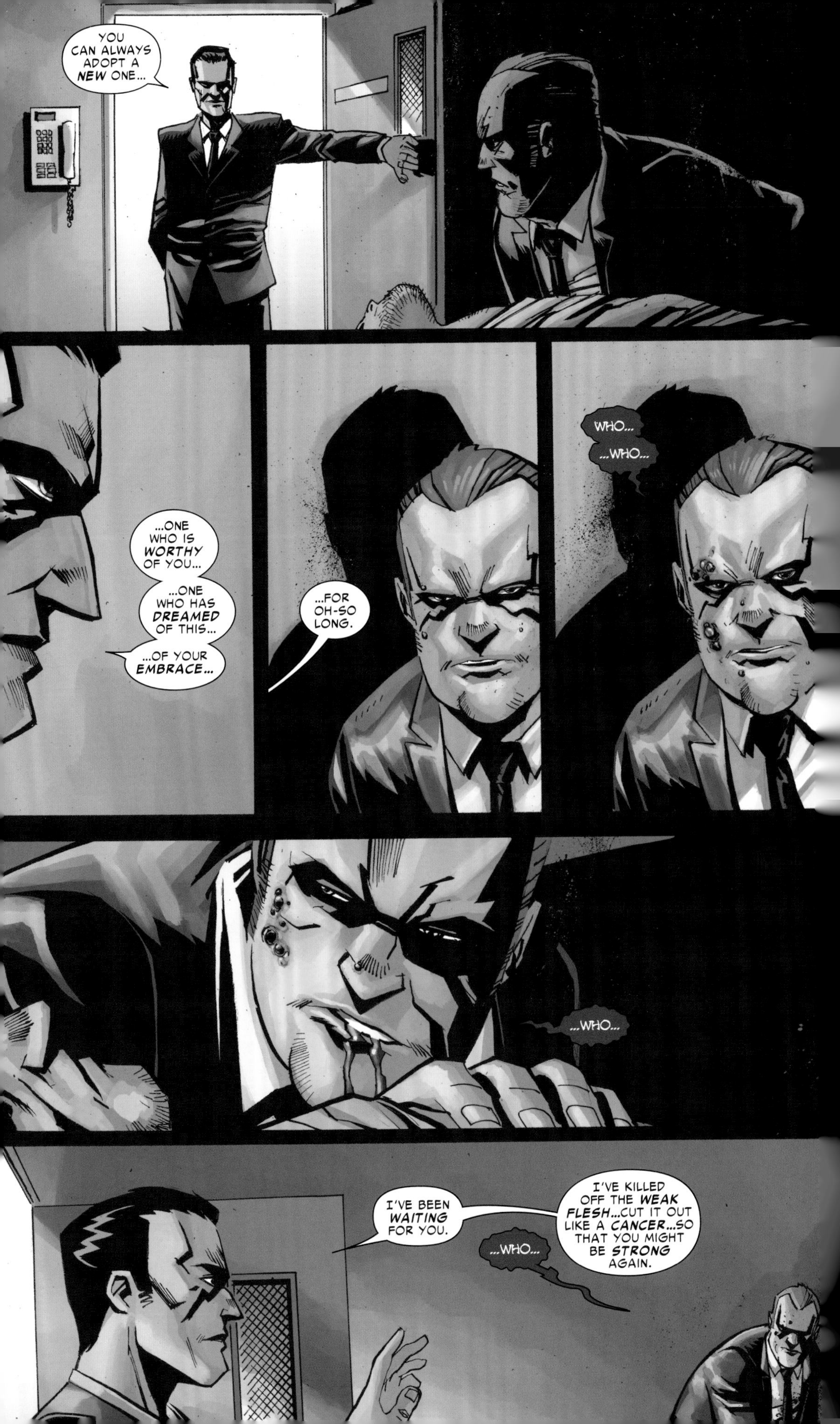
YOU CAN ALWAYS ADOPT A NEW ONE...
...ONE WHO IS WORTHY OF YOU...
...ONE WHO HAS DREAMED OF THIS...
...OF YOUR EMBRACE...
...FOR OH-SO LONG.
WHO...
...WHO...
...WHO...
I'VE BEEN WAITING FOR YOU.
...WHO...
I'VE KILLED OFF THE WEAK FLESH...CUT IT OUT LIKE A CANCER...SO THAT YOU MIGHT BE STRONG AGAIN.

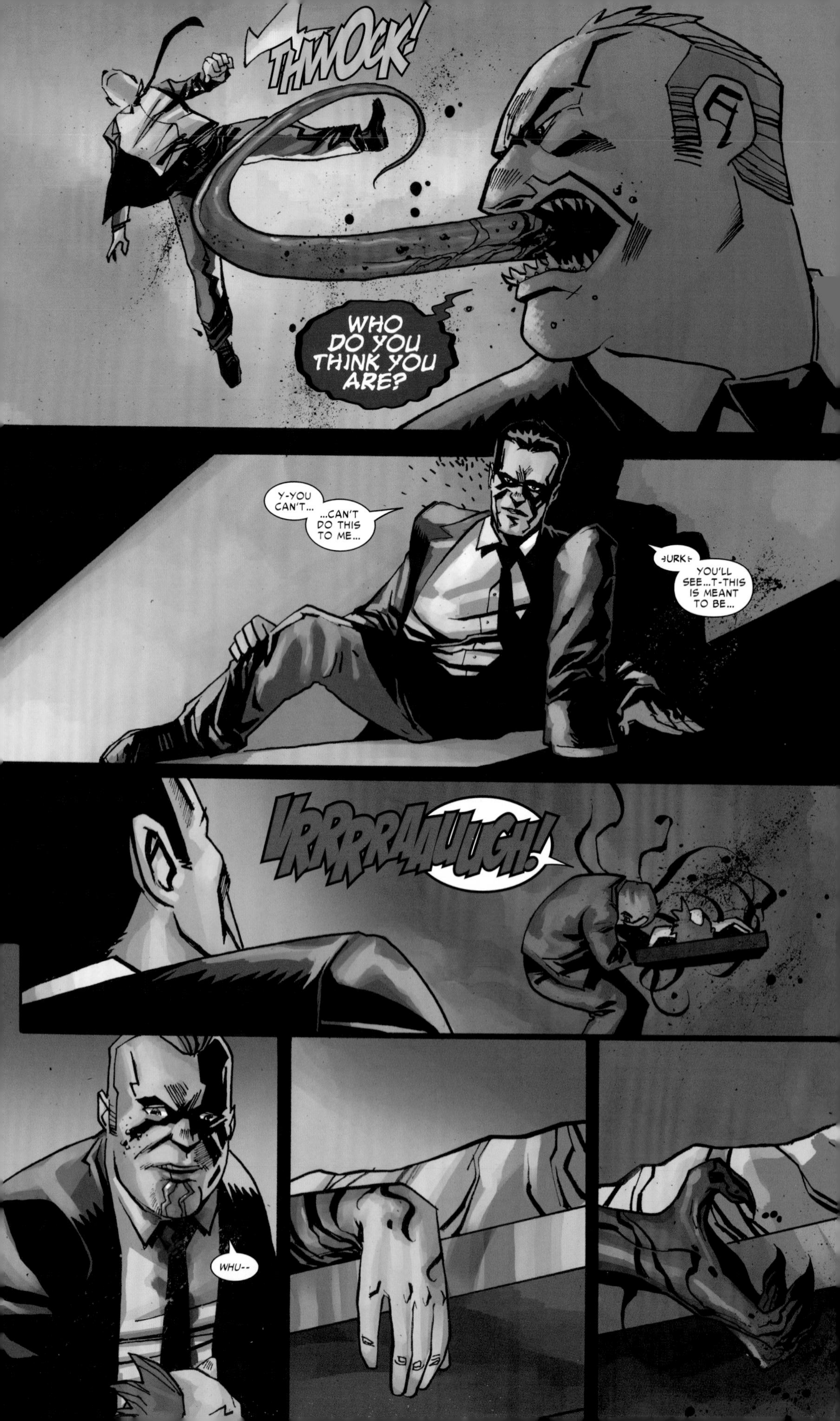
THWOCK!
WHO DO YOU THINK YOU ARE?
Y-YOU CAN'T...
...CAN'T DO THIS TO ME...
URK
YOU'LL SEE...T-THIS IS MEANT TO BE...
VRRRRAAUUGH!
WHU--

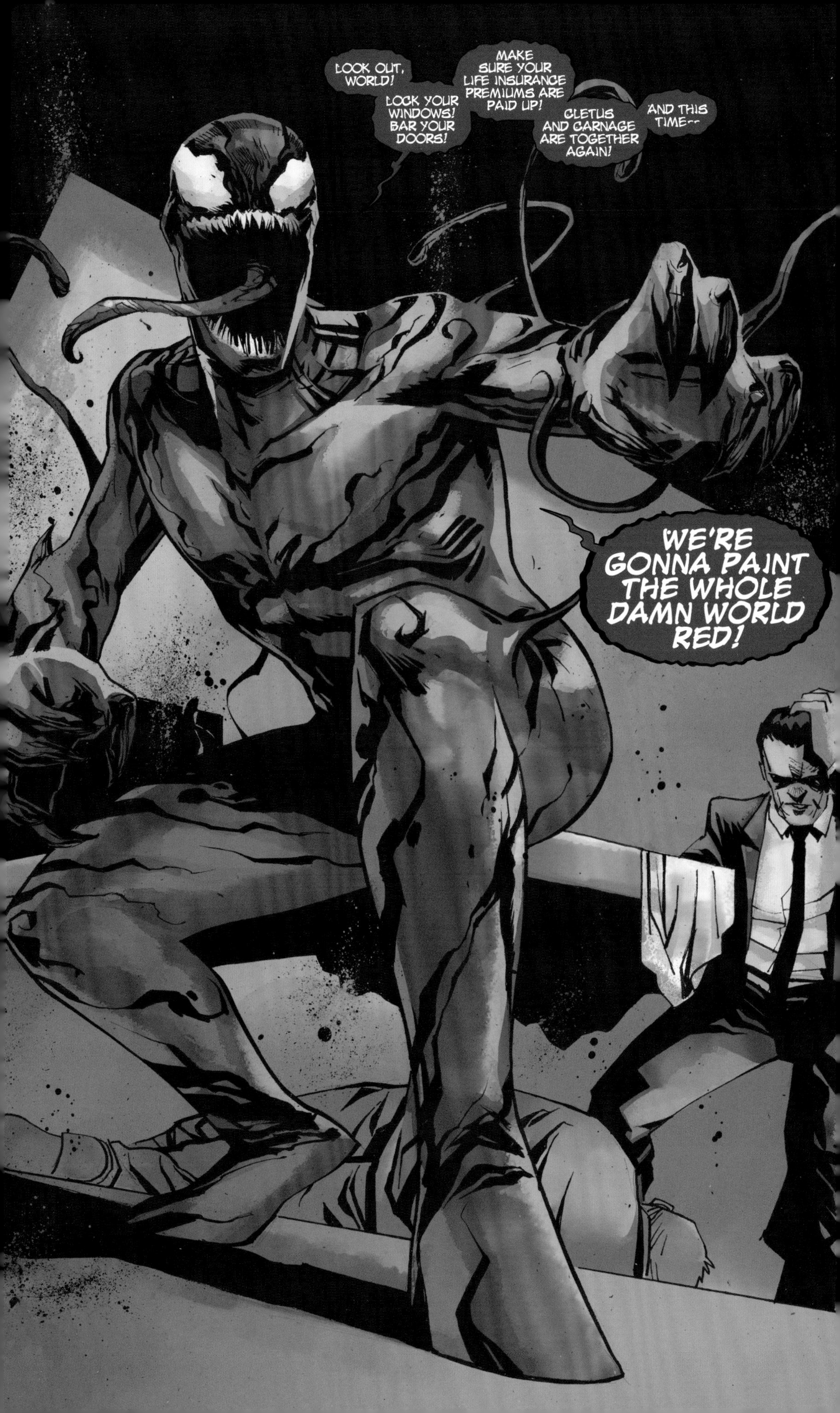
LOOK OUT, WORLD!
LOCK YOUR WINDOWS! BAR YOUR DOORS!
MAKE SURE YOUR LIFE INSURANCE PREMIUMS ARE PAID UP!
CLETUS AND CARNAGE ARE TOGETHER AGAIN!
AND THIS TIME--
WE'RE GONNA PAINT THE WHOLE DAMN WORLD RED!

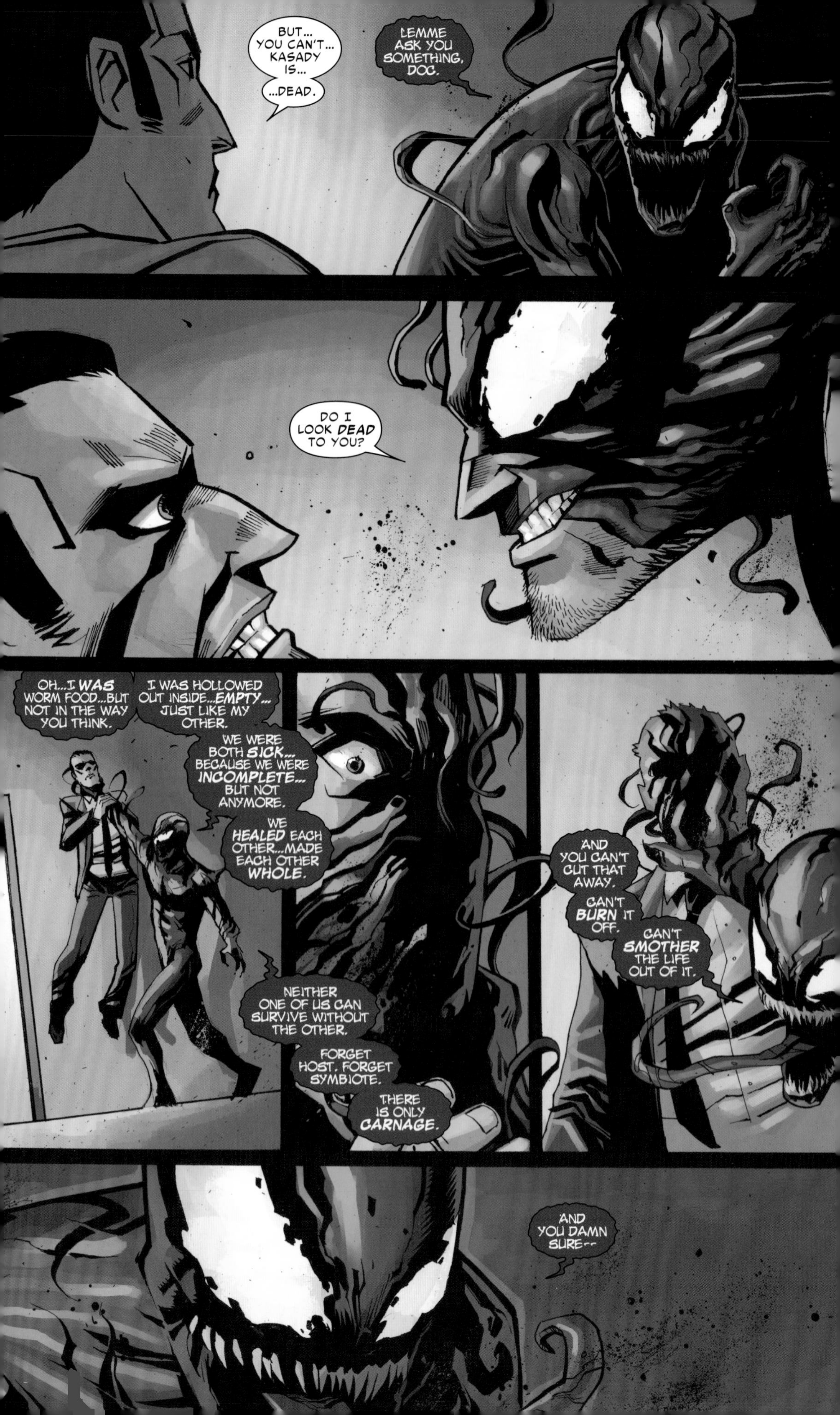
BUT... YOU CAN'T... KASADY IS...
...DEAD.
LEMME ASK YOU SOMETHING, DOC.
DO I LOOK DEAD TO YOU?
OH...I WAS WORM FOOD...BUT NOT IN THE WAY YOU THINK.
I WAS HOLLOWED OUT INSIDE...EMPTY... JUST LIKE MY OTHER.
WE WERE BOTH SICK... BECAUSE WE WERE INCOMPLETE... BUT NOT ANYMORE.
WE HEALED EACH OTHER...MADE EACH OTHER WHOLE.
NEITHER ONE OF US CAN SURVIVE WITHOUT THE OTHER.
FORGET HOST. FORGET SYMBIOTE.
THERE IS ONLY CARNAGE.
AND YOU CAN'T CUT THAT AWAY.
CAN'T BURN IT OFF.
CAN'T SMOTHER THE LIFE OUT OF IT.
AND YOU DAMN SURE--

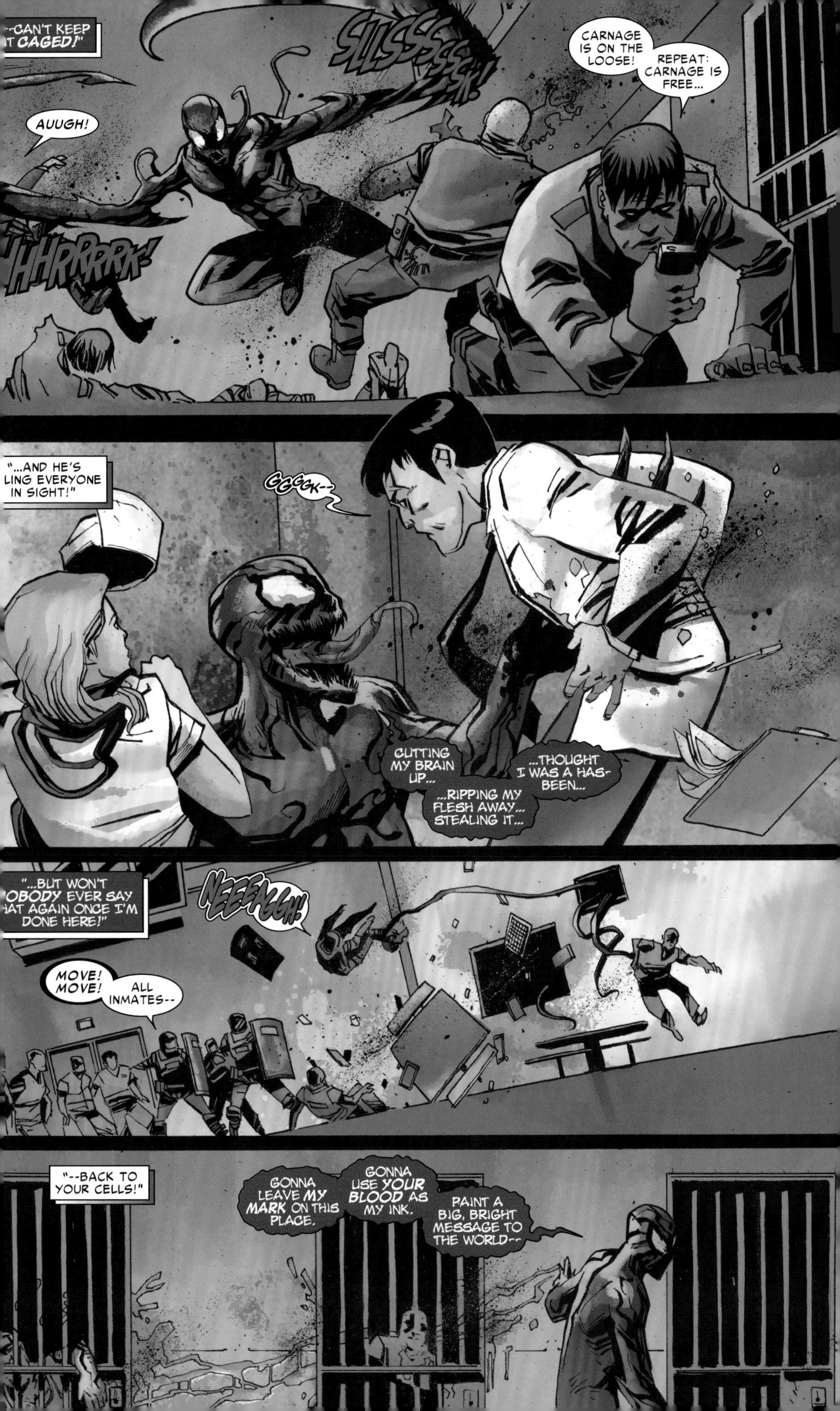

--CAN'T KEEP
IT CAGED!"
SLLSSSSSSK!
CARNAGE IS ON THE LOOSE!
REPEAT: CARNAGE IS FREE...
AUUGH!
HHRRRRK!
"...AND HE'S
LING EVERYONE IN SIGHT!"
GGGGK--
CUTTING MY BRAIN UP...
...RIPPING MY FLESH AWAY... STEALING IT...
...THOUGHT I WAS A HAS-BEEN...
"...BUT WON'T
OBODY EVER SAY
HAT AGAIN ONCE I'M DONE HERE!"
NEEEAGGH!
MOVE! MOVE!
ALL INMATES--
"--BACK TO YOUR CELLS!"
GONNA LEAVE MY MARK ON THIS PLACE.
GONNA USE YOUR BLOOD AS MY INK.
PAINT A BIG, BRIGHT MESSAGE TO THE WORLD--

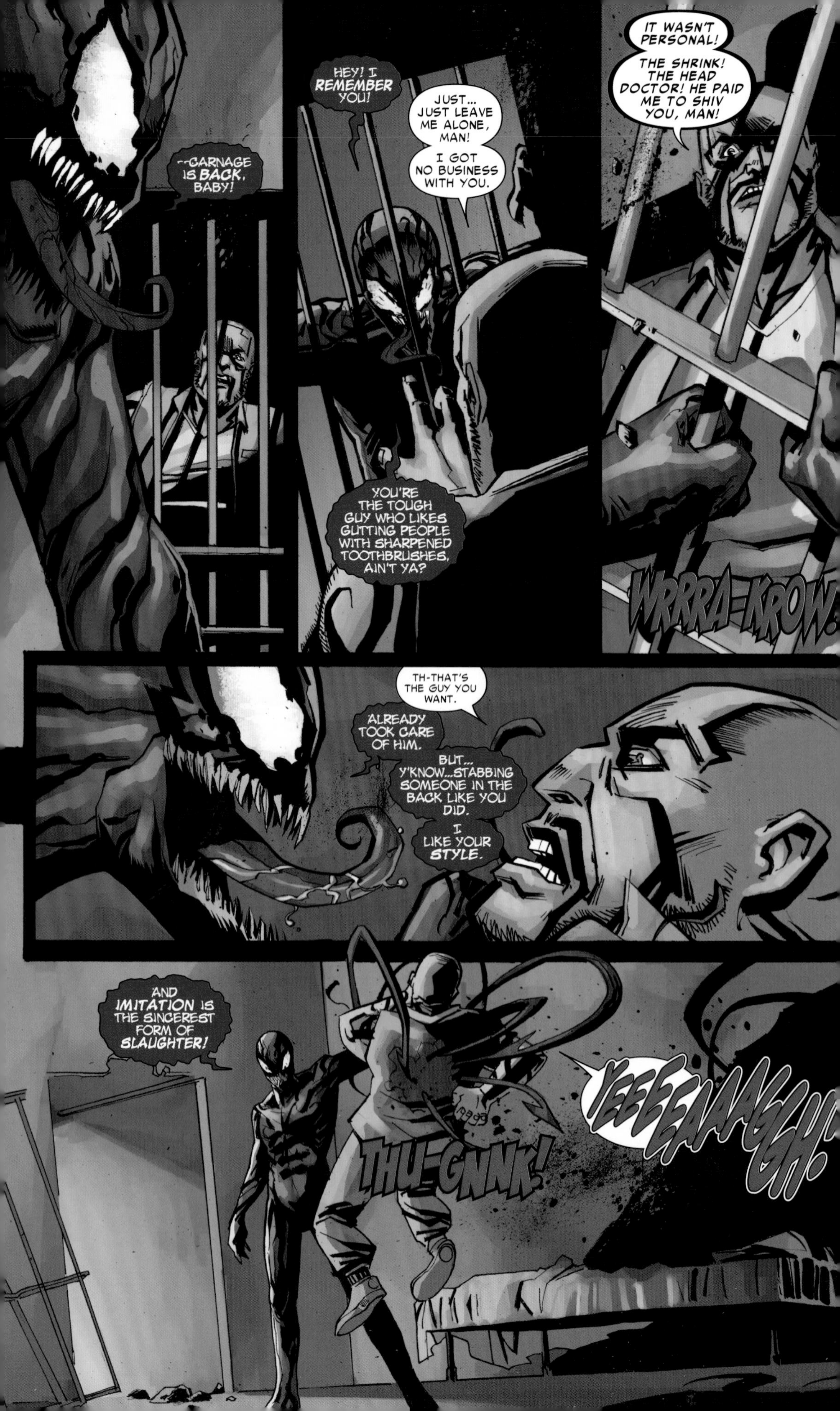
--CARNAGE IS BACK, BABY!
HEY! I REMEMBER YOU!
JUST... JUST LEAVE ME ALONE, MAN!
I GOT NO BUSINESS WITH YOU.
YOU'RE THE TOUGH GUY WHO LIKES GUTTING PEOPLE WITH SHARPENED TOOTHBRUSHES, AIN'T YA?
IT WASN'T PERSONAL!
THE SHRINK! THE HEAD DOCTOR! HE PAID ME TO SHIV YOU, MAN!
WRRRA-KROW!
TH-THAT'S THE GUY YOU WANT.
ALREADY TOOK CARE OF HIM.
BUT... Y'KNOW...STABBING SOMEONE IN THE BACK LIKE YOU DID.
I LIKE YOUR STYLE.
AND IMITATION IS THE SINCEREST FORM OF SLAUGHTER!
THU-GNNK!
YEEEEAAAGGH!

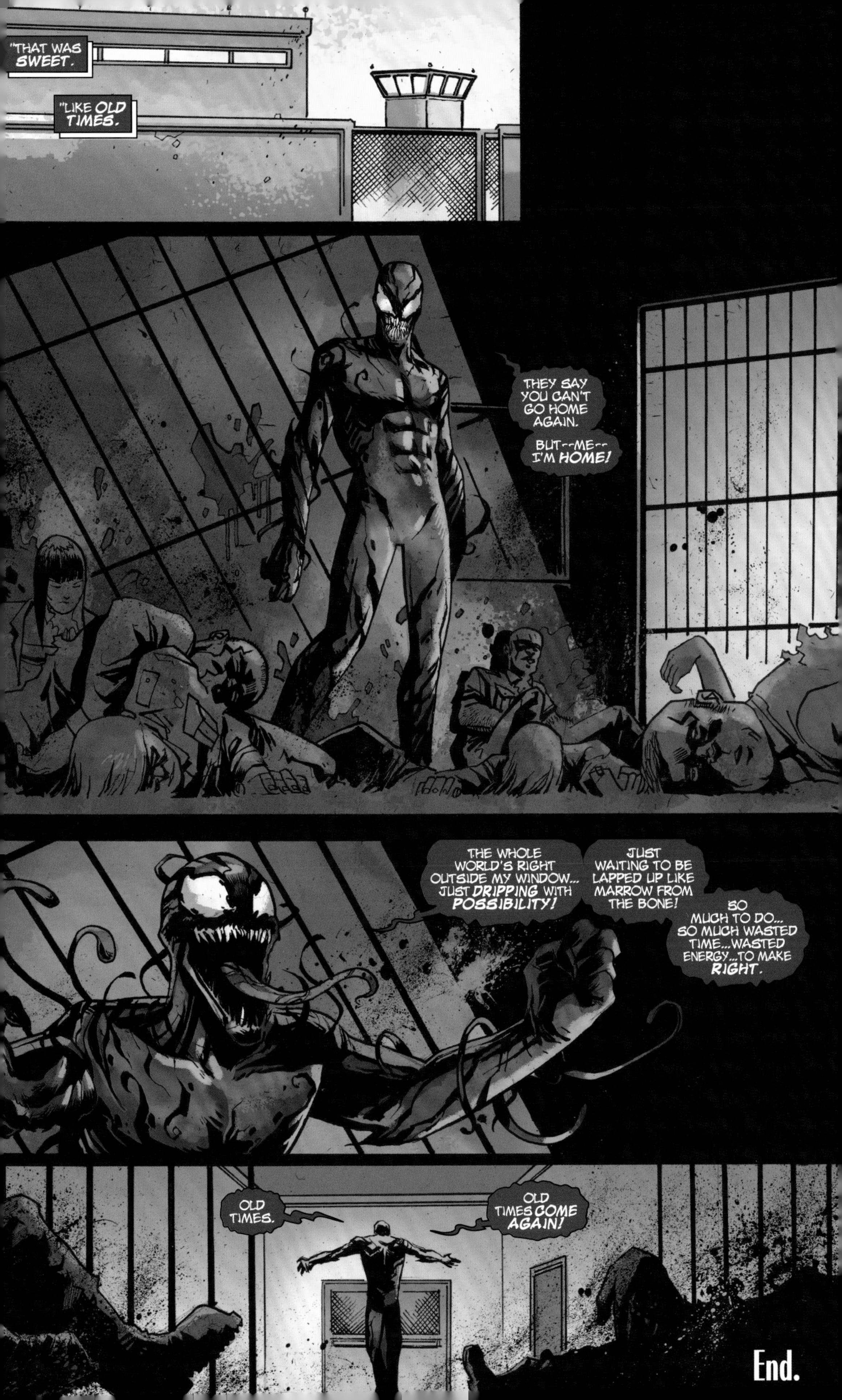
"THAT WAS SWEET.
"LIKE OLD TIMES.
THEY SAY YOU CAN'T GO HOME AGAIN.
BUT--ME--I'M HOME!
THE WHOLE WORLD'S RIGHT OUTSIDE MY WINDOW... JUST DRIPPING WITH POSSIBILITY!
JUST WAITING TO BE LAPPED UP LIKE MARROW FROM THE BONE!
SO MUCH TO DO... SO MUCH WASTED TIME...WASTED ENERGY...TO MAKE RIGHT.
OLD TIMES.
OLD TIMES COME AGAIN!
End.

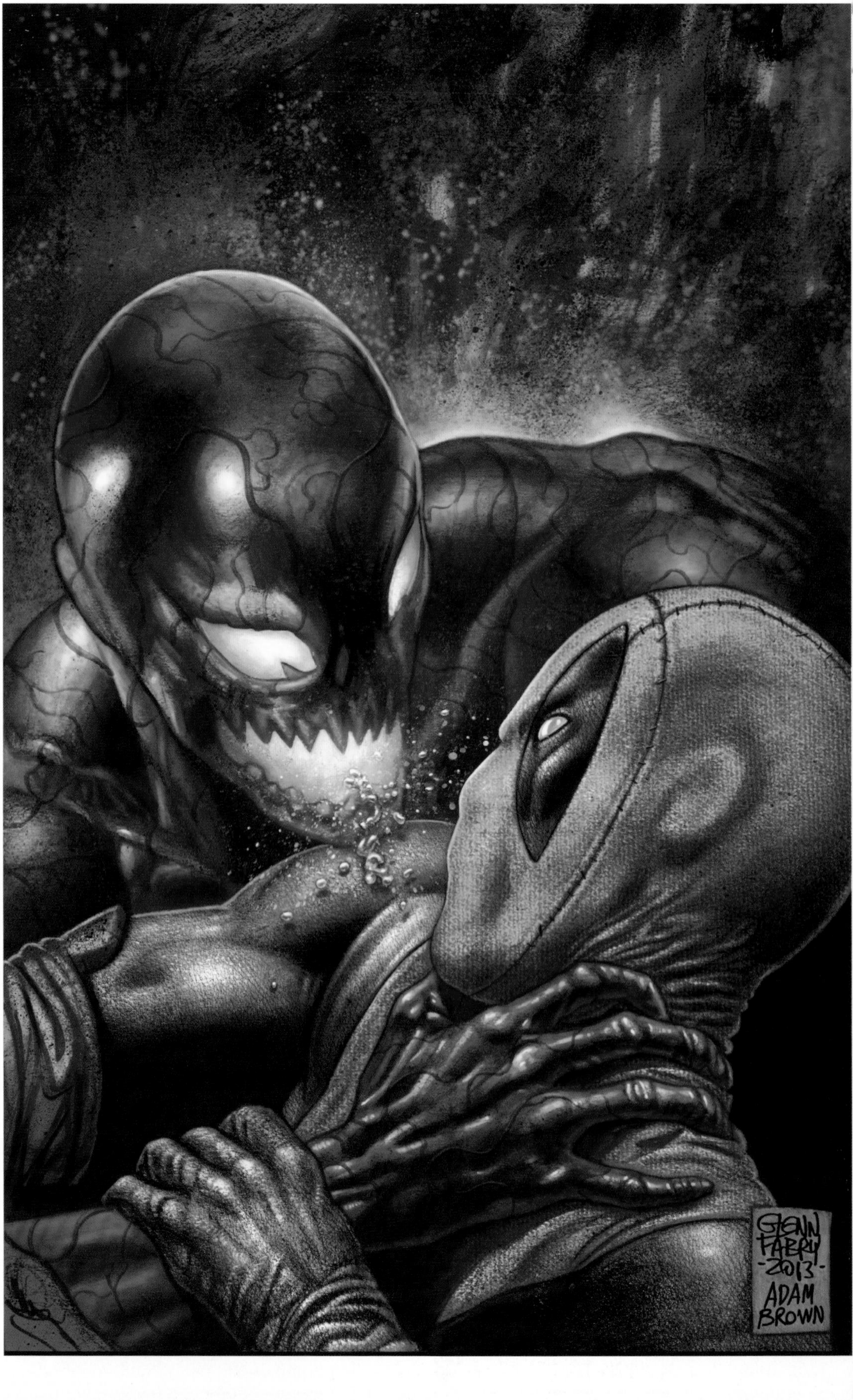
GLENN FABRY -2013- ADAM BROWN

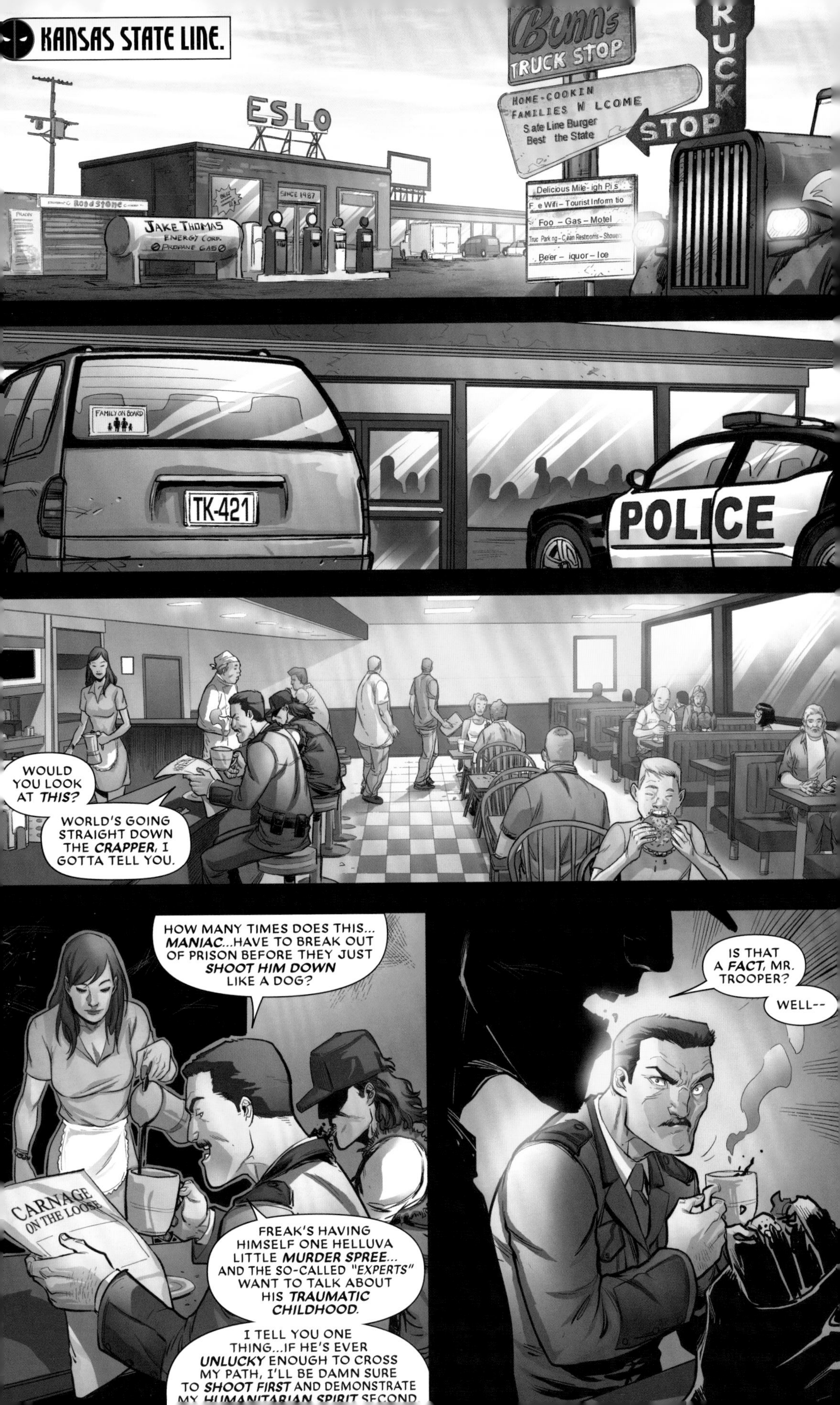
KANSAS STATE LINE.
Bunn's TRUCK STOP
HOME-COOKIN
FAMILIES W LCOME
Sate Line Burger
Best the State
TRUCK STOP
ESLO
JAKE THOMAS ENERGY CORP. PROPANE GAS
SINCE 1987
Delicious Mile- igh Pi s
F e Wifi – Tourist Inform tio
Foo – Gas – Motel
Beer – iquor – Ice
FAMILY ON BOARD
TK-421
POLICE
WOULD YOU LOOK AT *THIS?*
WORLD'S GOING STRAIGHT DOWN THE *CRAPPER,* I GOTTA TELL YOU.
HOW MANY TIMES DOES THIS... *MANIAC*...HAVE TO BREAK OUT OF PRISON BEFORE THEY JUST *SHOOT HIM DOWN* LIKE A DOG?
CARNAGE ON THE LOOSE
FREAK'S HAVING HIMSELF ONE HELLUVA LITTLE *MURDER SPREE*... AND THE SO-CALLED "*EXPERTS*" WANT TO TALK ABOUT HIS *TRAUMATIC CHILDHOOD.*
I TELL YOU ONE THING...IF HE'S EVER *UNLUCKY* ENOUGH TO CROSS MY PATH, I'LL BE DAMN SURE TO *SHOOT FIRST* AND DEMONSTRATE MY *HUMANITARIAN SPIRIT* SECOND.
IS THAT A *FACT*, MR. TROOPER?
WELL--

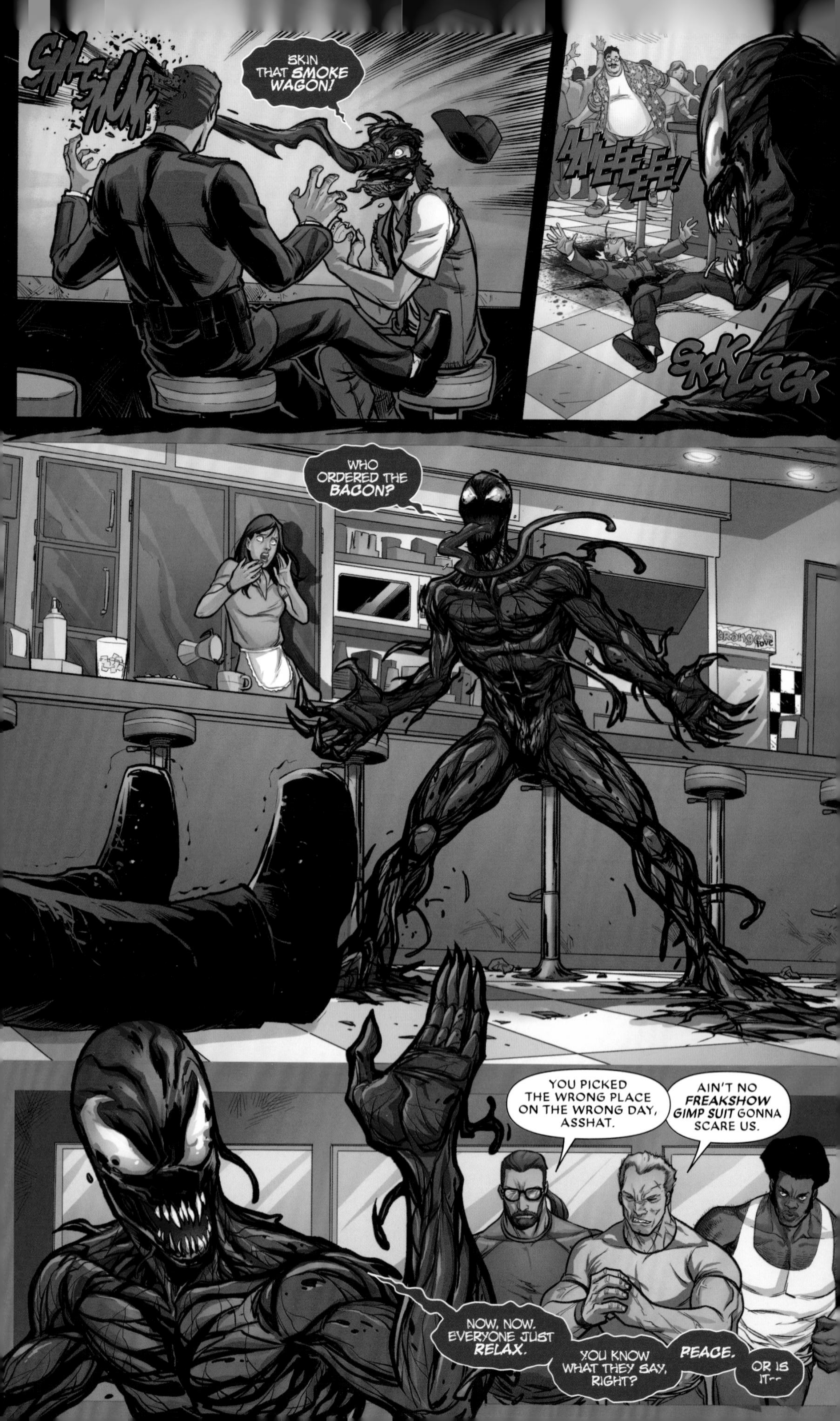
SH-SHUNK
SKIN THAT SMOKE WAGON!
AAIEEEEEEEE!
SKKLGGK
WHO ORDERED THE BACON?
YOU PICKED THE WRONG PLACE ON THE WRONG DAY, ASSHAT.
AIN'T NO FREAKSHOW GIMP SUIT GONNA SCARE US.
NOW, NOW. EVERYONE JUST RELAX.
YOU KNOW WHAT THEY SAY, RIGHT?
PEACE.
OR IS IT--

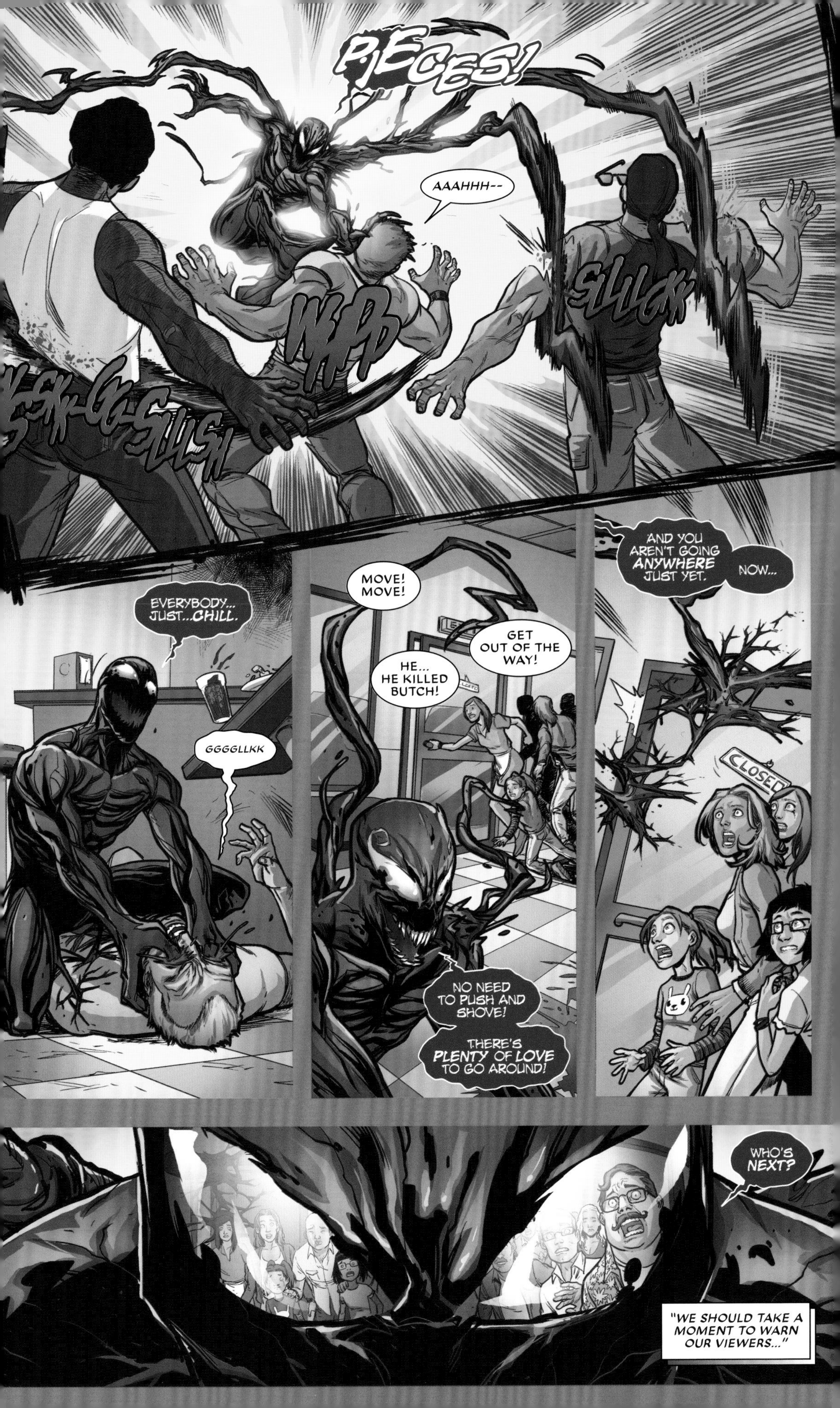
PIECES!
AAAHHH--
WAP
SLLLGK
SK-SK-GG-SLLSH
EVERYBODY... JUST...CHILL.
GGGGLLKK
MOVE! MOVE!
GET OUT OF THE WAY!
HE... HE KILLED BUTCH!
NO NEED TO PUSH AND SHOVE!
THERE'S PLENTY OF LOVE TO GO AROUND!
AND YOU AREN'T GOING ANYWHERE JUST YET.
NOW...
CLOSED
WHO'S NEXT?
"WE SHOULD TAKE A MOMENT TO WARN OUR VIEWERS..."

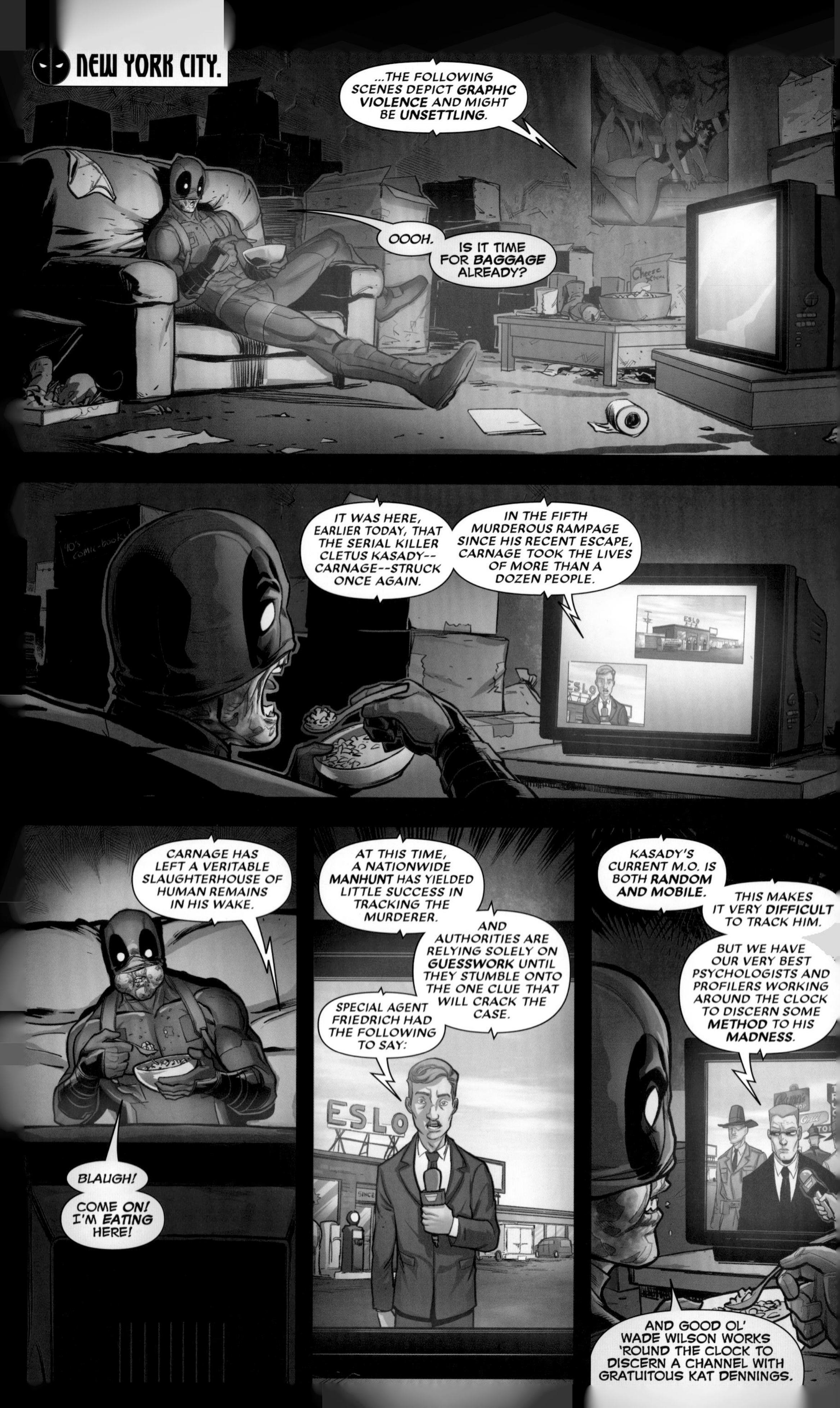
NEW YORK CITY.
...THE FOLLOWING SCENES DEPICT GRAPHIC VIOLENCE AND MIGHT BE UNSETTLING.
OOOH.
IS IT TIME FOR BAGGAGE ALREADY?
IT WAS HERE, EARLIER TODAY, THAT THE SERIAL KILLER CLETUS KASADY--CARNAGE--STRUCK ONCE AGAIN.
IN THE FIFTH MURDEROUS RAMPAGE SINCE HIS RECENT ESCAPE, CARNAGE TOOK THE LIVES OF MORE THAN A DOZEN PEOPLE.
CARNAGE HAS LEFT A VERITABLE SLAUGHTERHOUSE OF HUMAN REMAINS IN HIS WAKE.
BLAUGH!
COME ON! I'M EATING HERE!
AT THIS TIME, A NATIONWIDE MANHUNT HAS YIELDED LITTLE SUCCESS IN TRACKING THE MURDERER.
AND AUTHORITIES ARE RELYING SOLELY ON GUESSWORK UNTIL THEY STUMBLE ONTO THE ONE CLUE THAT WILL CRACK THE CASE.
SPECIAL AGENT FRIEDRICH HAD THE FOLLOWING TO SAY:
KASADY'S CURRENT M.O. IS BOTH RANDOM AND MOBILE.
THIS MAKES IT VERY DIFFICULT TO TRACK HIM.
BUT WE HAVE OUR VERY BEST PSYCHOLOGISTS AND PROFILERS WORKING AROUND THE CLOCK TO DISCERN SOME METHOD TO HIS MADNESS.
AND GOOD OL' WADE WILSON WORKS 'ROUND THE CLOCK TO DISCERN A CHANNEL WITH GRATUITOUS KAT DENNINGS.

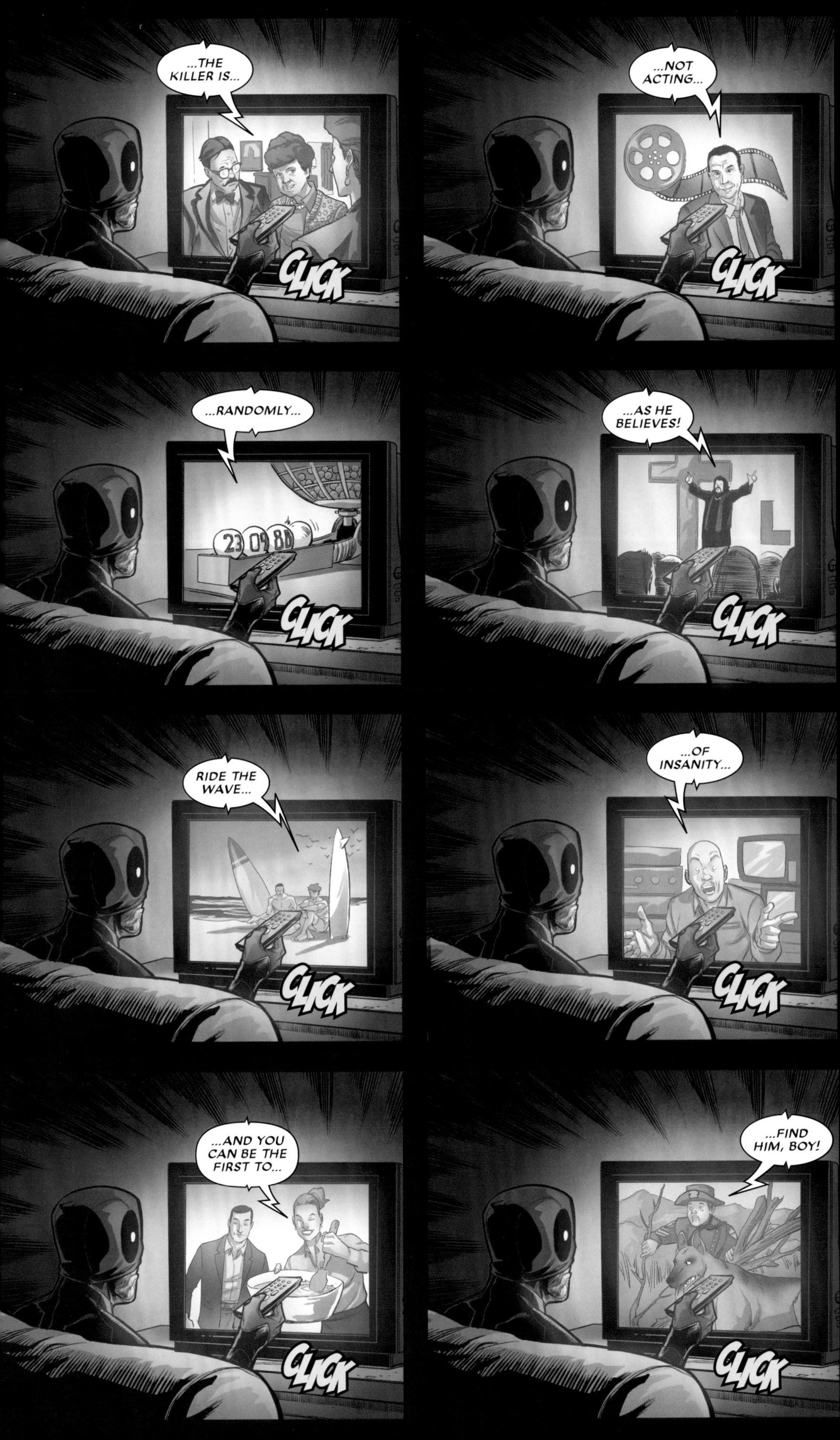
...THE KILLER IS...
CLICK
...NOT ACTING...
CLICK
...RANDOMLY...
CLICK
...AS HE BELIEVES!
CLICK
RIDE THE WAVE...
CLICK
...OF INSANITY...
CLICK
...AND YOU CAN BE THE FIRST TO...
CLICK
...FIND HIM, BOY!
CLICK

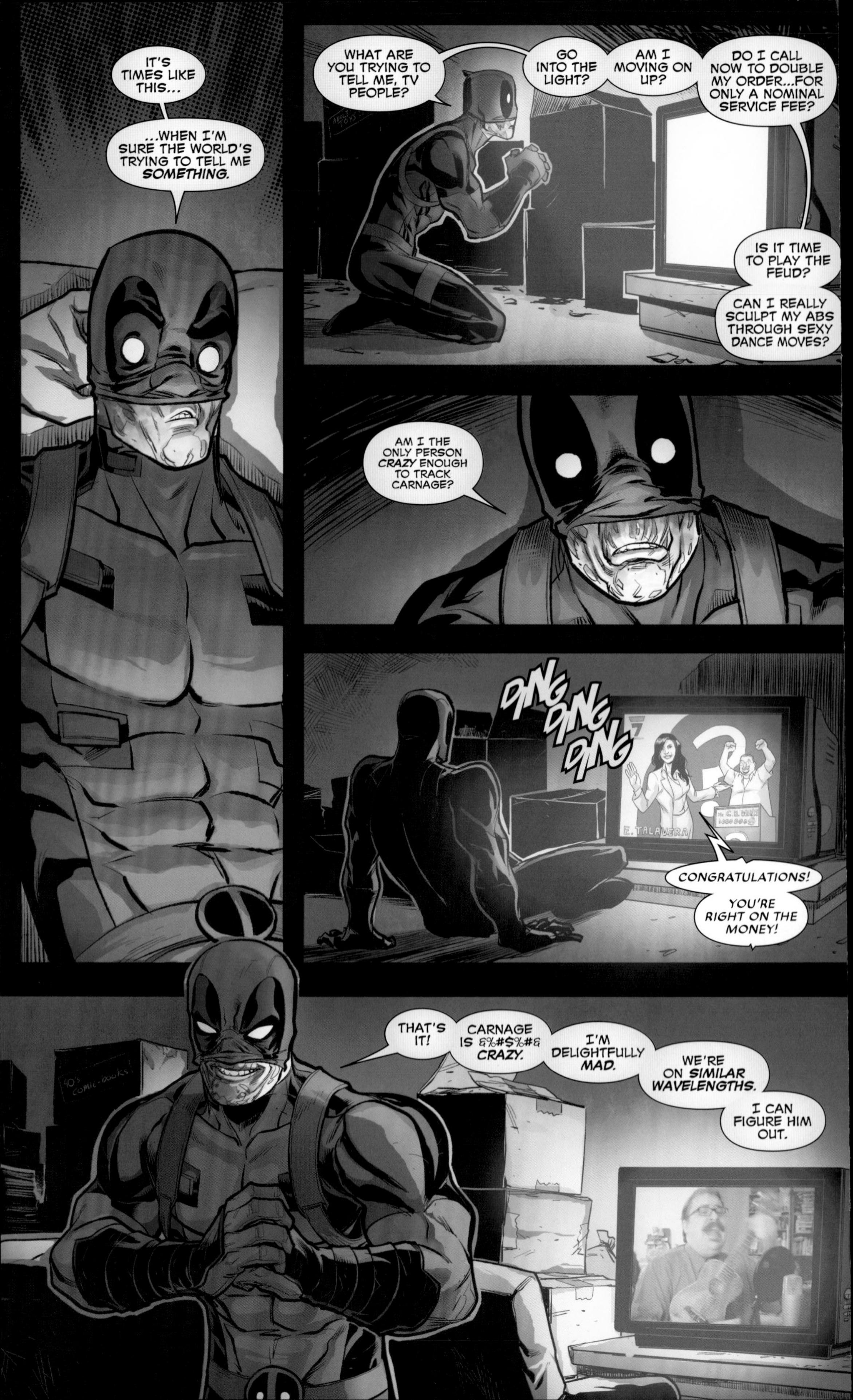

IT'S TIMES LIKE THIS...
...WHEN I'M SURE THE WORLD'S TRYING TO TELL ME SOMETHING.
WHAT ARE YOU TRYING TO TELL ME, TV PEOPLE?
GO INTO THE LIGHT?
AM I MOVING ON UP?
DO I CALL NOW TO DOUBLE MY ORDER...FOR ONLY A NOMINAL SERVICE FEE?
IS IT TIME TO PLAY THE FEUD?
CAN I REALLY SCULPT MY ABS THROUGH SEXY DANCE MOVES?
AM I THE ONLY PERSON CRAZY ENOUGH TO TRACK CARNAGE?
DING DING DING
E. TALAVERA
CONGRATULATIONS!
YOU'RE RIGHT ON THE MONEY!
THAT'S IT!
CARNAGE IS &%#$%#& CRAZY.
I'M DELIGHTFULLY MAD.
WE'RE ON SIMILAR WAVELENGTHS.
I CAN FIGURE HIM OUT.
90'S COMIC-BOOKS

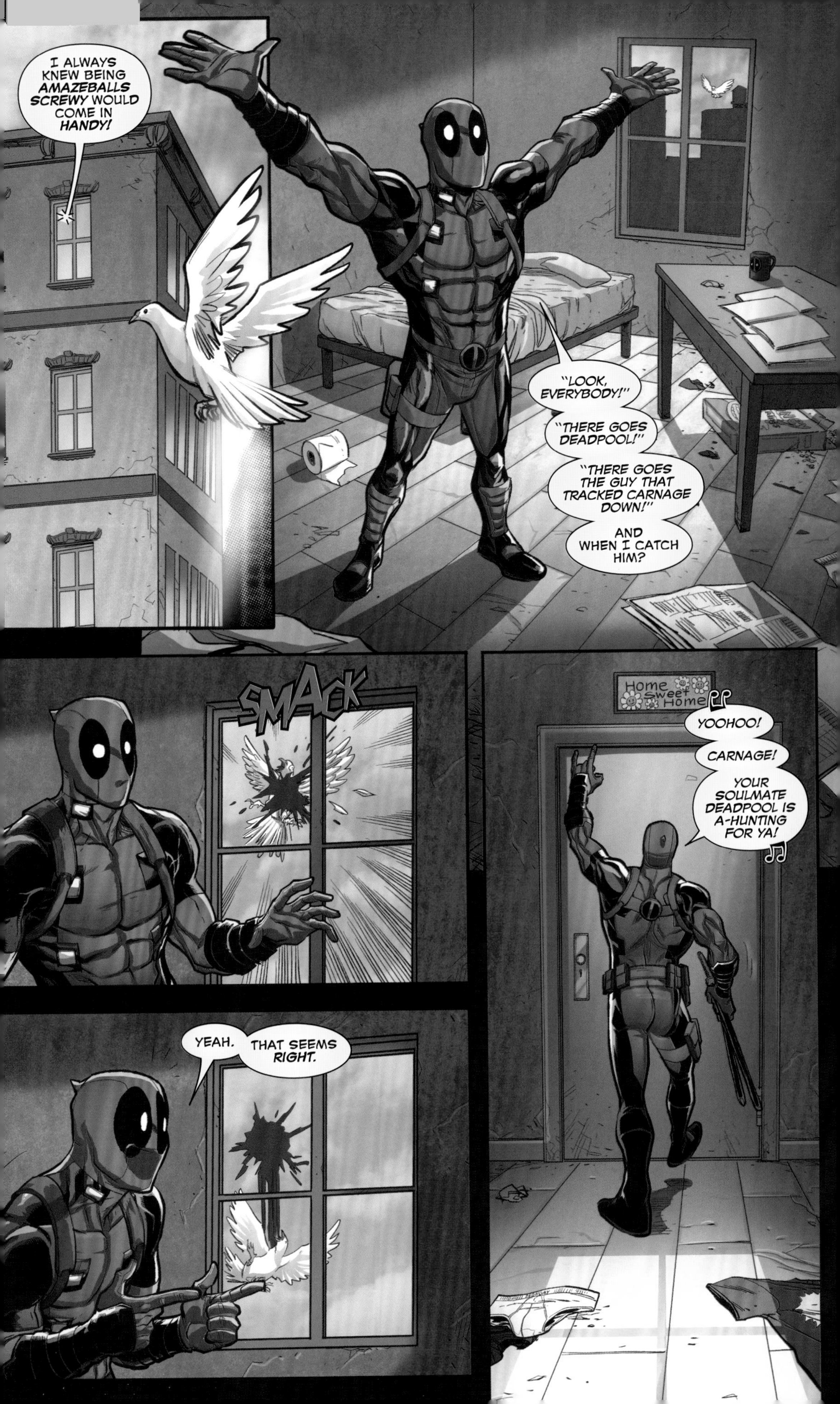
I ALWAYS KNEW BEING AMAZEBALLS SCREWY WOULD COME IN HANDY!
"LOOK, EVERYBODY!"
"THERE GOES DEADPOOL!"
"THERE GOES THE GUY THAT TRACKED CARNAGE DOWN!"
AND WHEN I CATCH HIM?
SMACK
YEAH.
THAT SEEMS RIGHT.
Home Sweet Home
YOOHOO!
CARNAGE!
YOUR SOULMATE DEADPOOL IS A-HUNTING FOR YA!

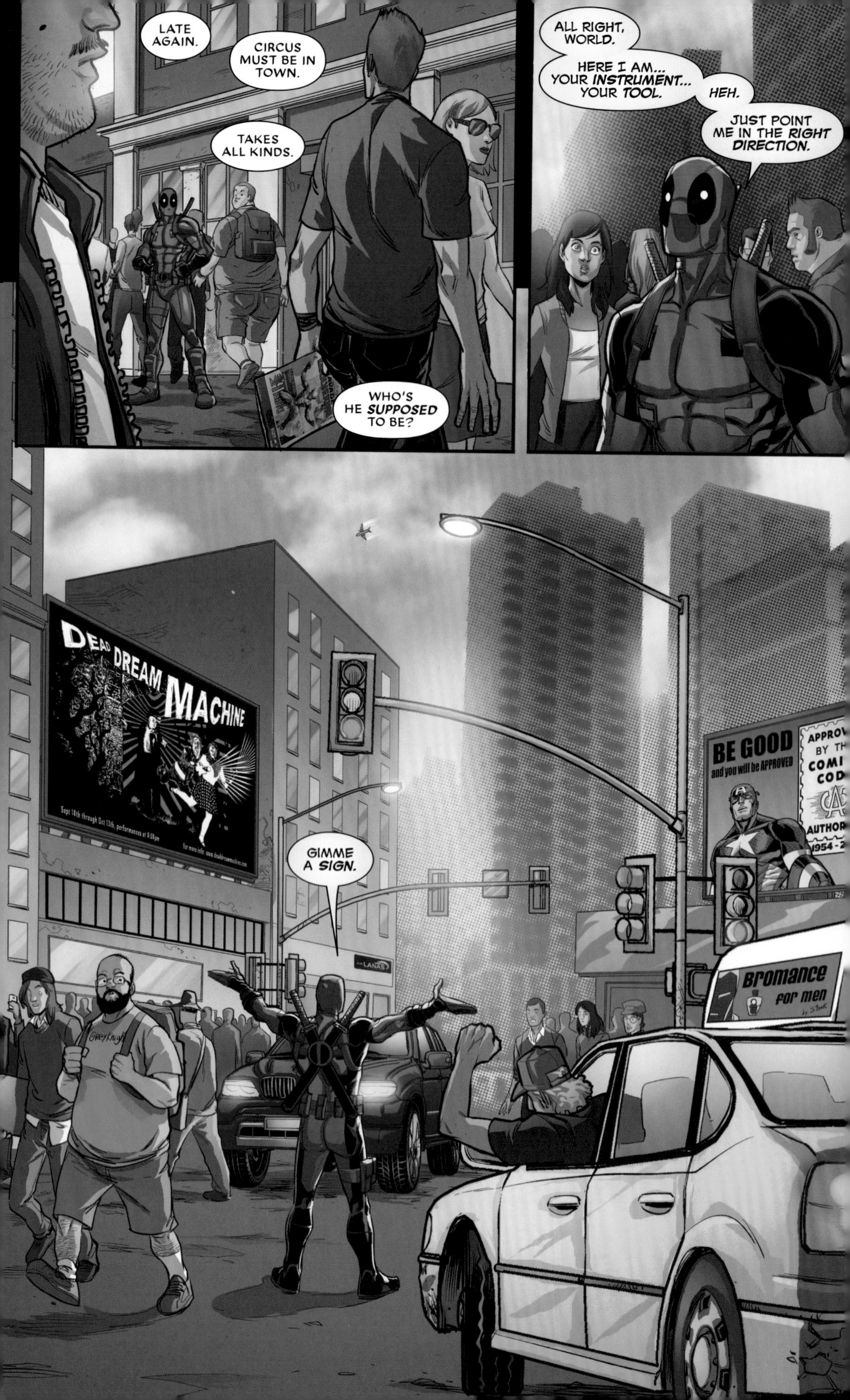
LATE AGAIN.
CIRCUS MUST BE IN TOWN.
TAKES ALL KINDS.
WHO'S HE *SUPPOSED* TO BE?
ALL RIGHT, WORLD.
HERE I AM... YOUR *INSTRUMENT*... YOUR *TOOL*.
HEH.
JUST POINT ME IN THE *RIGHT DIRECTION*.
DEAD DREAM MACHINE
GIMME A *SIGN*.
BE GOOD
and you will be APPROVED
Bromance
for men

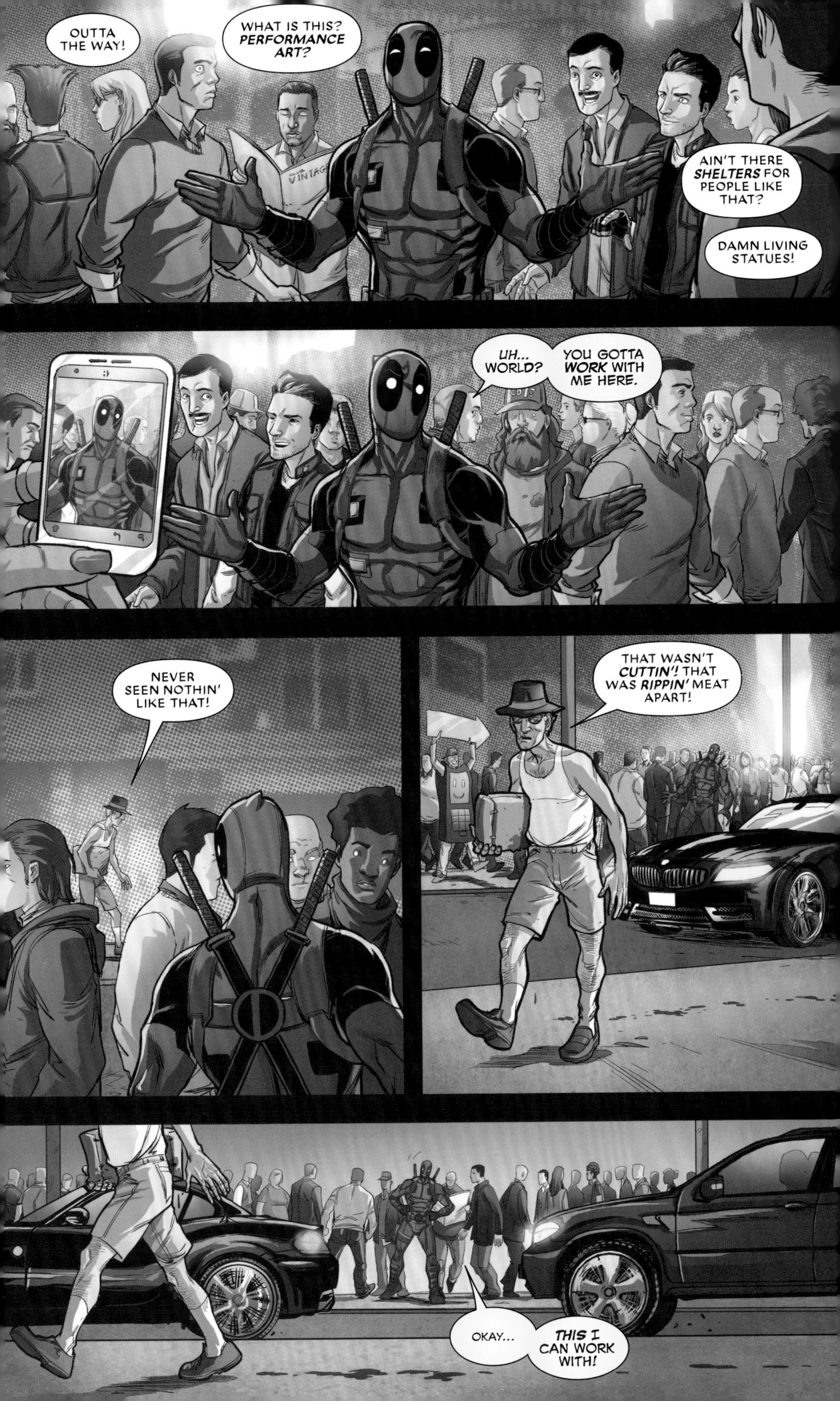
OUTTA THE WAY!
WHAT IS THIS? PERFORMANCE ART?
VINTAGE
AIN'T THERE SHELTERS FOR PEOPLE LIKE THAT?
DAMN LIVING STATUES!
UH... WORLD?
YOU GOTTA WORK WITH ME HERE.
NEVER SEEN NOTHIN' LIKE THAT!
THAT WASN'T CUTTIN'! THAT WAS RIPPIN' MEAT APART!
OKAY...
THIS I CAN WORK WITH!

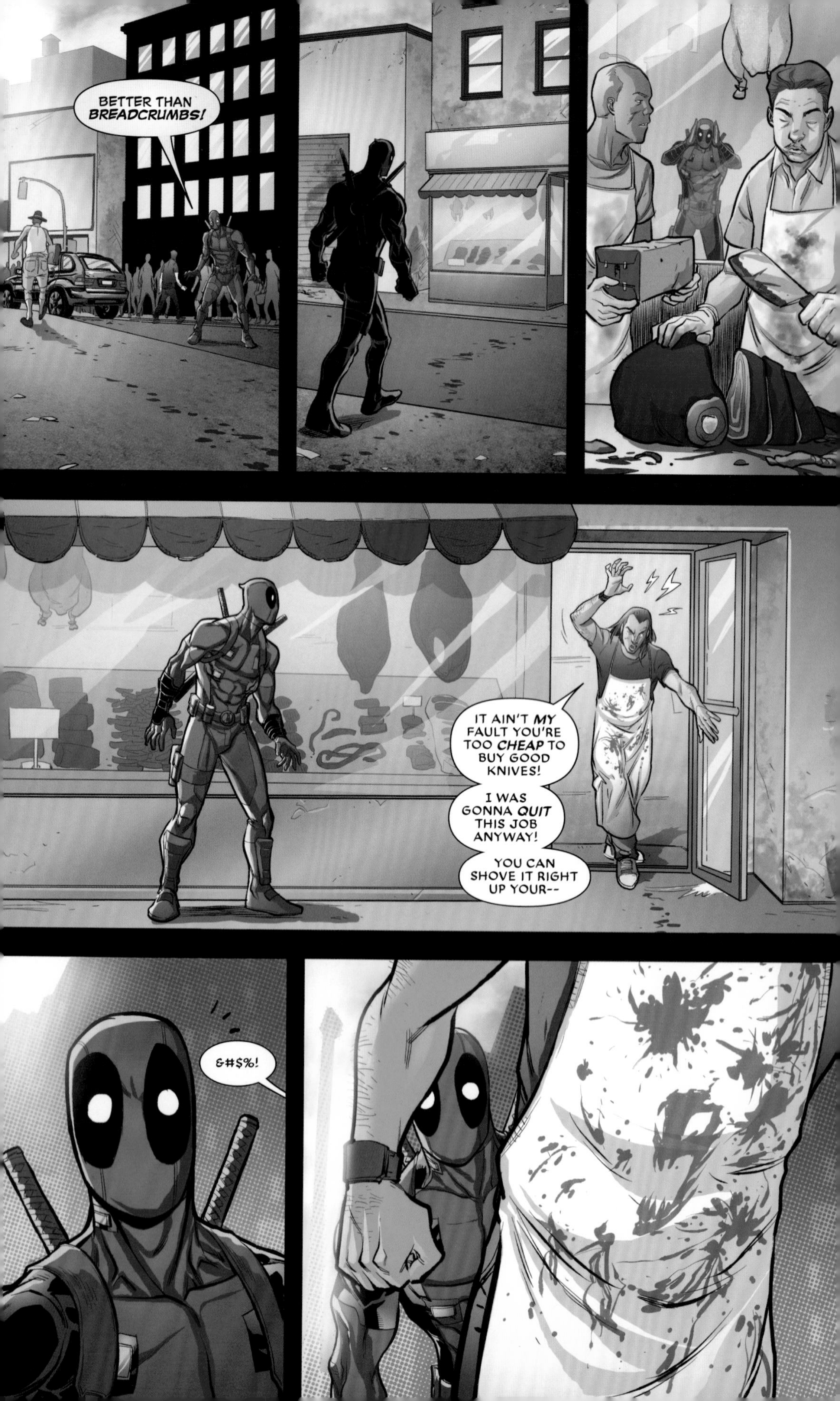
BETTER THAN BREADCRUMBS!
IT AIN'T MY FAULT YOU'RE TOO CHEAP TO BUY GOOD KNIVES!
I WAS GONNA QUIT THIS JOB ANYWAY!
YOU CAN SHOVE IT RIGHT UP YOUR--
&#$%!

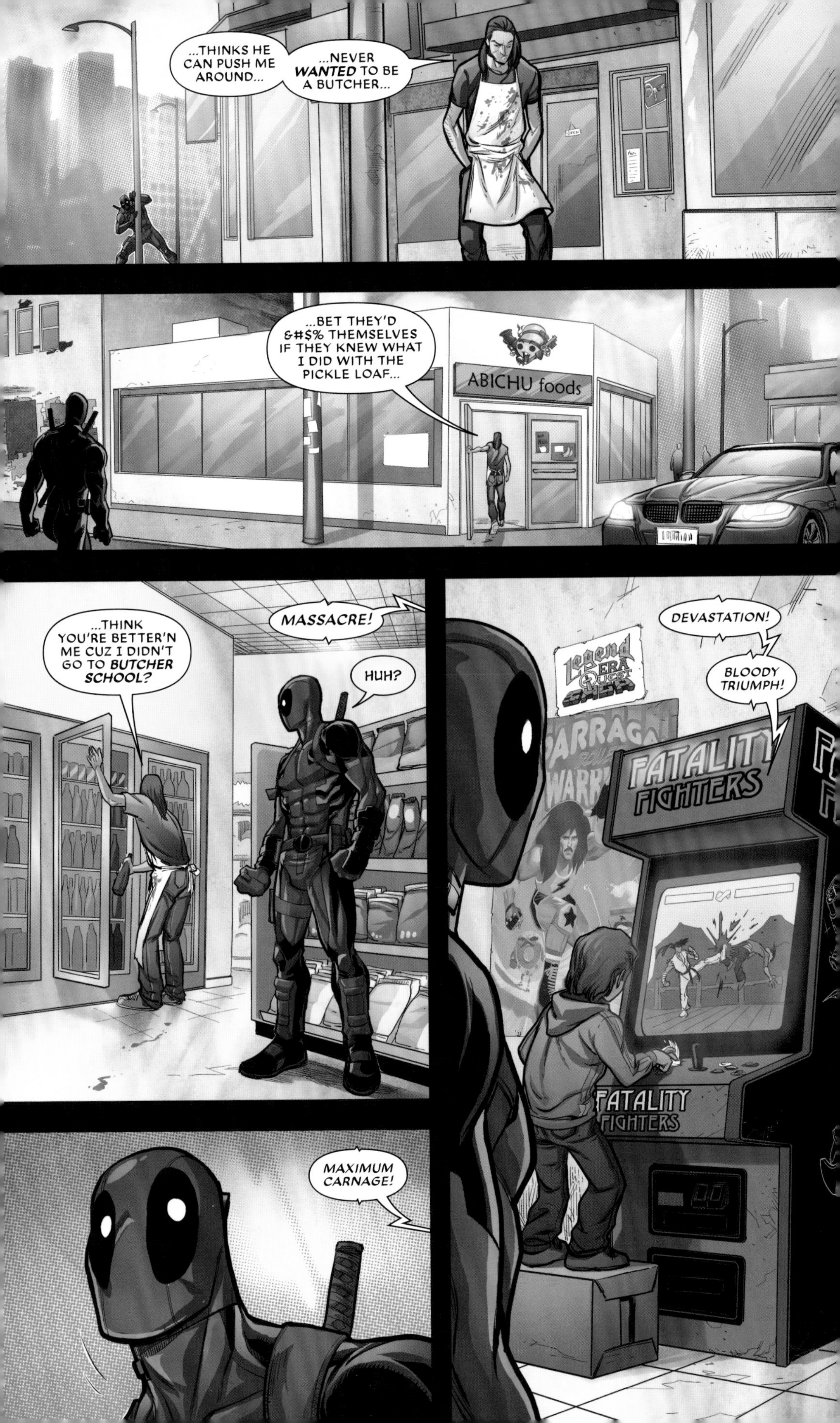
...THINKS HE CAN PUSH ME AROUND...
...NEVER *WANTED* TO BE A BUTCHER...
...BET THEY'D &#$% THEMSELVES IF THEY KNEW WHAT I DID WITH THE PICKLE LOAF...
ABICHU foods
...THINK YOU'RE BETTER'N ME CUZ I DIDN'T GO TO *BUTCHER SCHOOL?*
MASSACRE!
HUH?
DEVASTATION!
BLOODY TRIUMPH!
FATALITY FIGHTERS
FATALITY FIGHTERS
MAXIMUM CARNAGE!

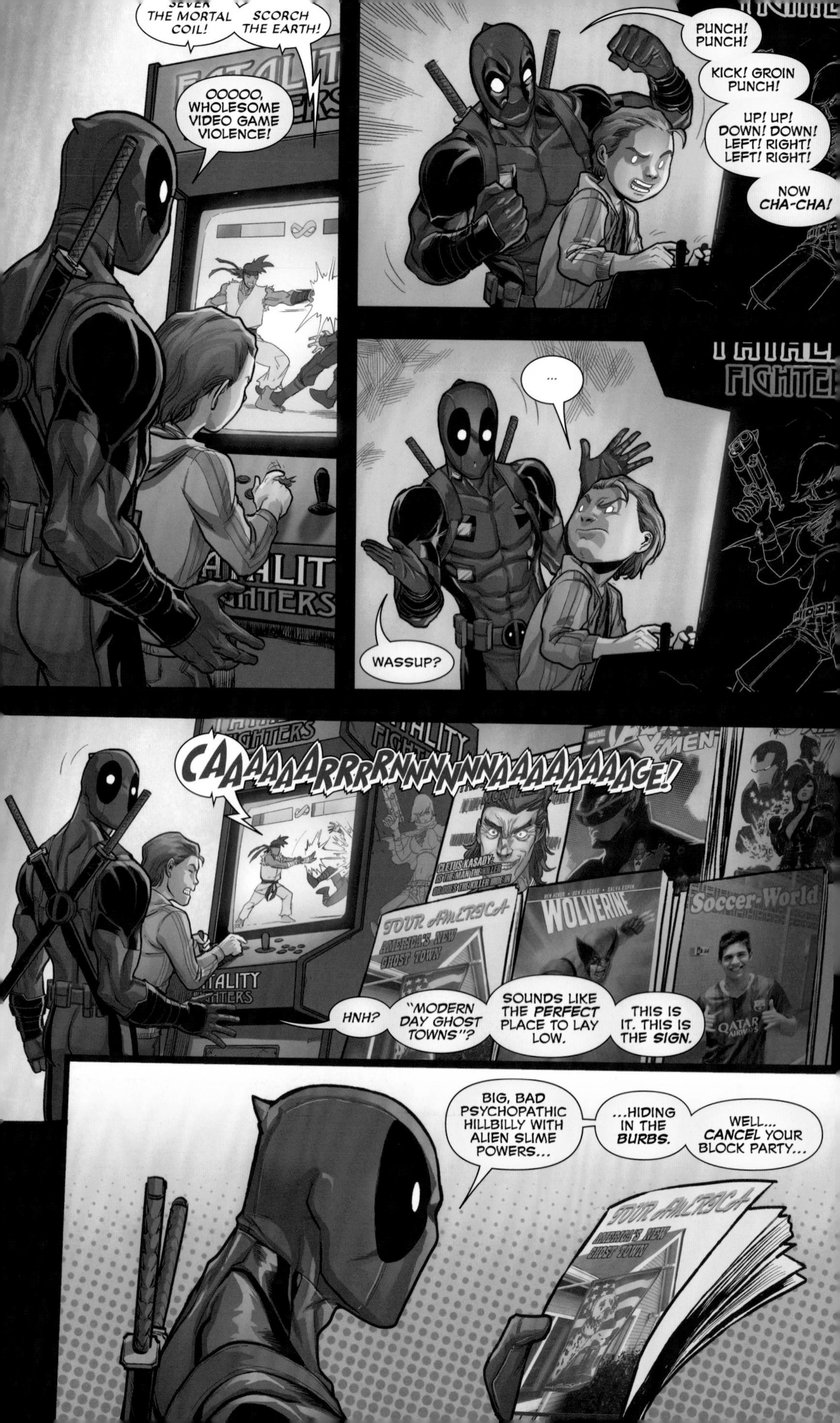
SEVER THE MORTAL COIL!
SCORCH THE EARTH!
OOOOO, WHOLESOME VIDEO GAME VIOLENCE!
FATALITY FIGHTERS
PUNCH! PUNCH!
KICK! GROIN PUNCH!
UP! UP! DOWN! DOWN! LEFT! RIGHT! LEFT! RIGHT!
NOW CHA-CHA!
...
WASSUP?
CAAAAAARRRRNNNNNNAAAAAAAAAGE!
WOLVERINE
Soccer-World
YOUR AMERICA
AMERICA'S NEW GHOST TOWN
HNH?
"MODERN DAY GHOST TOWNS"?
SOUNDS LIKE THE PERFECT PLACE TO LAY LOW.
THIS IS IT. THIS IS THE SIGN.
BIG, BAD PSYCHOPATHIC HILLBILLY WITH ALIEN SLIME POWERS...
...HIDING IN THE BURBS.
WELL... CANCEL YOUR BLOCK PARTY...

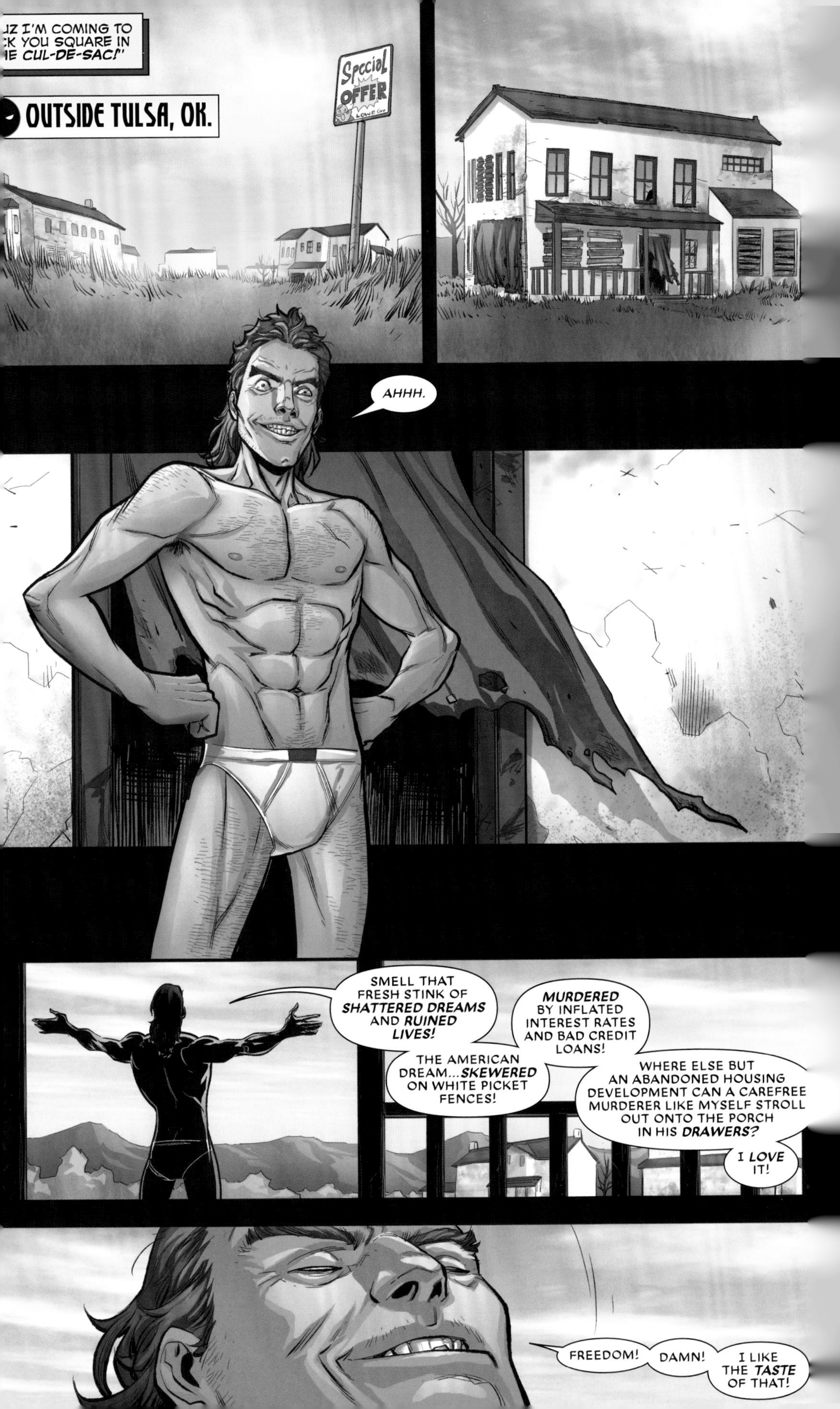

…UZ I'M COMING TO …CK YOU SQUARE IN …E CUL-DE-SAC!"
OUTSIDE TULSA, OK.
Special OFFER
AHHH.
SMELL THAT FRESH STINK OF SHATTERED DREAMS AND RUINED LIVES!
MURDERED BY INFLATED INTEREST RATES AND BAD CREDIT LOANS!
THE AMERICAN DREAM... SKEWERED ON WHITE PICKET FENCES!
WHERE ELSE BUT AN ABANDONED HOUSING DEVELOPMENT CAN A CAREFREE MURDERER LIKE MYSELF STROLL OUT ONTO THE PORCH IN HIS DRAWERS?
I LOVE IT!
FREEDOM!
DAMN!
I LIKE THE TASTE OF THAT!

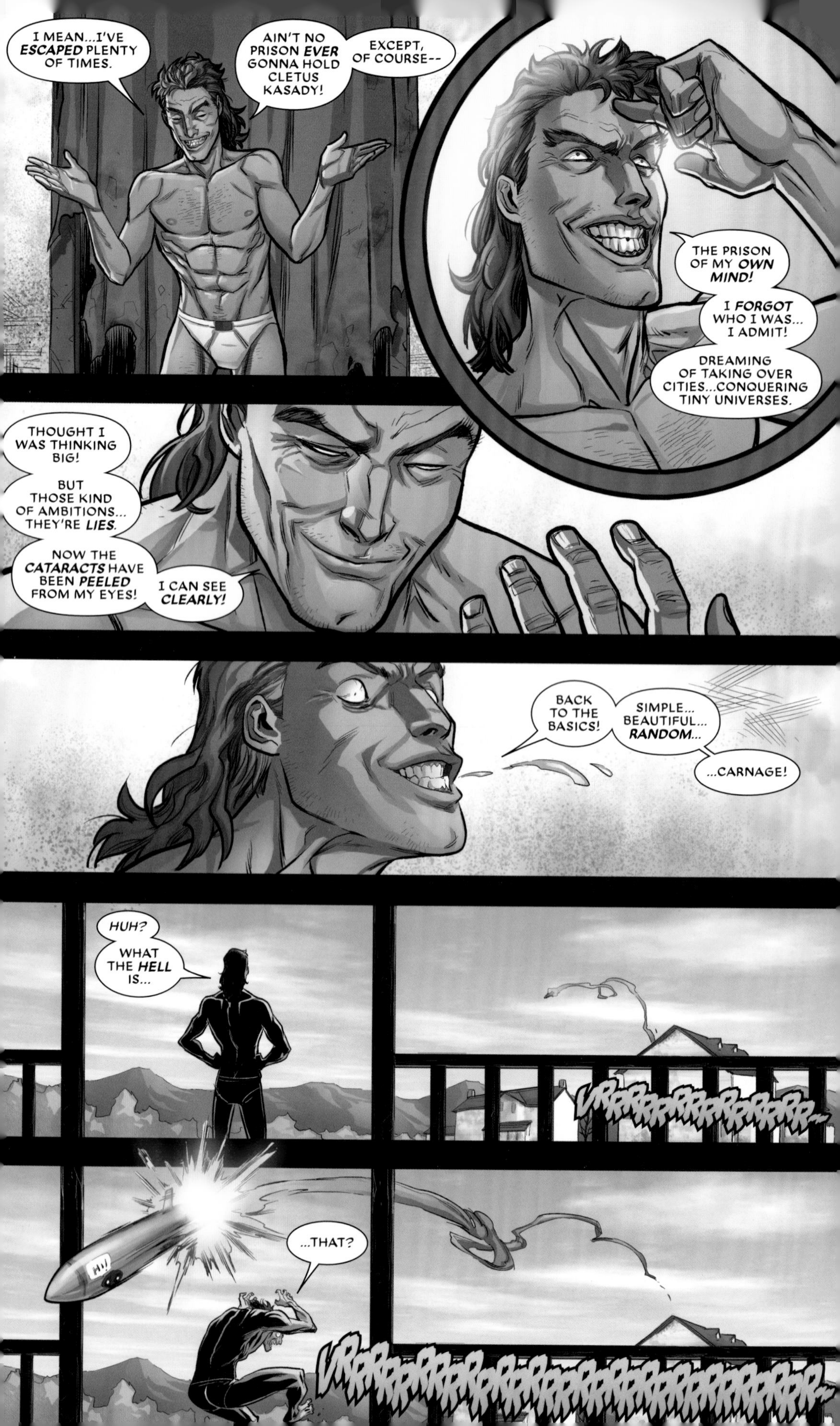
I MEAN...I'VE ESCAPED PLENTY OF TIMES.
AIN'T NO PRISON EVER GONNA HOLD CLETUS KASADY!
EXCEPT, OF COURSE--
THE PRISON OF MY OWN MIND!
I FORGOT WHO I WAS... I ADMIT!
DREAMING OF TAKING OVER CITIES...CONQUERING TINY UNIVERSES.
THOUGHT I WAS THINKING BIG!
BUT THOSE KIND OF AMBITIONS... THEY'RE LIES.
NOW THE CATARACTS HAVE BEEN PEELED FROM MY EYES!
I CAN SEE CLEARLY!
BACK TO THE BASICS!
SIMPLE... BEAUTIFUL... RANDOM...
...CARNAGE!
HUH?
WHAT THE HELL IS...
VRRRRRRRRRRRRRRRR--
...THAT?
HI!
VRRRRRRRRRRRRRRRRRRRRRRRRRRRRRRRRRRR--

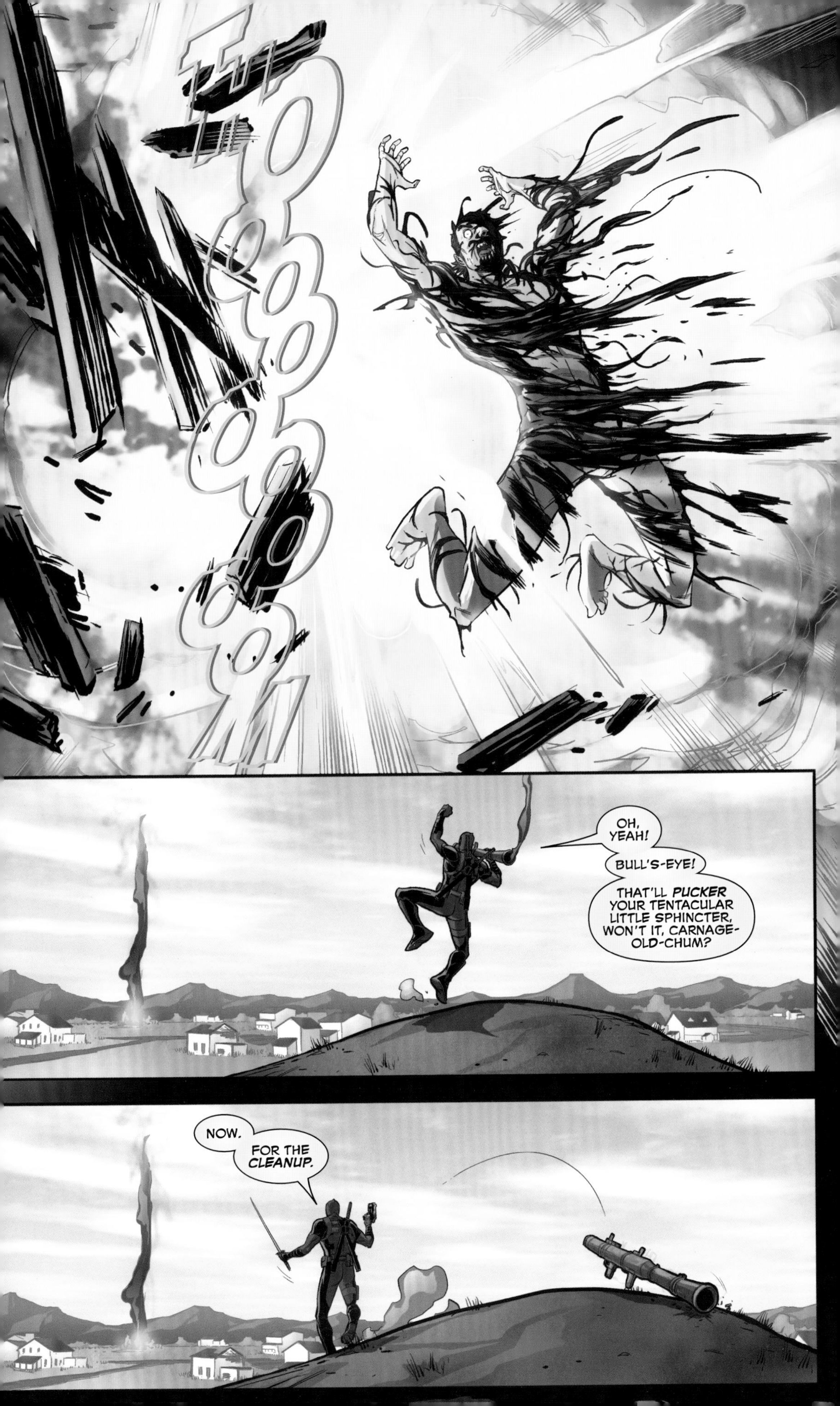

FOOOOOOOOM
OH, YEAH!
BULL'S-EYE!
THAT'LL *PUCKER* YOUR TENTACULAR LITTLE SPHINCTER, WON'T IT, CARNAGE-OLD-CHUM?
NOW.
FOR THE *CLEANUP.*

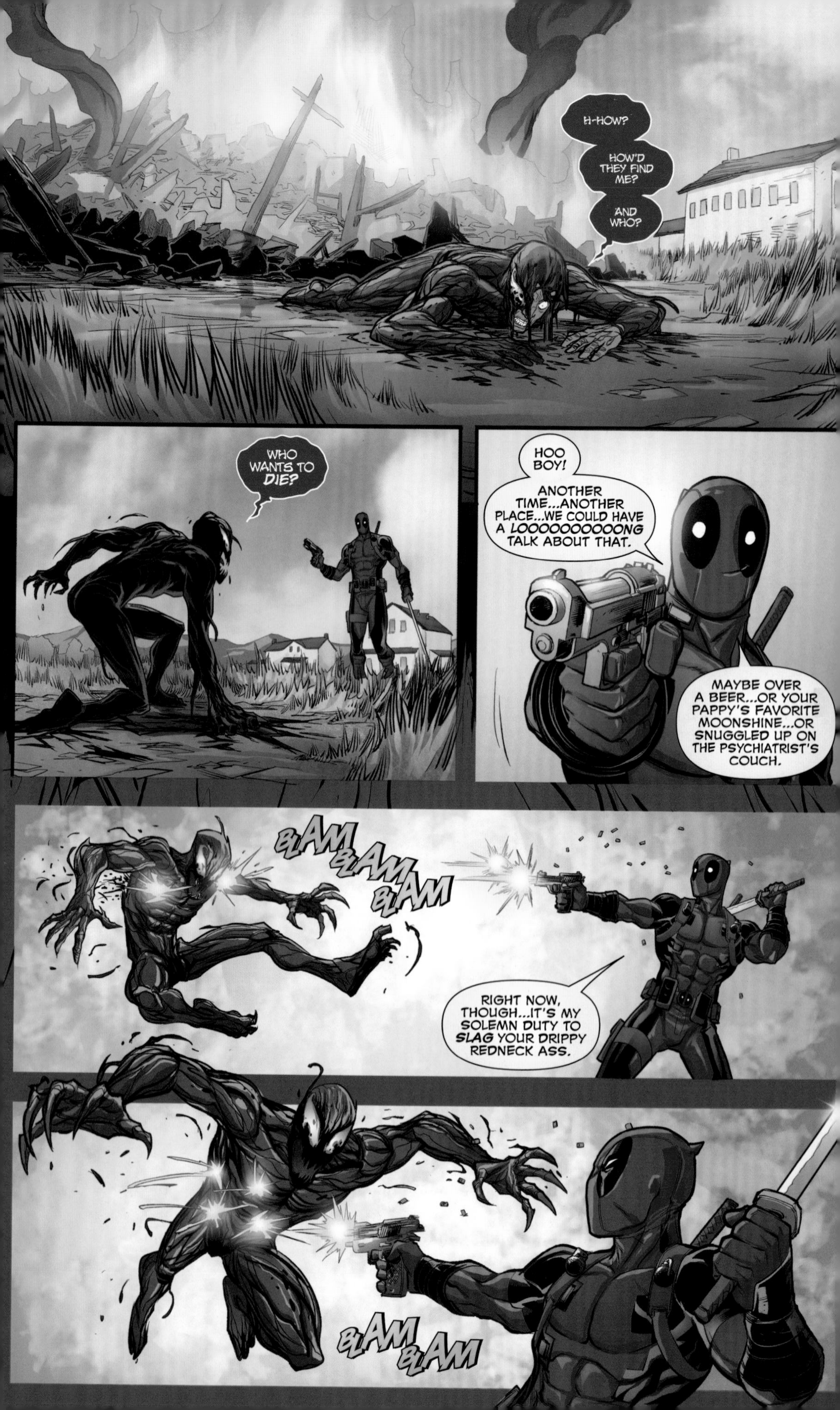
H-HOW?
HOW'D THEY FIND ME?
AND WHO?
WHO WANTS TO DIE?
HOO BOY!
ANOTHER TIME...ANOTHER PLACE...WE COULD HAVE A LOOOOOOOOOONG TALK ABOUT THAT.
MAYBE OVER A BEER...OR YOUR PAPPY'S FAVORITE MOONSHINE...OR SNUGGLED UP ON THE PSYCHIATRIST'S COUCH.
BLAM BLAM BLAM
RIGHT NOW, THOUGH...IT'S MY SOLEMN DUTY TO SLAG YOUR DRIPPY REDNECK ASS.
BLAM BLAM

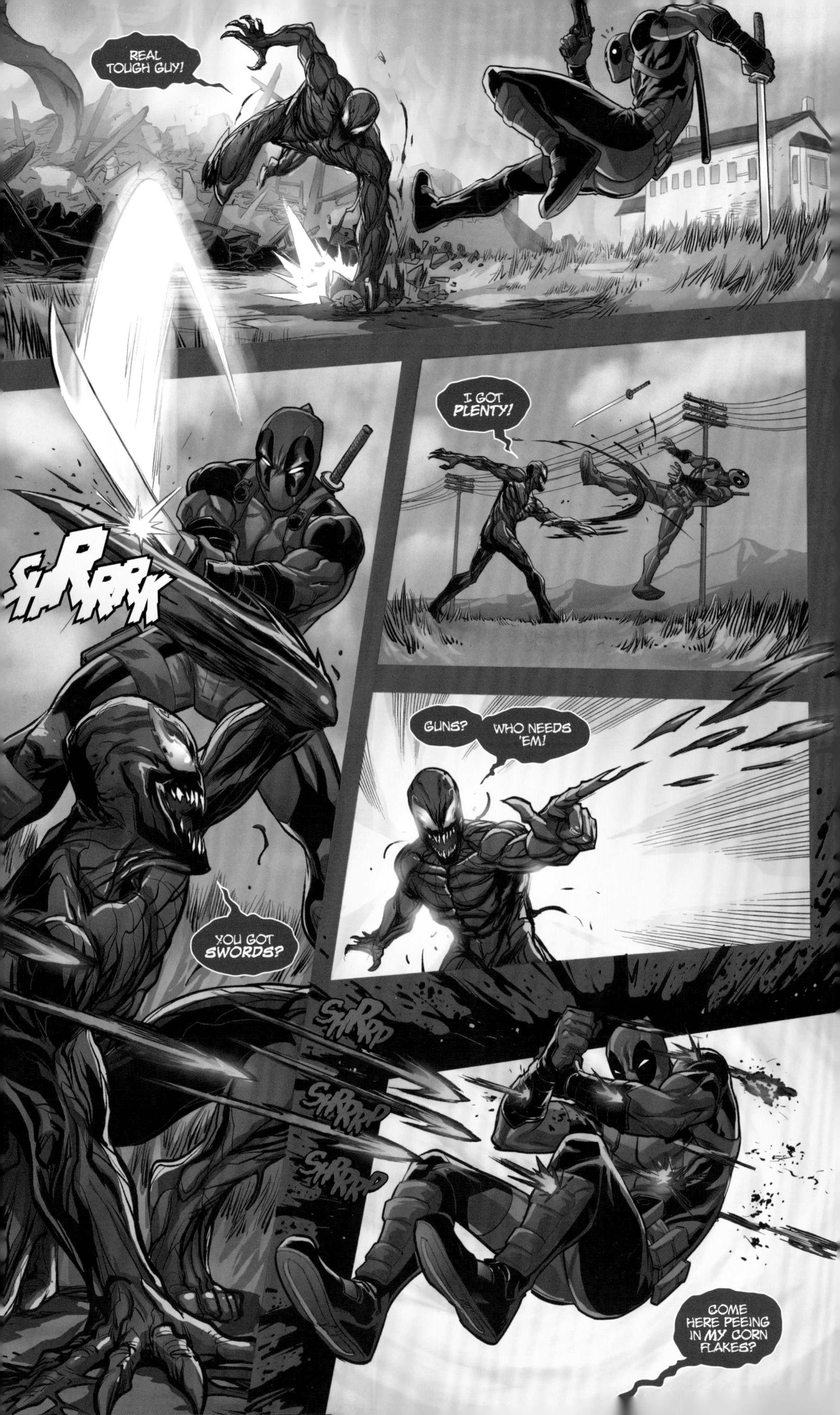
REAL TOUGH GUY!
SHRRRK
YOU GOT SWORDS?
I GOT PLENTY!
GUNS?
WHO NEEDS 'EM!
SHRRP
SHRRRP
SHRRRP
COME HERE PEEING IN MY CORN FLAKES?

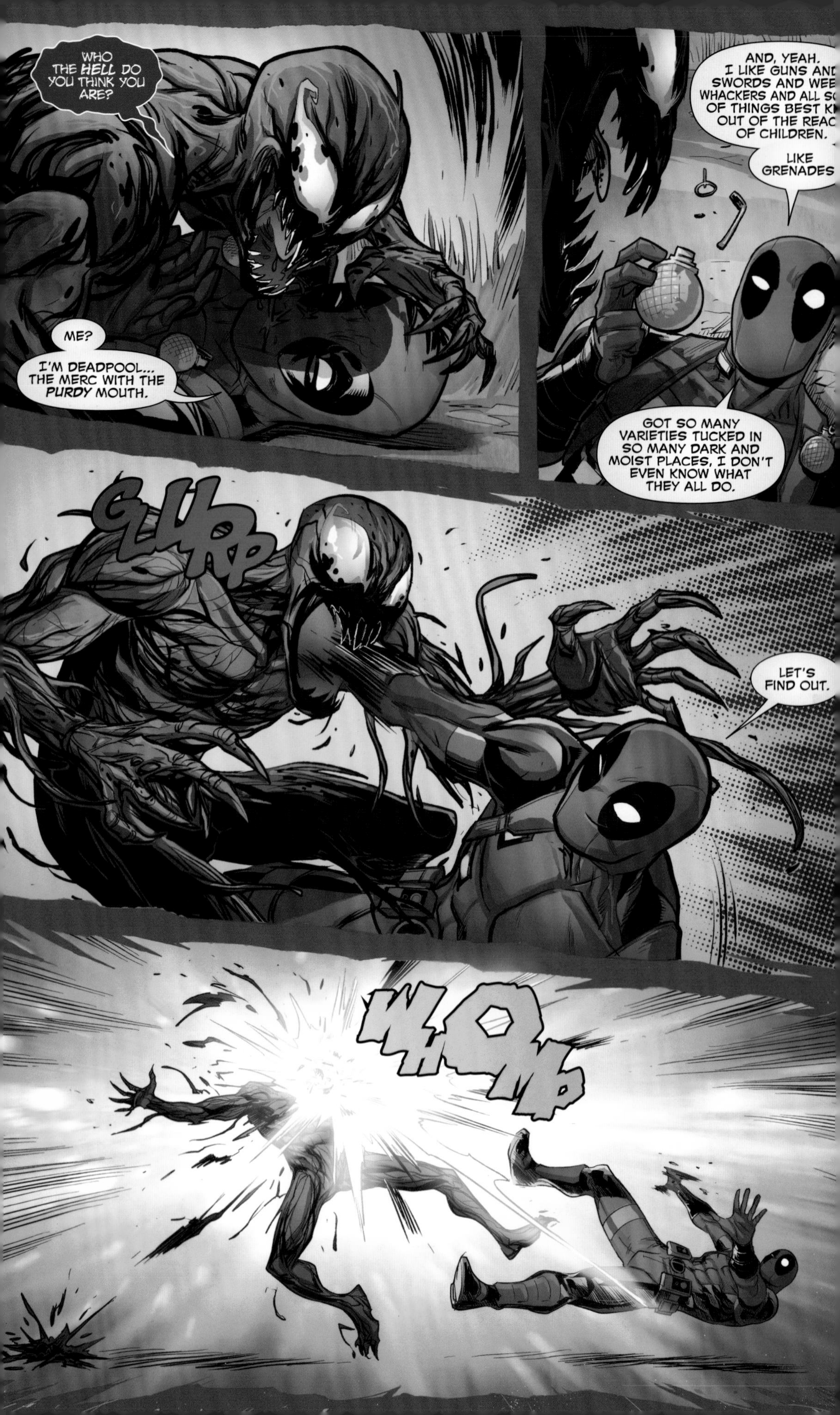
WHO THE HELL DO YOU THINK YOU ARE?
ME?
I'M DEADPOOL... THE MERC WITH THE PURDY MOUTH.
AND, YEAH. I LIKE GUNS AND SWORDS AND WEE WHACKERS AND ALL S OF THINGS BEST K OUT OF THE REAC OF CHILDREN.
LIKE GRENADES
GOT SO MANY VARIETIES TUCKED IN SO MANY DARK AND MOIST PLACES, I DON'T EVEN KNOW WHAT THEY ALL DO.
GLURP
LET'S FIND OUT.
WHOMB

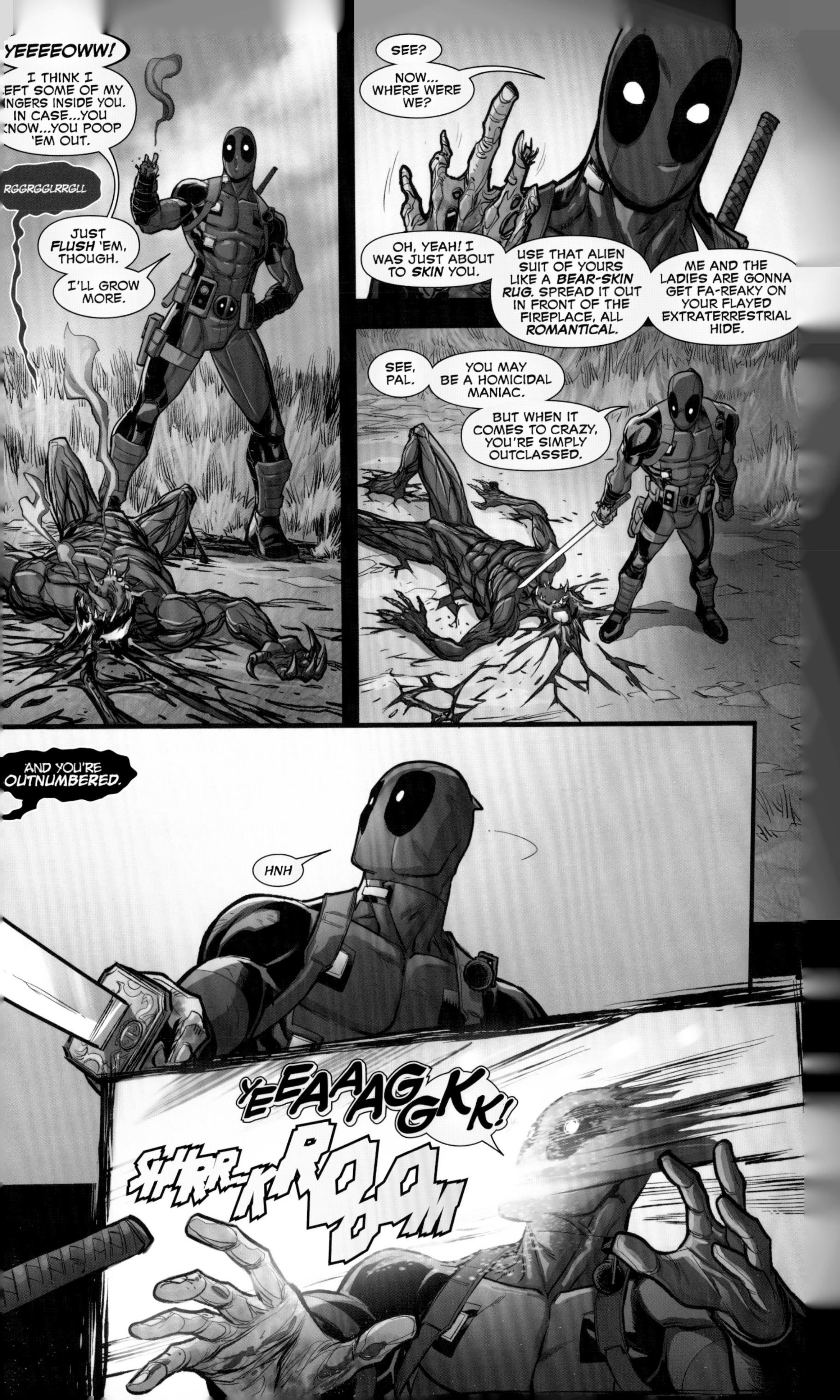

YEEEEOWW!
I THINK I EFT SOME OF MY NGERS INSIDE YOU. IN CASE...YOU NOW...YOU POOP 'EM OUT.
RGGRGGLRRGLL
JUST FLUSH 'EM, THOUGH.
I'LL GROW MORE.
SEE?
NOW... WHERE WERE WE?
OH, YEAH! I WAS JUST ABOUT TO SKIN YOU.
USE THAT ALIEN SUIT OF YOURS LIKE A BEAR-SKIN RUG. SPREAD IT OUT IN FRONT OF THE FIREPLACE, ALL ROMANTICAL.
ME AND THE LADIES ARE GONNA GET FA-REAKY ON YOUR FLAYED EXTRATERRESTRIAL HIDE.
SEE, PAL.
YOU MAY BE A HOMICIDAL MANIAC.
BUT WHEN IT COMES TO CRAZY, YOU'RE SIMPLY OUTCLASSED.
AND YOU'RE OUTNUMBERED.
HNH
YEEAAAGGKKK!
SHRR-KROOM

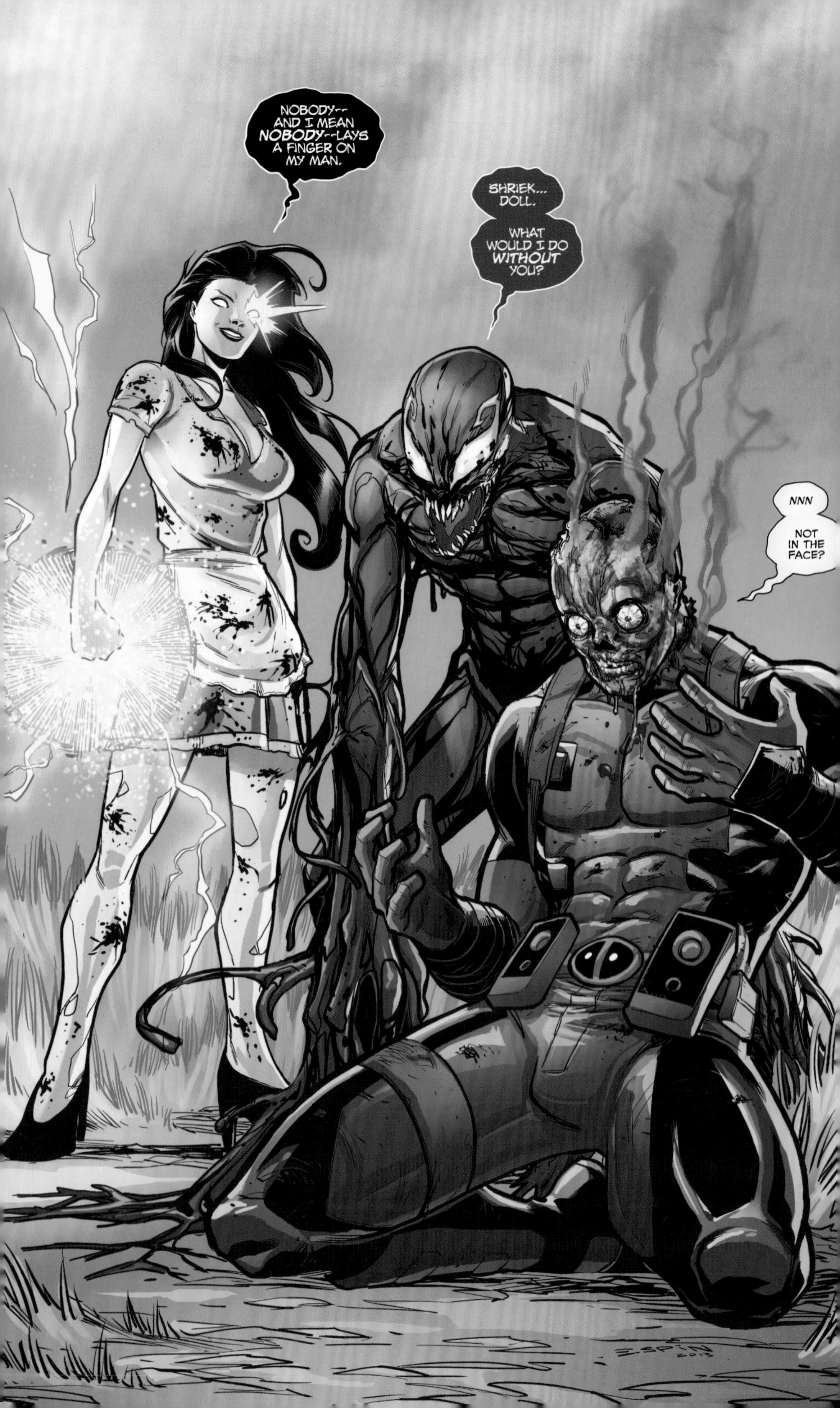
NOBODY-- AND I MEAN NOBODY--LAYS A FINGER ON MY MAN.
SHRIEK... DOLL.
WHAT WOULD I DO WITHOUT YOU?
NNN
NOT IN THE FACE?

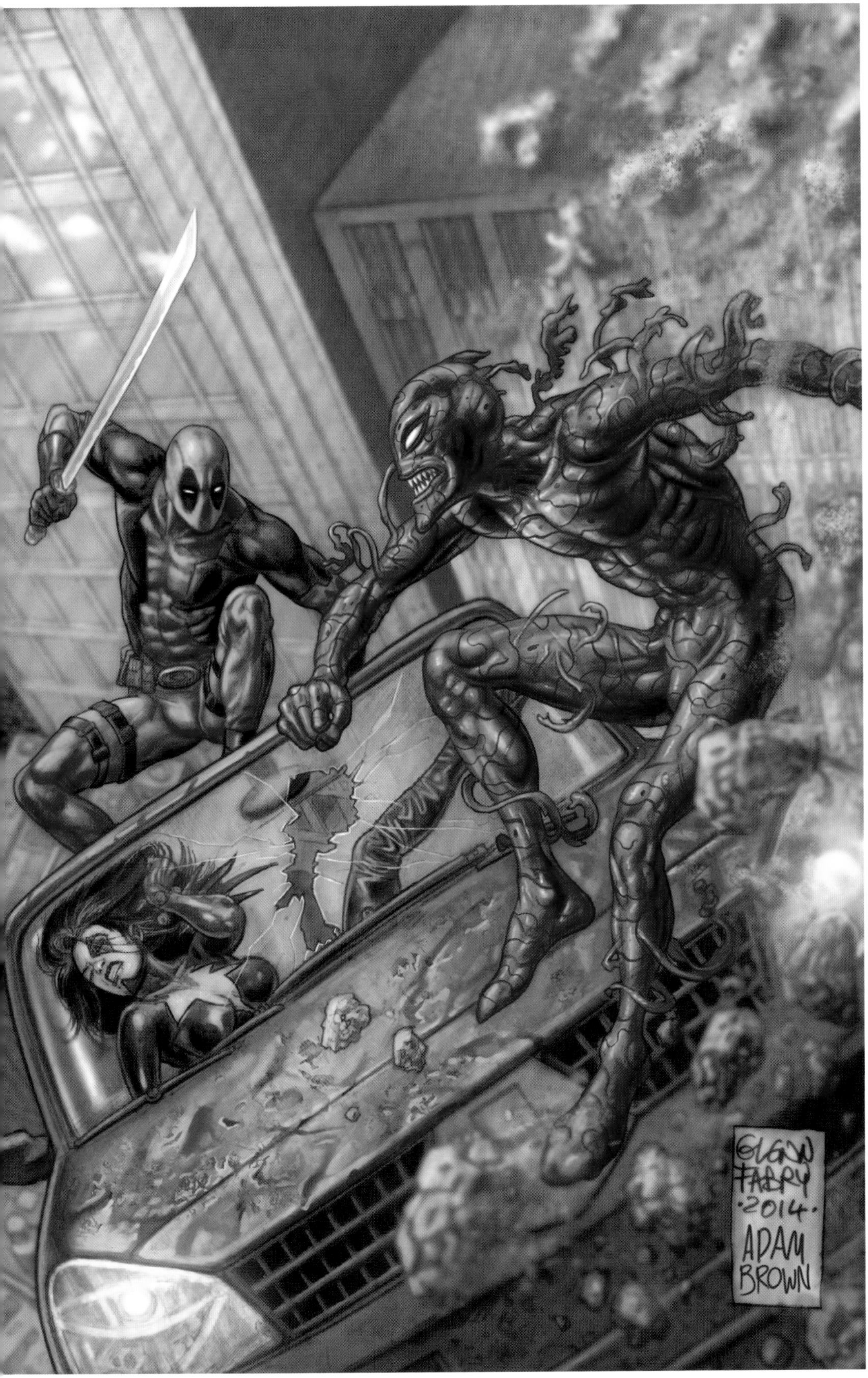
GLENN FABRY
·2014·
ADAM BROWN

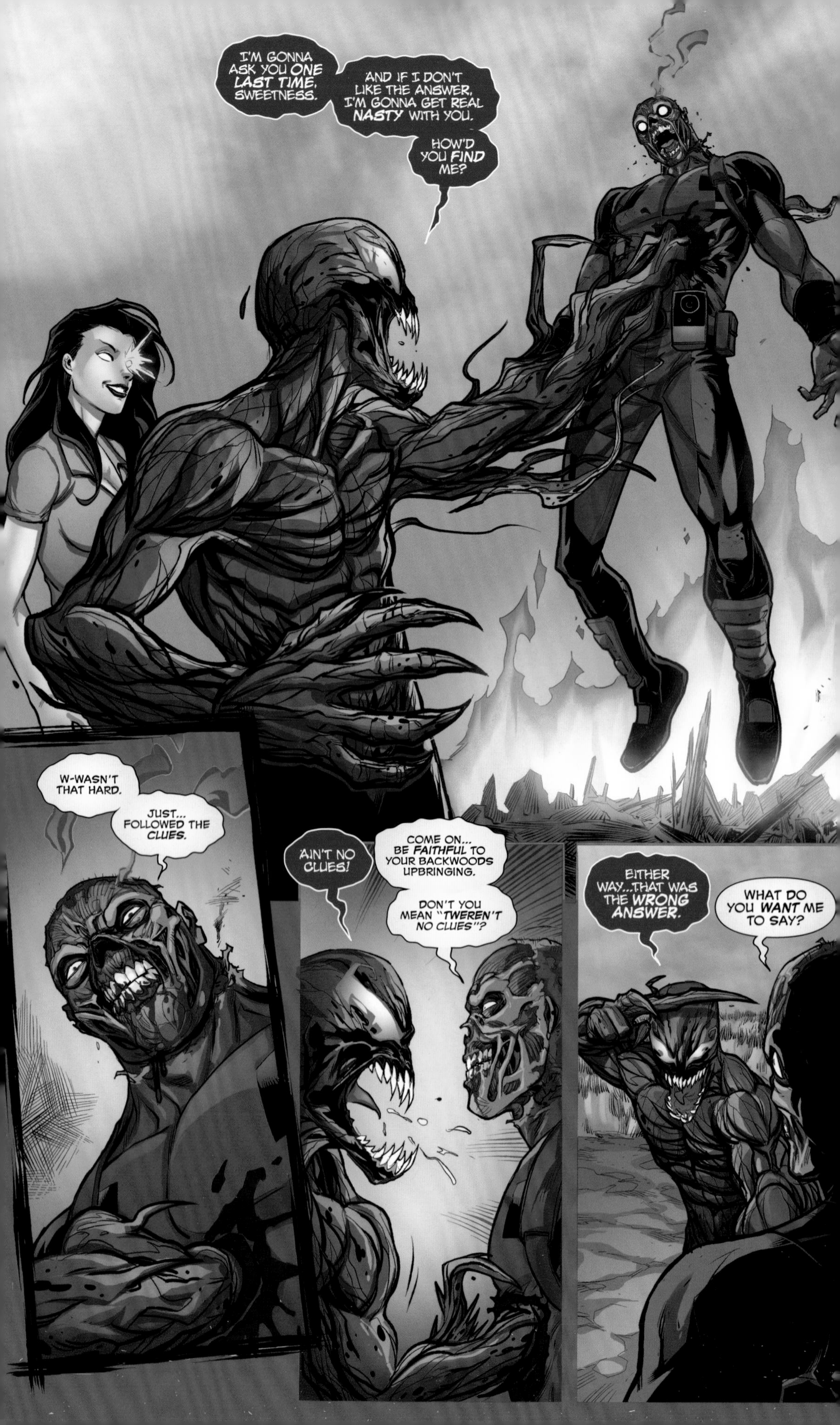
I'M GONNA ASK YOU ONE LAST TIME, SWEETNESS.
AND IF I DON'T LIKE THE ANSWER, I'M GONNA GET REAL NASTY WITH YOU.
HOW'D YOU FIND ME?
W-WASN'T THAT HARD.
JUST... FOLLOWED THE CLUES.
AIN'T NO CLUES!
COME ON... BE FAITHFUL TO YOUR BACKWOODS UPBRINGING.
DON'T YOU MEAN "TWEREN'T NO CLUES"?
EITHER WAY...THAT WAS THE WRONG ANSWER.
WHAT DO YOU WANT ME TO SAY?

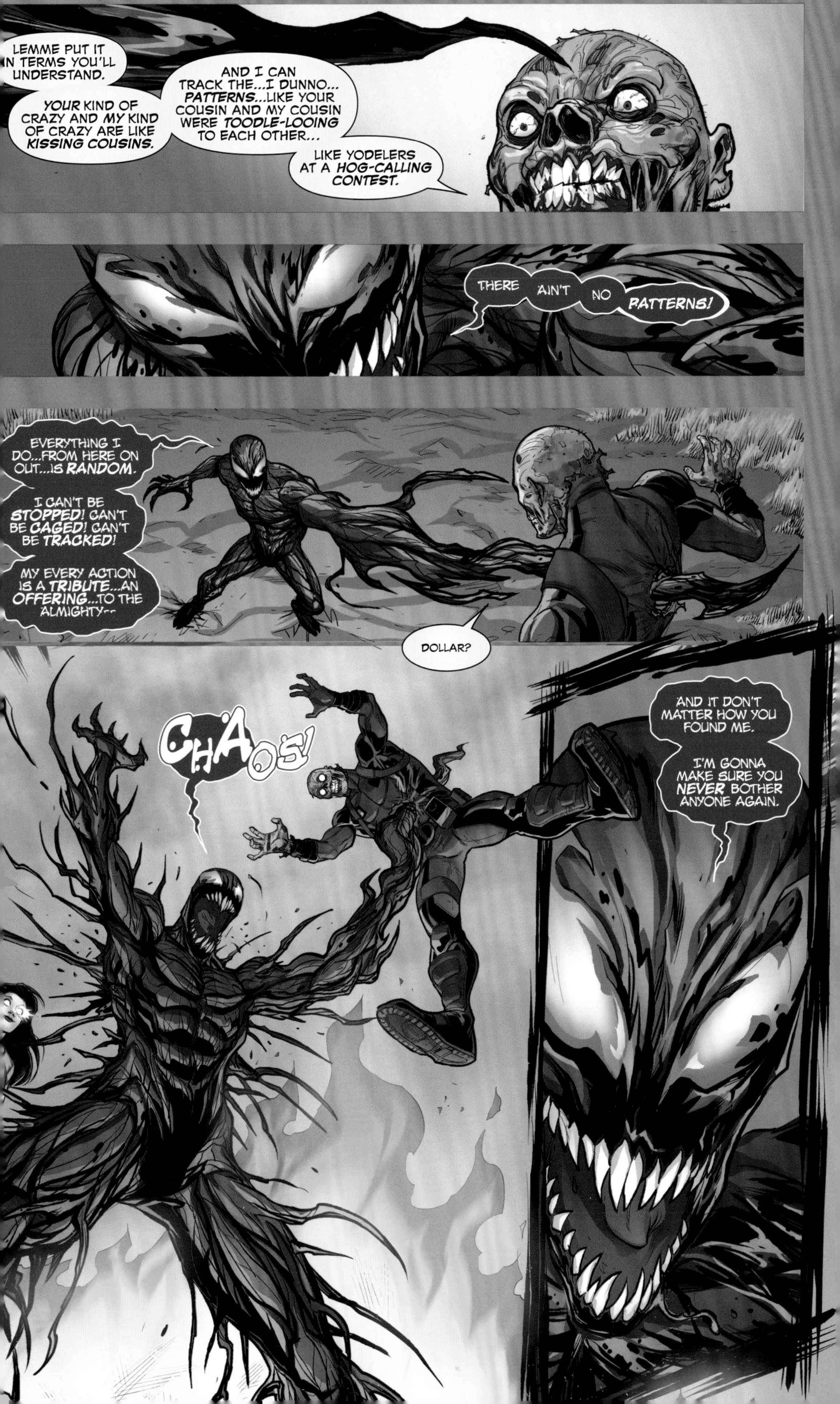
LEMME PUT IT IN TERMS YOU'LL UNDERSTAND.
YOUR KIND OF CRAZY AND MY KIND OF CRAZY ARE LIKE KISSING COUSINS.
AND I CAN TRACK THE...I DUNNO... PATTERNS...LIKE YOUR COUSIN AND MY COUSIN WERE TOODLE-LOOING TO EACH OTHER...
LIKE YODELERS AT A HOG-CALLING CONTEST.
THERE AIN'T NO PATTERNS!
EVERYTHING I DO...FROM HERE ON OUT...IS RANDOM.
I CAN'T BE STOPPED! CAN'T BE CAGED! CAN'T BE TRACKED!
MY EVERY ACTION IS A TRIBUTE...AN OFFERING...TO THE ALMIGHTY--
DOLLAR?
CHAOS!
AND IT DON'T MATTER HOW YOU FOUND ME.
I'M GONNA MAKE SURE YOU NEVER BOTHER ANYONE AGAIN.

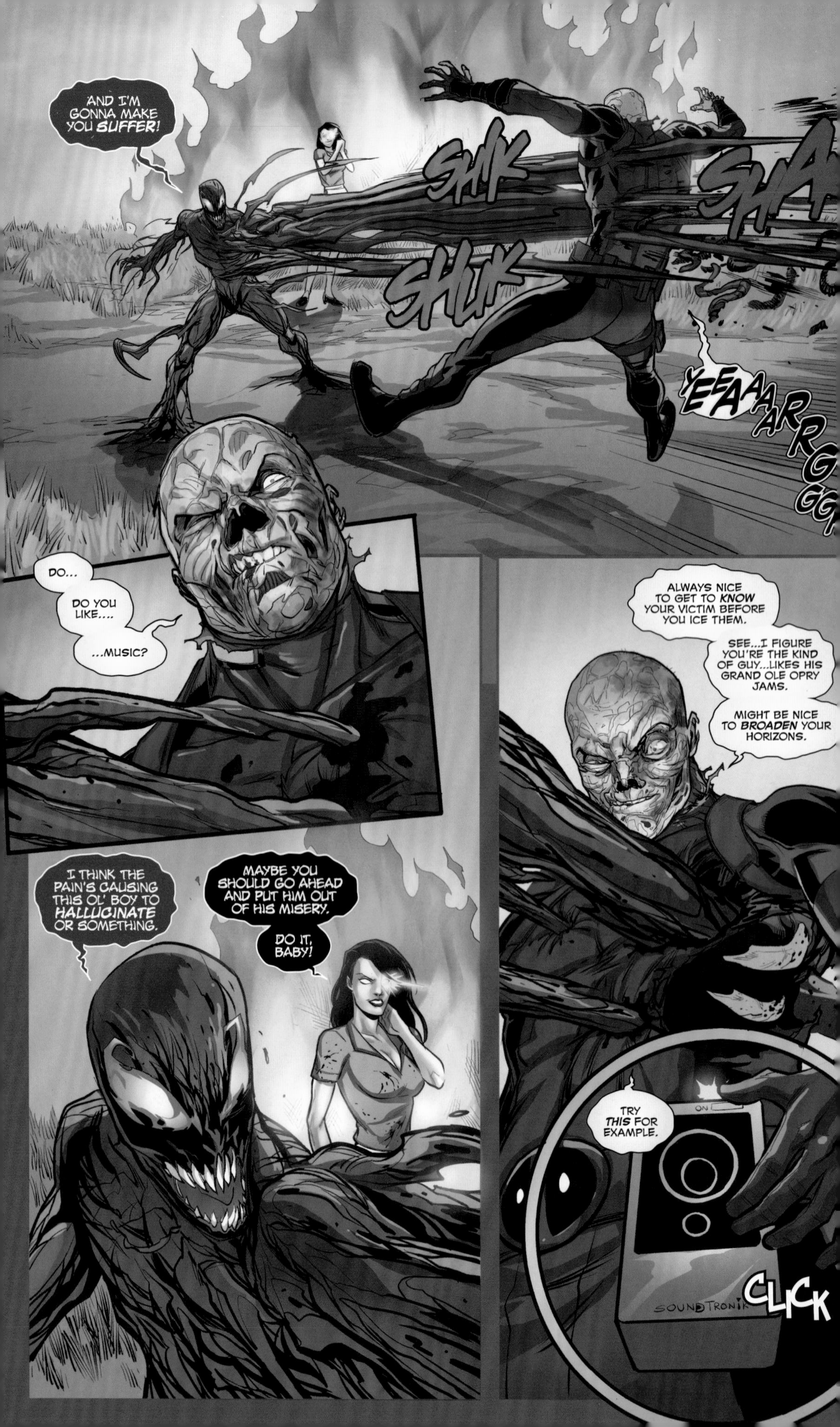
AND I'M GONNA MAKE YOU SUFFER!
SHIK
SHAK
SHUK
YEEAAAARRGGG
DO...
DO YOU LIKE....
...MUSIC?
I THINK THE PAIN'S CAUSING THIS OL' BOY TO HALLUCINATE OR SOMETHING.
MAYBE YOU SHOULD GO AHEAD AND PUT HIM OUT OF HIS MISERY.
DO IT, BABY!
ALWAYS NICE TO GET TO KNOW YOUR VICTIM BEFORE YOU ICE THEM.
SEE...I FIGURE YOU'RE THE KIND OF GUY...LIKES HIS GRAND OLE OPRY JAMS.
MIGHT BE NICE TO BROADEN YOUR HORIZONS.
TRY THIS FOR EXAMPLE.
ON
SOUNDTRONIK
CLICK

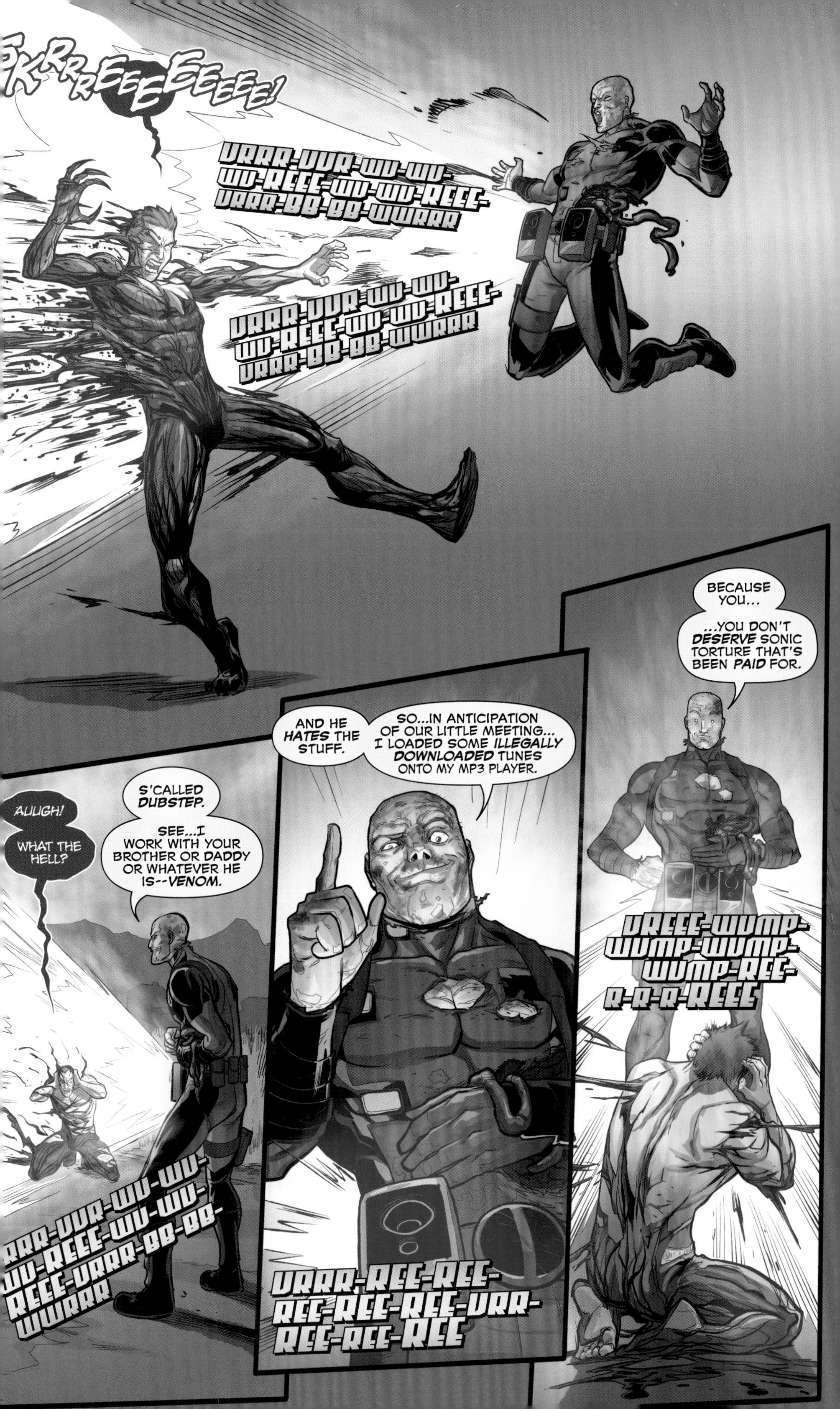
SKRRREEEEEEEEE!
VRRR-VVR-WV-WV-
WV-REEE-WV-WV-REEE-
VRRR-BB-BB-WWRRR
VRRR-VVR-WV-WV-
WV-REEE-WV-WV-REEE-
VRRR-BB-BB-WWRRR
AUUGH!
WHAT THE HELL?
S'CALLED DUBSTEP.
SEE...I WORK WITH YOUR BROTHER OR DADDY OR WHATEVER HE IS--VENOM.
RRR-VVR-WV-WV-
WV-REEE-WV-WV-
REEE-VRRR-BB-BB-
WWRRR
AND HE HATES THE STUFF.
SO...IN ANTICIPATION OF OUR LITTLE MEETING... I LOADED SOME ILLEGALLY DOWNLOADED TUNES ONTO MY MP3 PLAYER.
VRRR-REE-REE-
REE-REE-REE-VRR-
REE-REE-REE
BECAUSE YOU...
...YOU DON'T DESERVE SONIC TORTURE THAT'S BEEN PAID FOR.
VREEE-WVMP-
WVMP-WVMP-
WVMP-REE-
R-R-R-REEE

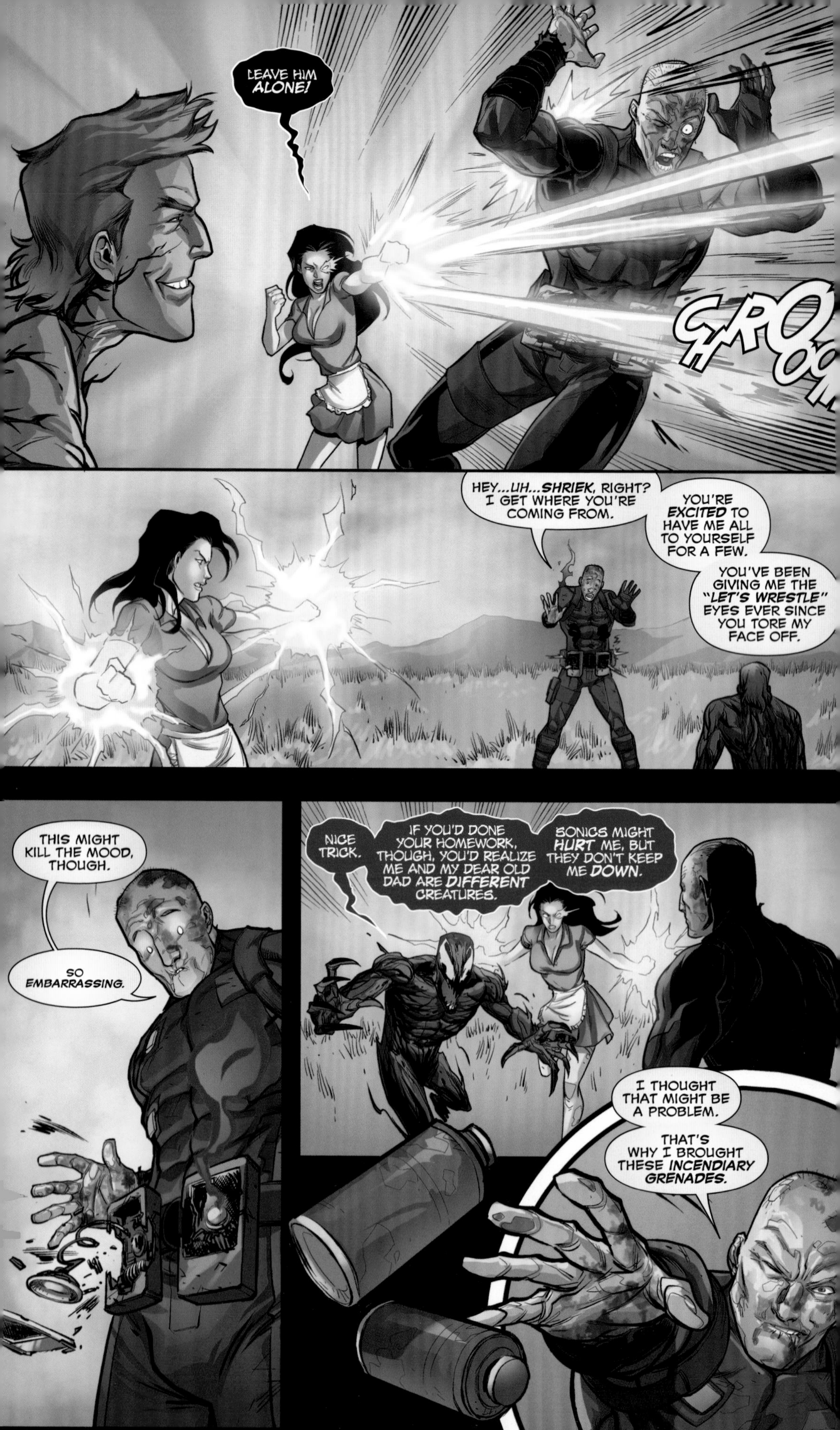

LEAVE HIM ALONE!
CHROOOOM
HEY...UH...SHRIEK, RIGHT? I GET WHERE YOU'RE COMING FROM.
YOU'RE EXCITED TO HAVE ME ALL TO YOURSELF FOR A FEW.
YOU'VE BEEN GIVING ME THE "LET'S WRESTLE" EYES EVER SINCE YOU TORE MY FACE OFF.
THIS MIGHT KILL THE MOOD, THOUGH.
SO EMBARRASSING.
NICE TRICK.
IF YOU'D DONE YOUR HOMEWORK, THOUGH, YOU'D REALIZE ME AND MY DEAR OLD DAD ARE DIFFERENT CREATURES.
SONICS MIGHT HURT ME, BUT THEY DON'T KEEP ME DOWN.
I THOUGHT THAT MIGHT BE A PROBLEM.
THAT'S WHY I BROUGHT THESE INCENDIARY GRENADES.

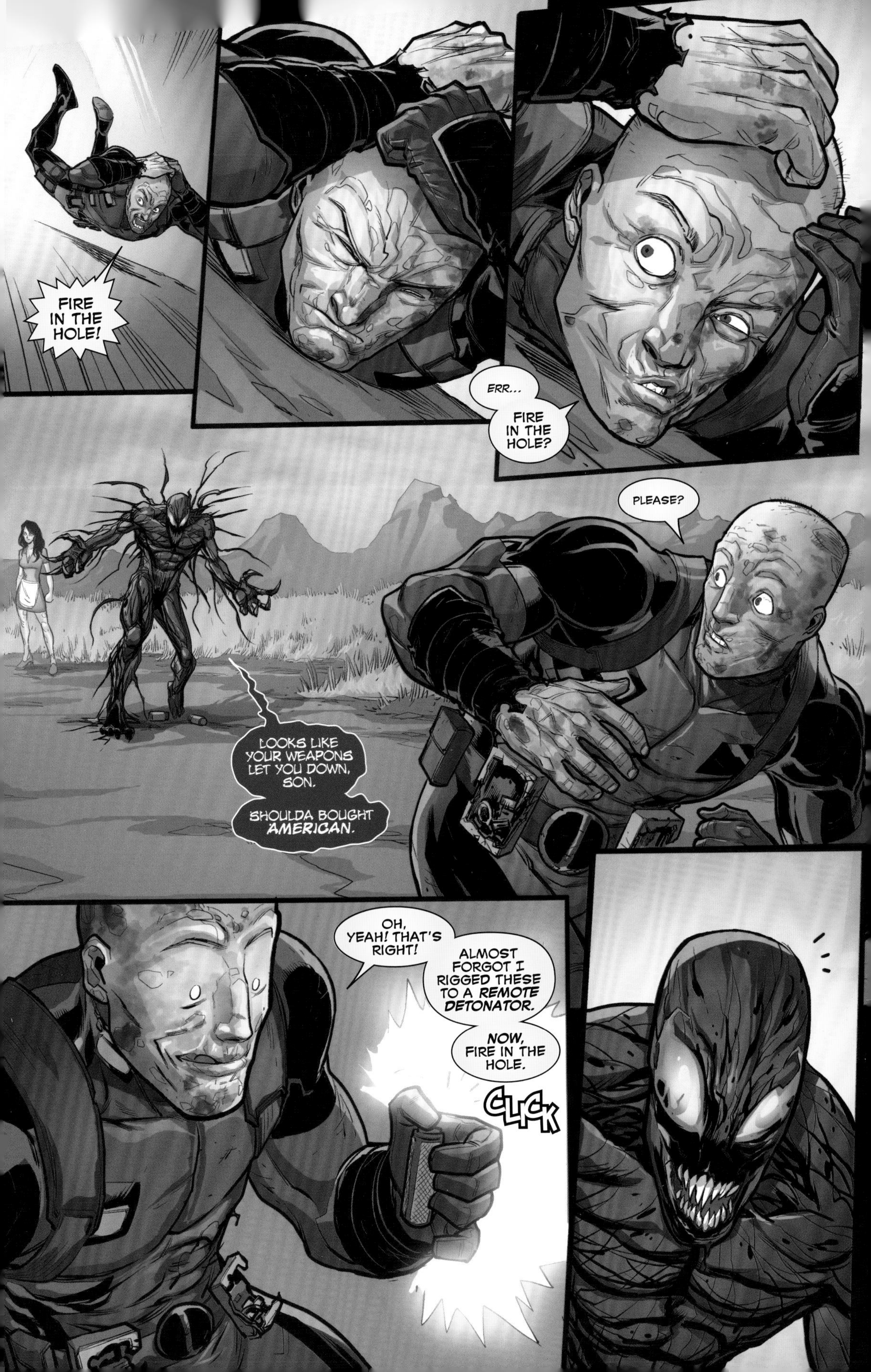
FIRE IN THE HOLE!
ERR...
FIRE IN THE HOLE?
PLEASE?
LOOKS LIKE YOUR WEAPONS LET YOU DOWN, SON.
SHOULDA BOUGHT AMERICAN.
OH, YEAH! THAT'S RIGHT!
ALMOST FORGOT I RIGGED THESE TO A REMOTE DETONATOR.
NOW, FIRE IN THE HOLE.
CLICK

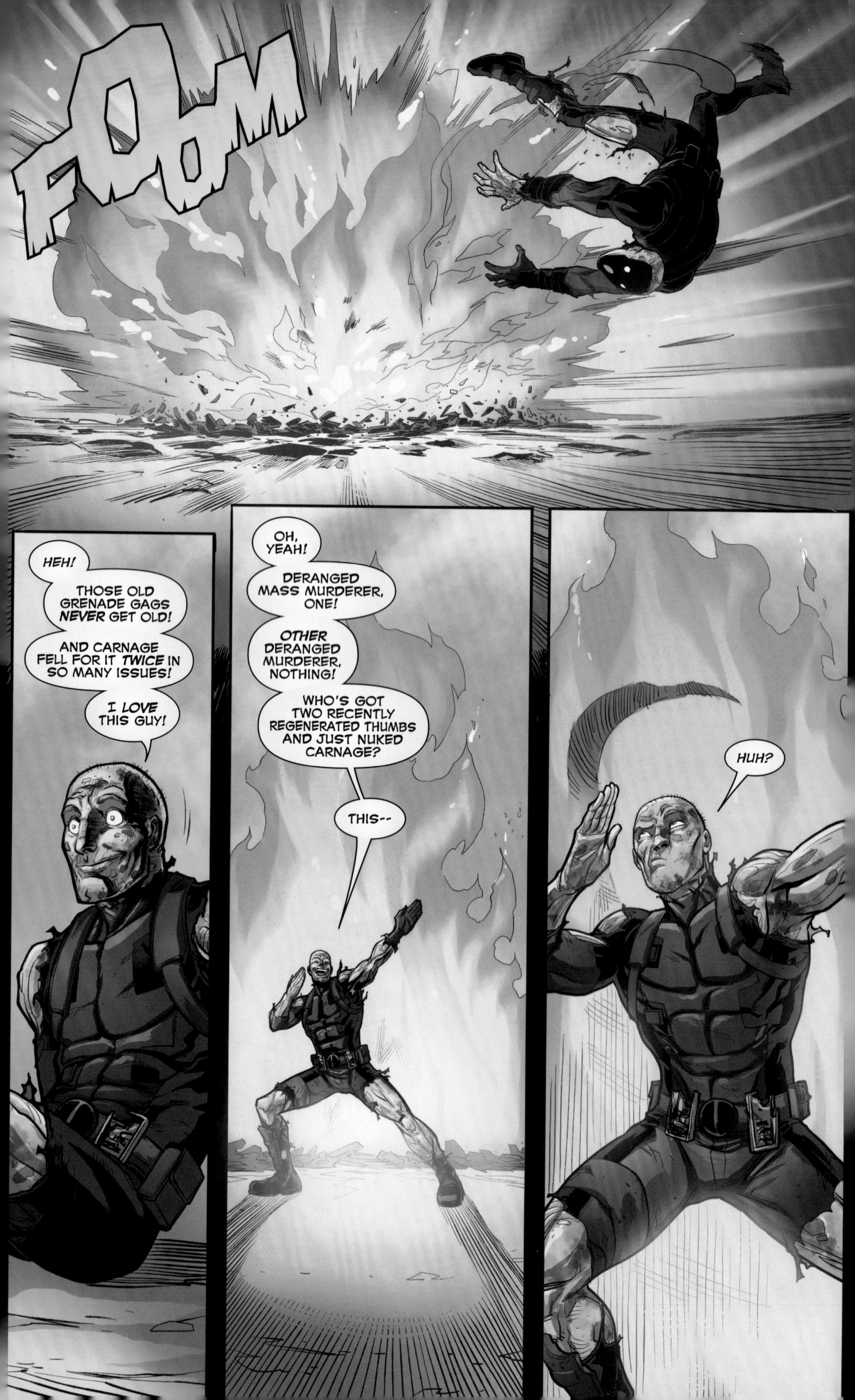
FOOM
HEH!
THOSE OLD GRENADE GAGS NEVER GET OLD!
AND CARNAGE FELL FOR IT TWICE IN SO MANY ISSUES!
I LOVE THIS GUY!
OH, YEAH!
DERANGED MASS MURDERER, ONE!
OTHER DERANGED MURDERER, NOTHING!
WHO'S GOT TWO RECENTLY REGENERATED THUMBS AND JUST NUKED CARNAGE?
THIS--
HUH?

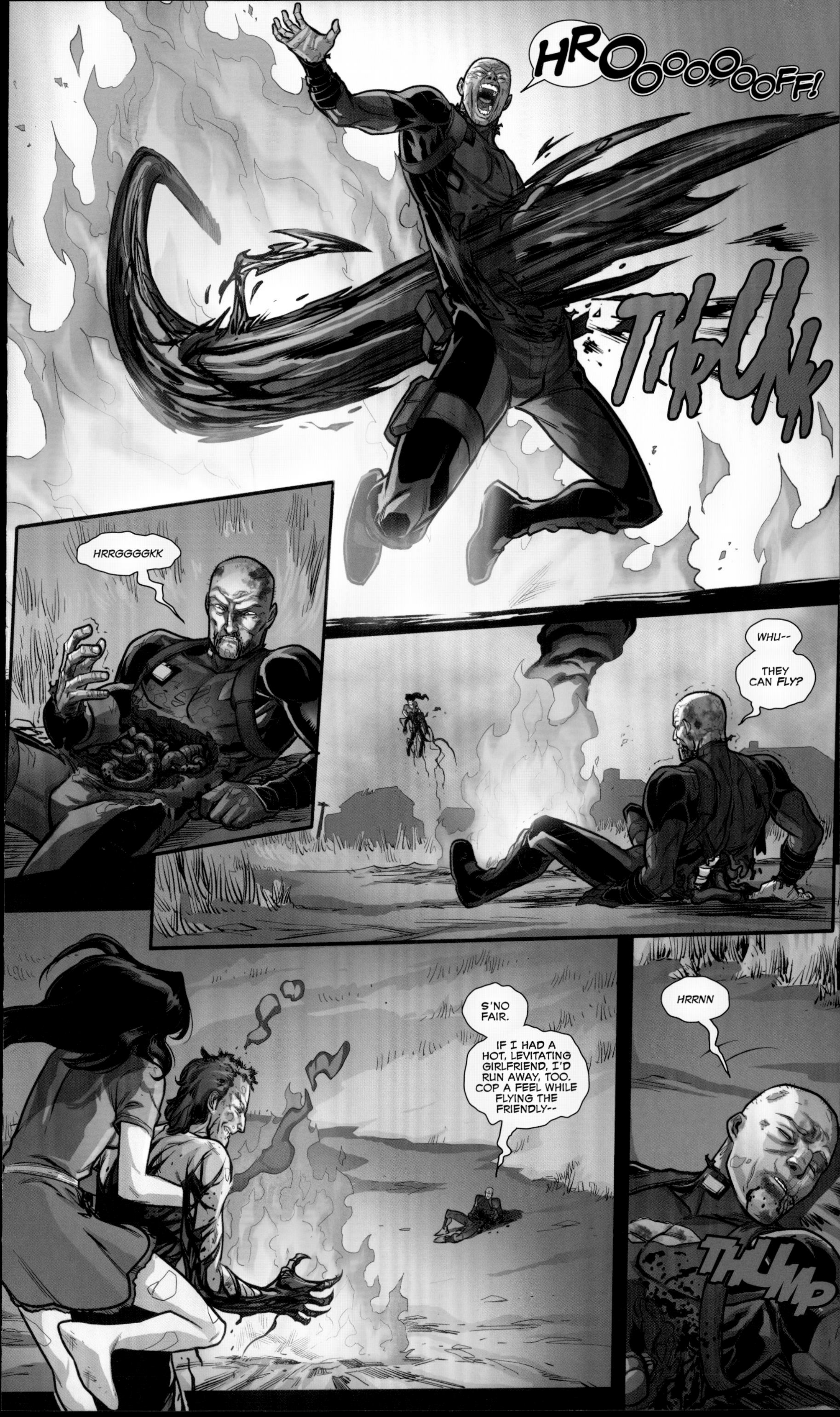
HROOOOOOOOFF!
THRUNK
HRRGGGGKK
WHU--
THEY CAN FLY?
S'NO FAIR.
IF I HAD A HOT, LEVITATING GIRLFRIEND, I'D RUN AWAY, TOO. COP A FEEL WHILE FLYING THE FRIENDLY--
HRRNN
THUMP

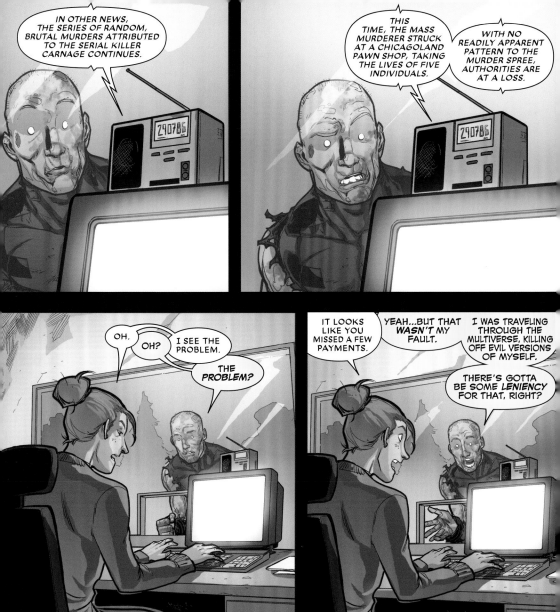

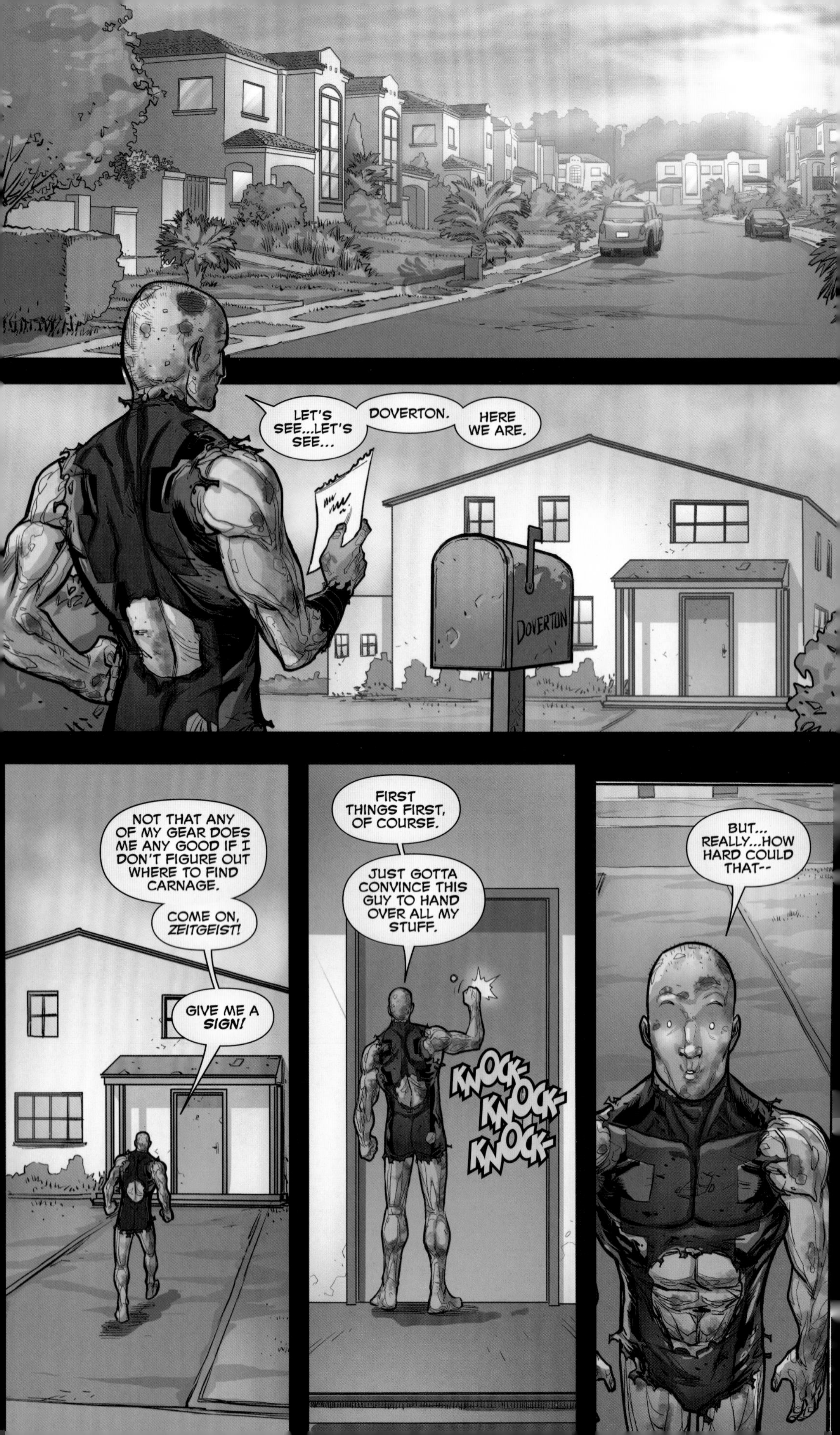
LET'S SEE...LET'S SEE...
DOVERTON.
HERE WE ARE.
DOVERTON
NOT THAT ANY OF MY GEAR DOES ME ANY GOOD IF I DON'T FIGURE OUT WHERE TO FIND CARNAGE.
COME ON, ZEITGEIST!
GIVE ME A SIGN!
FIRST THINGS FIRST, OF COURSE.
JUST GOTTA CONVINCE THIS GUY TO HAND OVER ALL MY STUFF.
KNOCK-KNOCK-KNOCK
BUT... REALLY...HOW HARD COULD THAT--

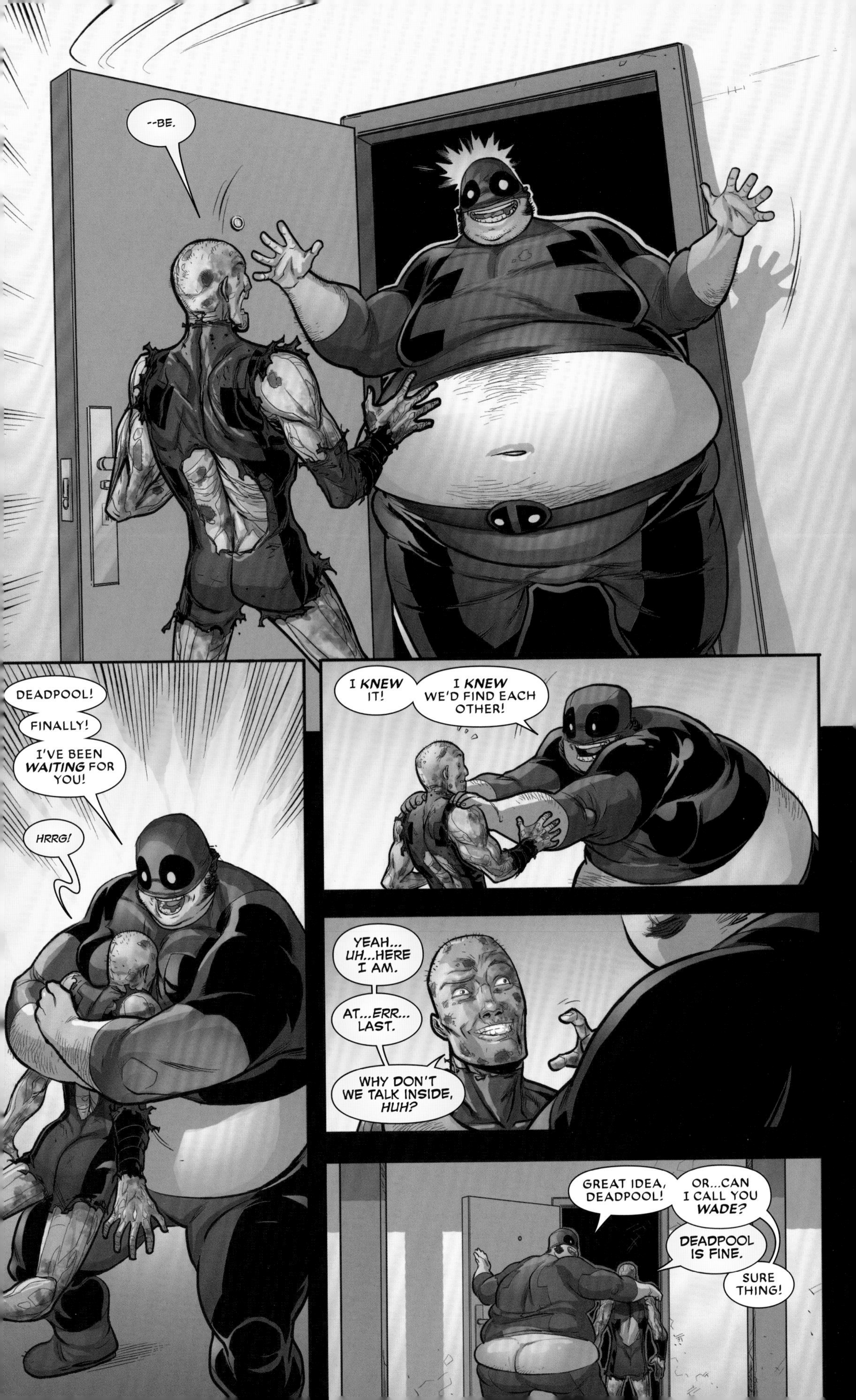
--BE.
DEADPOOL!
FINALLY!
I'VE BEEN WAITING FOR YOU!
HRRG!
I KNEW IT!
I KNEW WE'D FIND EACH OTHER!
YEAH... UH...HERE I AM.
AT...ERR... LAST.
WHY DON'T WE TALK INSIDE, HUH?
GREAT IDEA, DEADPOOL!
OR...CAN I CALL YOU WADE?
DEADPOOL IS FINE.
SURE THING!

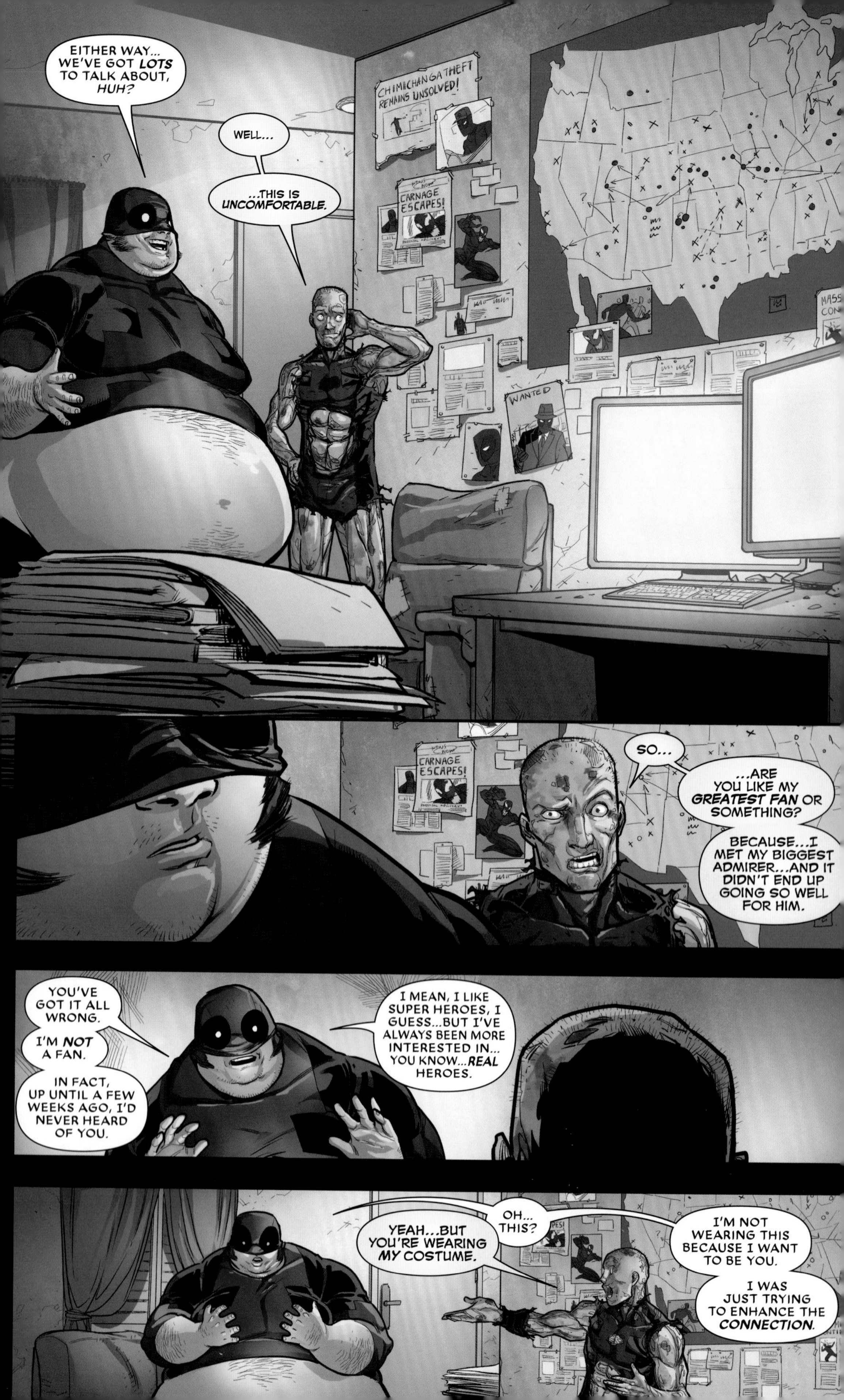
EITHER WAY... WE'VE GOT *LOTS* TO TALK ABOUT, *HUH?*
CHIMICHANGA THEFT REMAINS UNSOLVED!
CARNAGE ESCAPES!
WANTED
WELL...
...THIS IS *UNCOMFORTABLE.*
SO...
...ARE YOU LIKE MY *GREATEST FAN* OR SOMETHING?
BECAUSE...I MET MY BIGGEST ADMIRER...AND IT DIDN'T END UP GOING SO WELL FOR HIM.
YOU'VE GOT IT ALL WRONG.
I'M *NOT* A FAN.
IN FACT, UP UNTIL A FEW WEEKS AGO, I'D NEVER HEARD OF YOU.
I MEAN, I LIKE SUPER HEROES, I GUESS...BUT I'VE ALWAYS BEEN MORE INTERESTED IN... YOU KNOW...*REAL* HEROES.
YEAH...BUT YOU'RE WEARING *MY* COSTUME.
OH... THIS?
I'M NOT WEARING THIS BECAUSE I WANT TO BE YOU.
I WAS JUST TRYING TO ENHANCE THE *CONNECTION.*

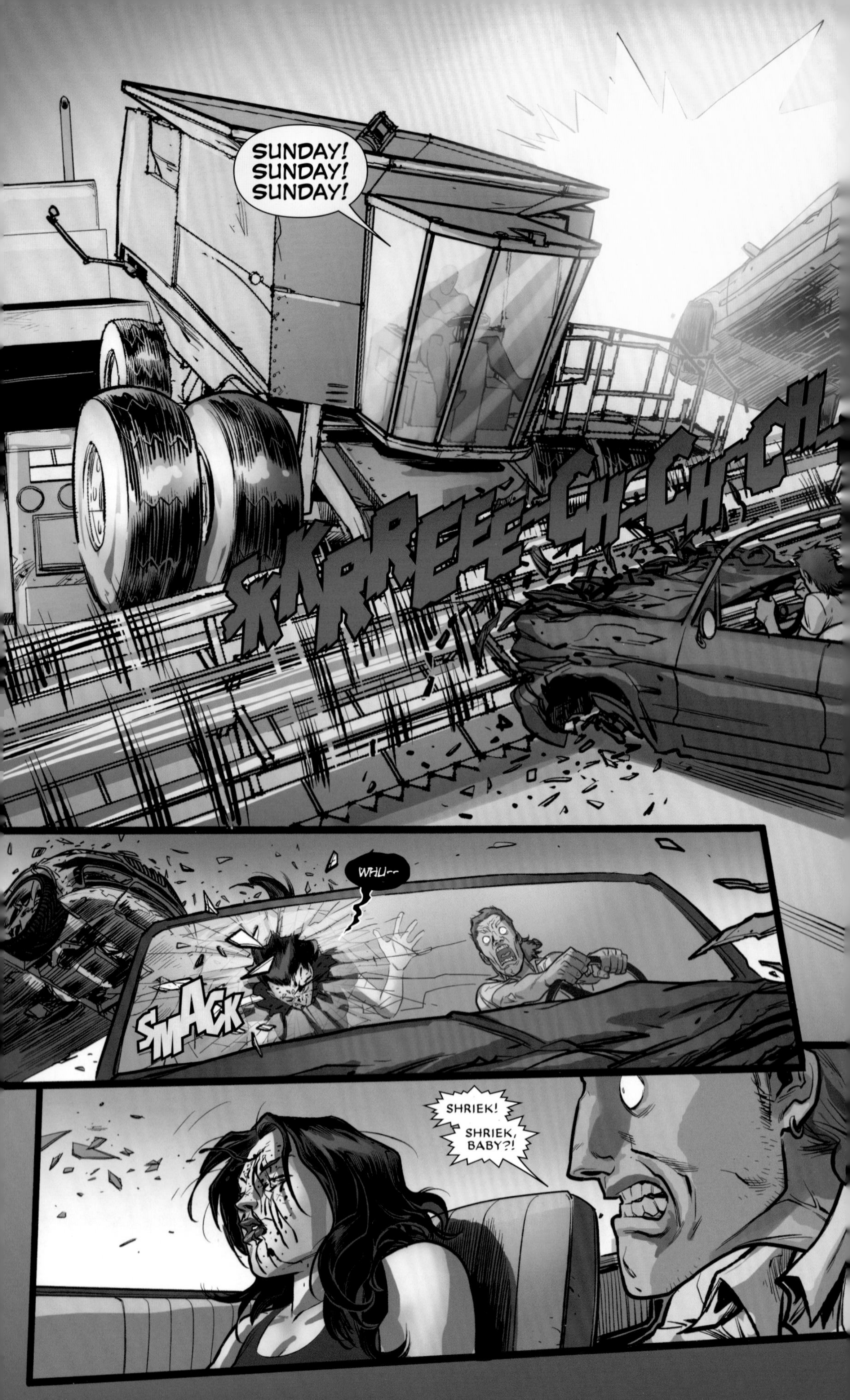
SUNDAY! SUNDAY! SUNDAY!
SKRREEE-CH-CH-CH
WHU--
SMACK
SHRIEK!
SHRIEK, BABY?!

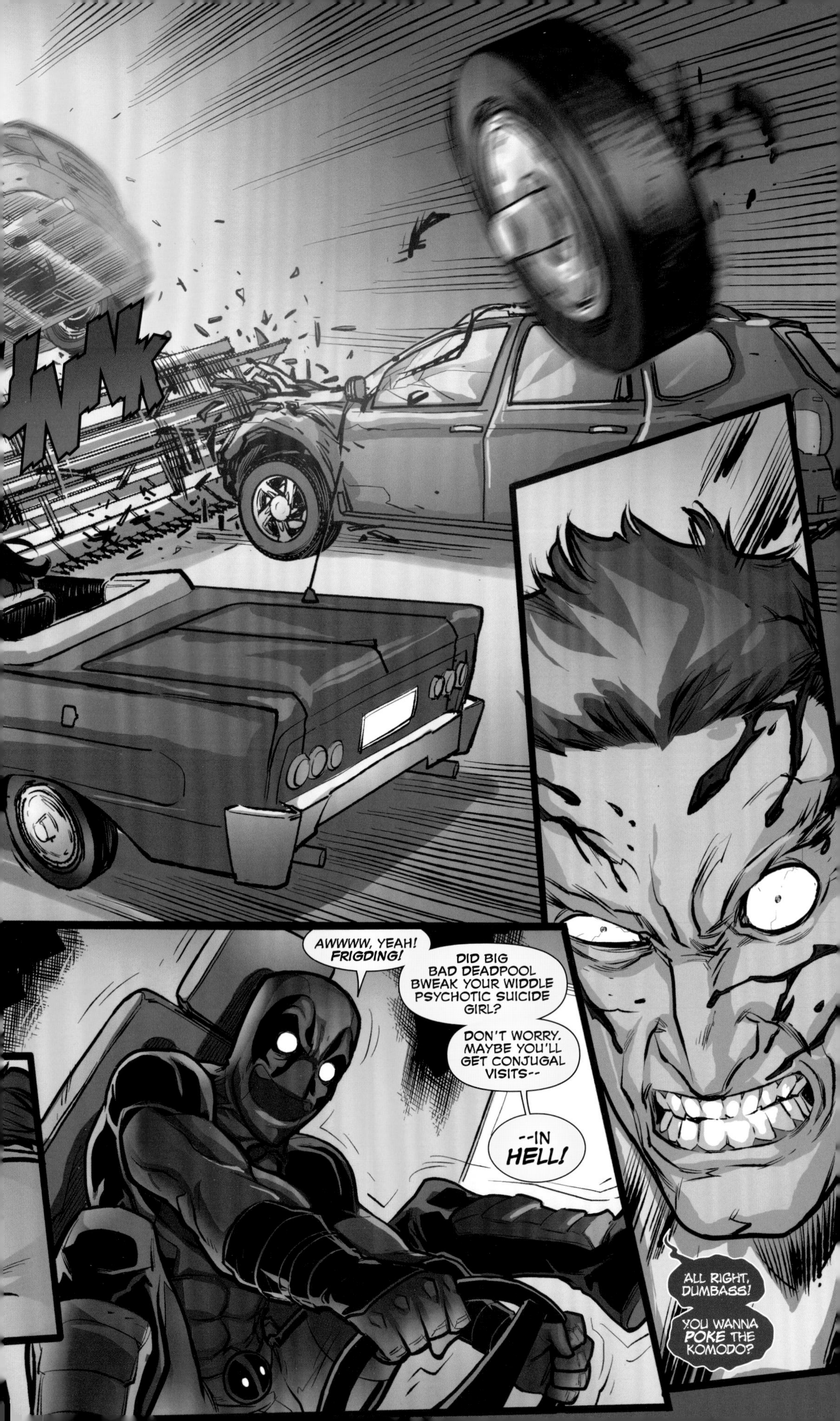

AWWWW, YEAH! FRIGDING!
DID BIG BAD DEADPOOL BWEAK YOUR WIDDLE PSYCHOTIC SUICIDE GIRL?
DON'T WORRY. MAYBE YOU'LL GET CONJUGAL VISITS--
--IN HELL!
ALL RIGHT, DUMBASS!
YOU WANNA POKE THE KOMODO?

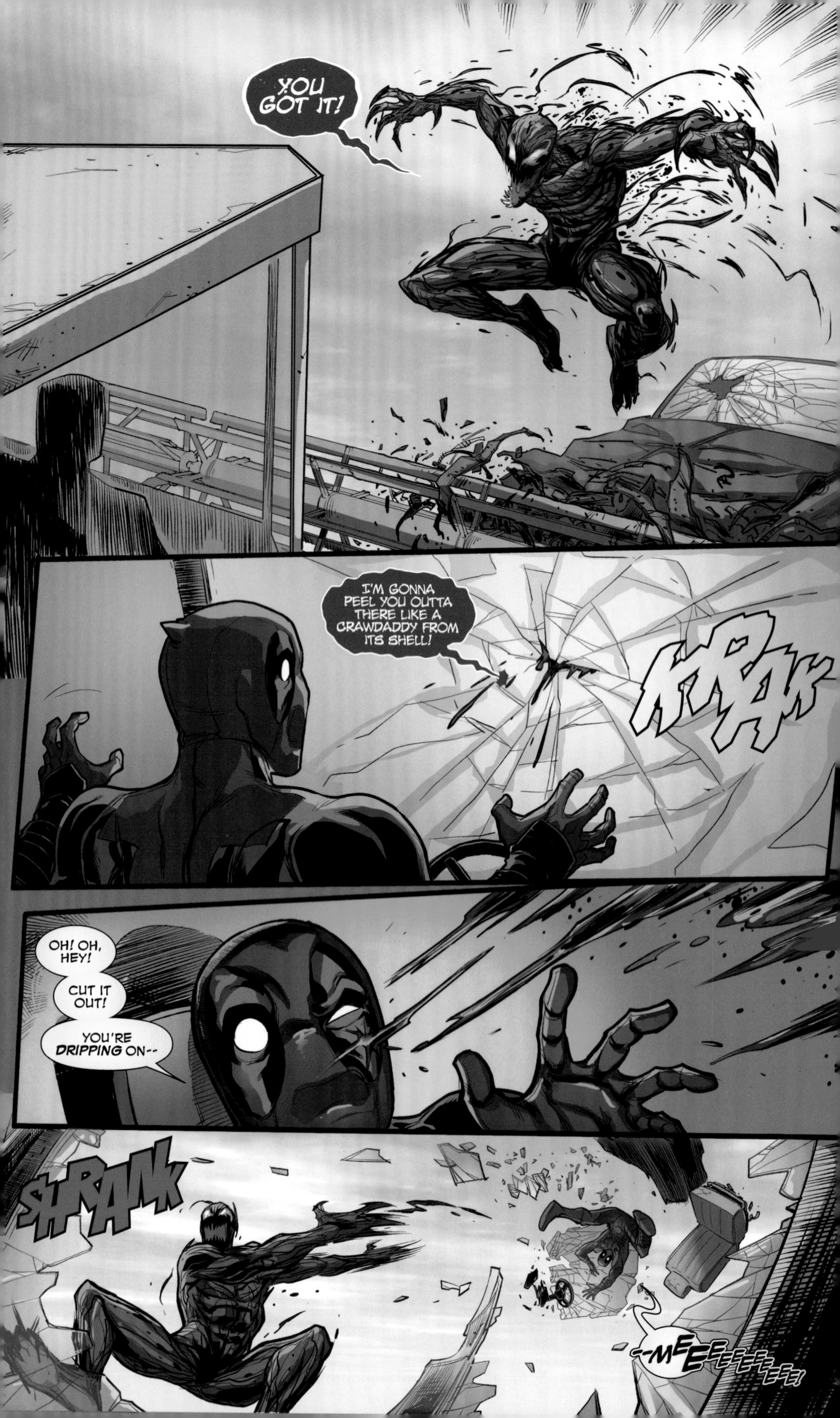
YOU GOT IT!
I'M GONNA PEEL YOU OUTTA THERE LIKE A CRAWDADDY FROM ITS SHELL!
KRAK
OH! OH, HEY!
CUT IT OUT!
YOU'RE DRIPPING ON--
SHRANK
--MEEEEEEEEEEE!

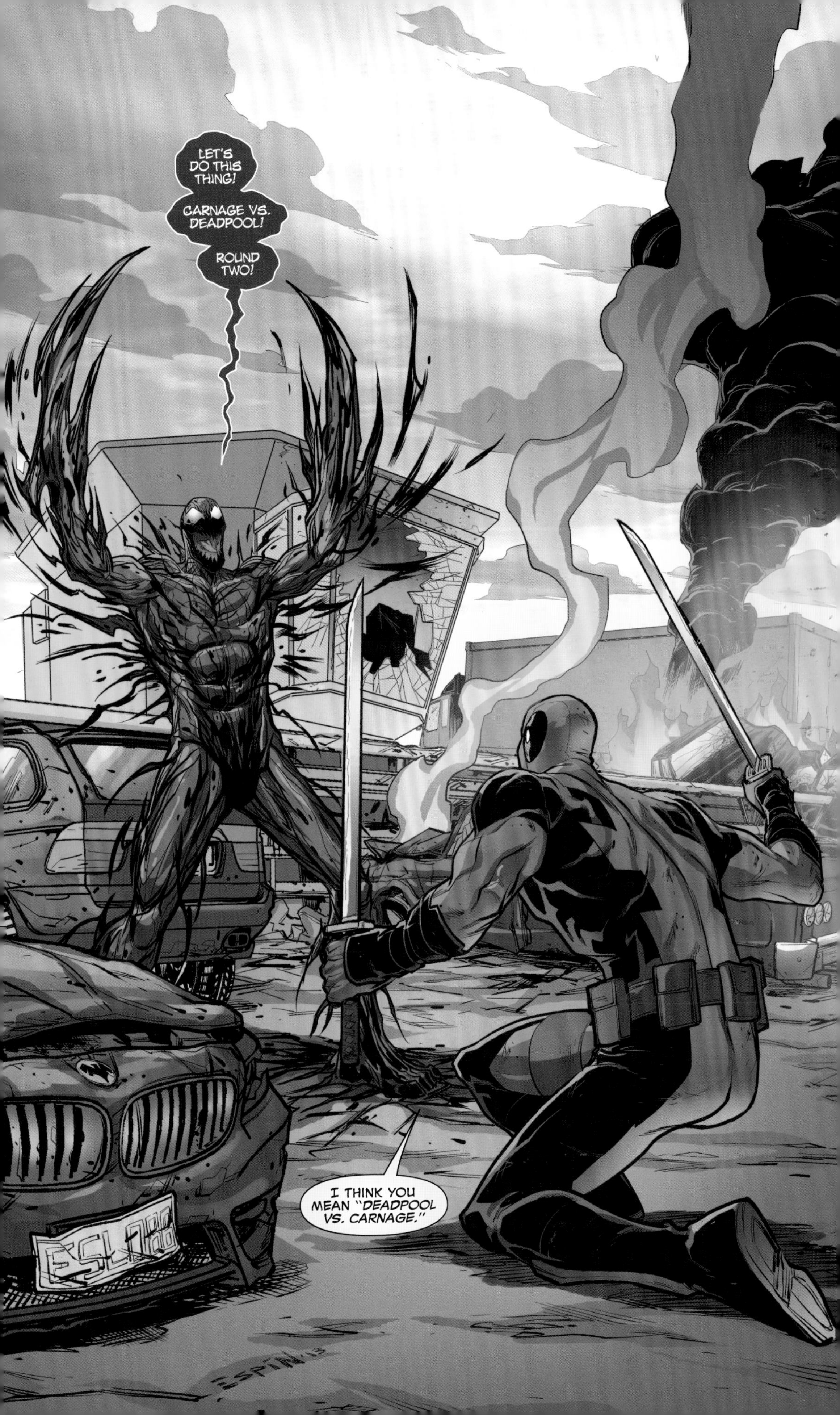
LET'S DO THIS THING!
CARNAGE VS. DEADPOOL!
ROUND TWO!
I THINK YOU MEAN "DEADPOOL VS. CARNAGE."
ESPIN '13

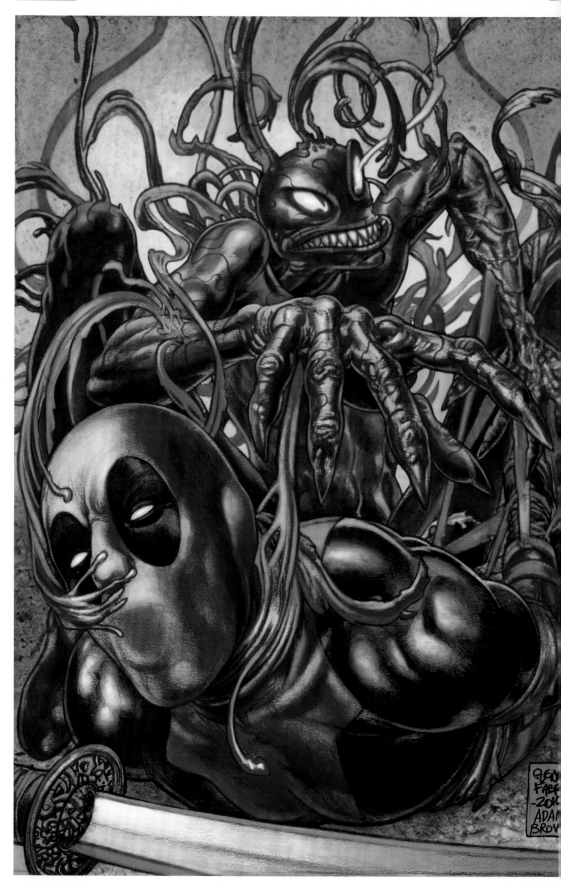

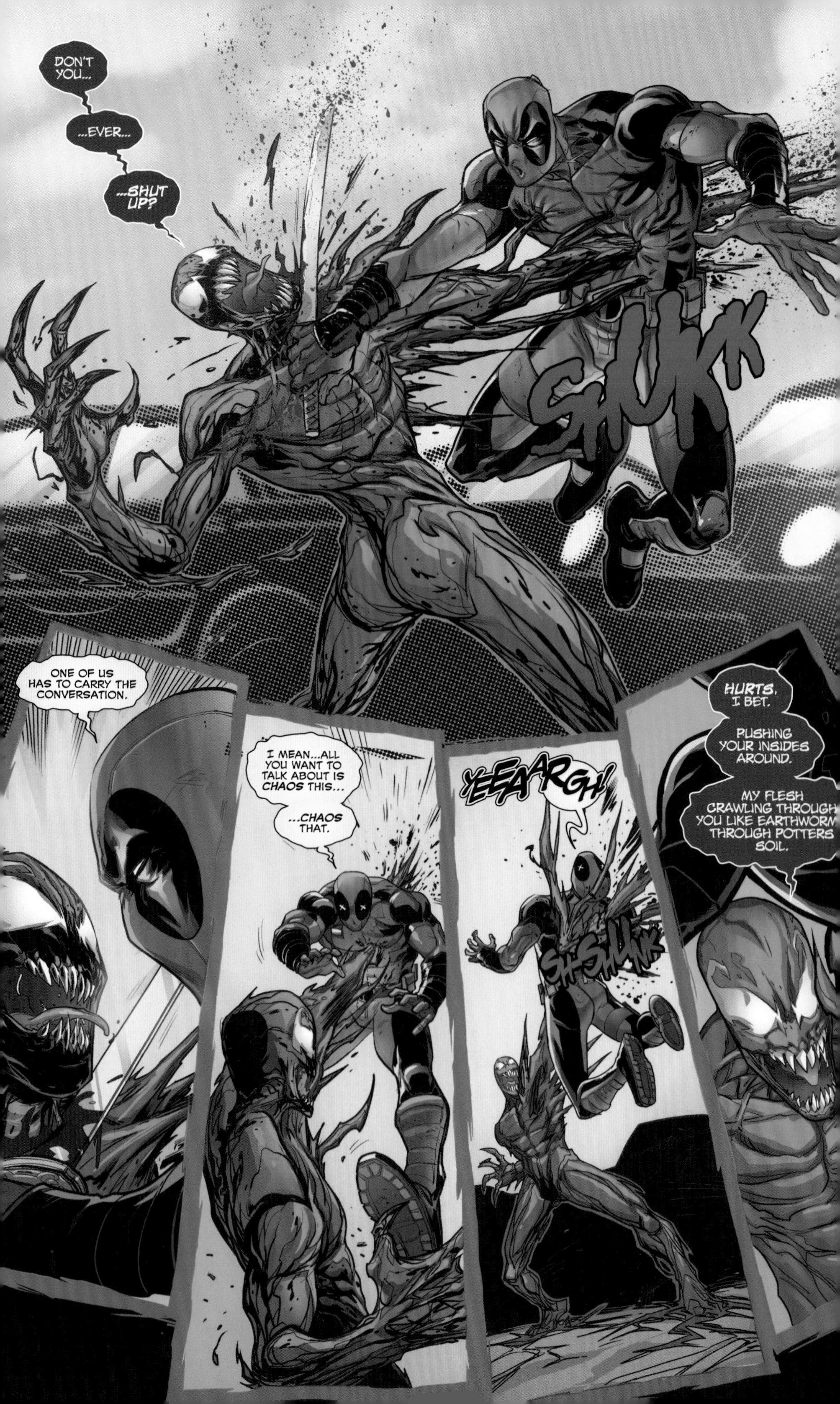
DON'T YOU...
...EVER...
...SHUT UP?
SHUKK
ONE OF US HAS TO CARRY THE CONVERSATION.
I MEAN...ALL YOU WANT TO TALK ABOUT IS CHAOS THIS...
...CHAOS THAT.
YEEAARGH!
SH-SHUNK
HURTS, I BET.
PUSHING YOUR INSIDES AROUND.
MY FLESH CRAWLING THROUGH YOU LIKE EARTHWORM THROUGH POTTERS SOIL.

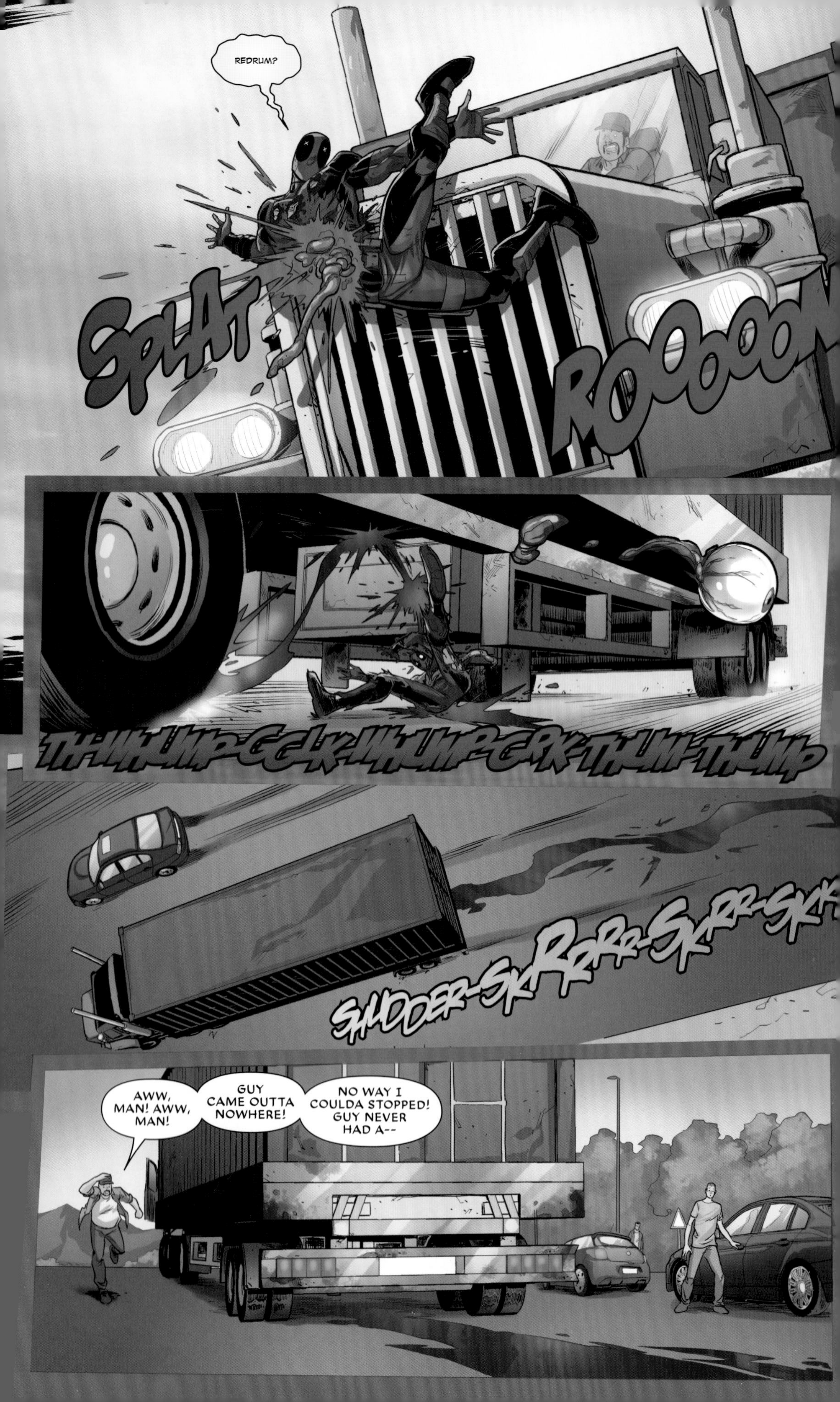

REDRUM?
SPLAT
ROOOOOM
TH-WHUMP-GGLK-WHUMP-GRK-THUM-THUMP
SHUDDER-SKRRRR-SKRR-SKR
AWW, MAN! AWW, MAN!
GUY CAME OUTTA NOWHERE!
NO WAY I COULDA STOPPED! GUY NEVER HAD A--

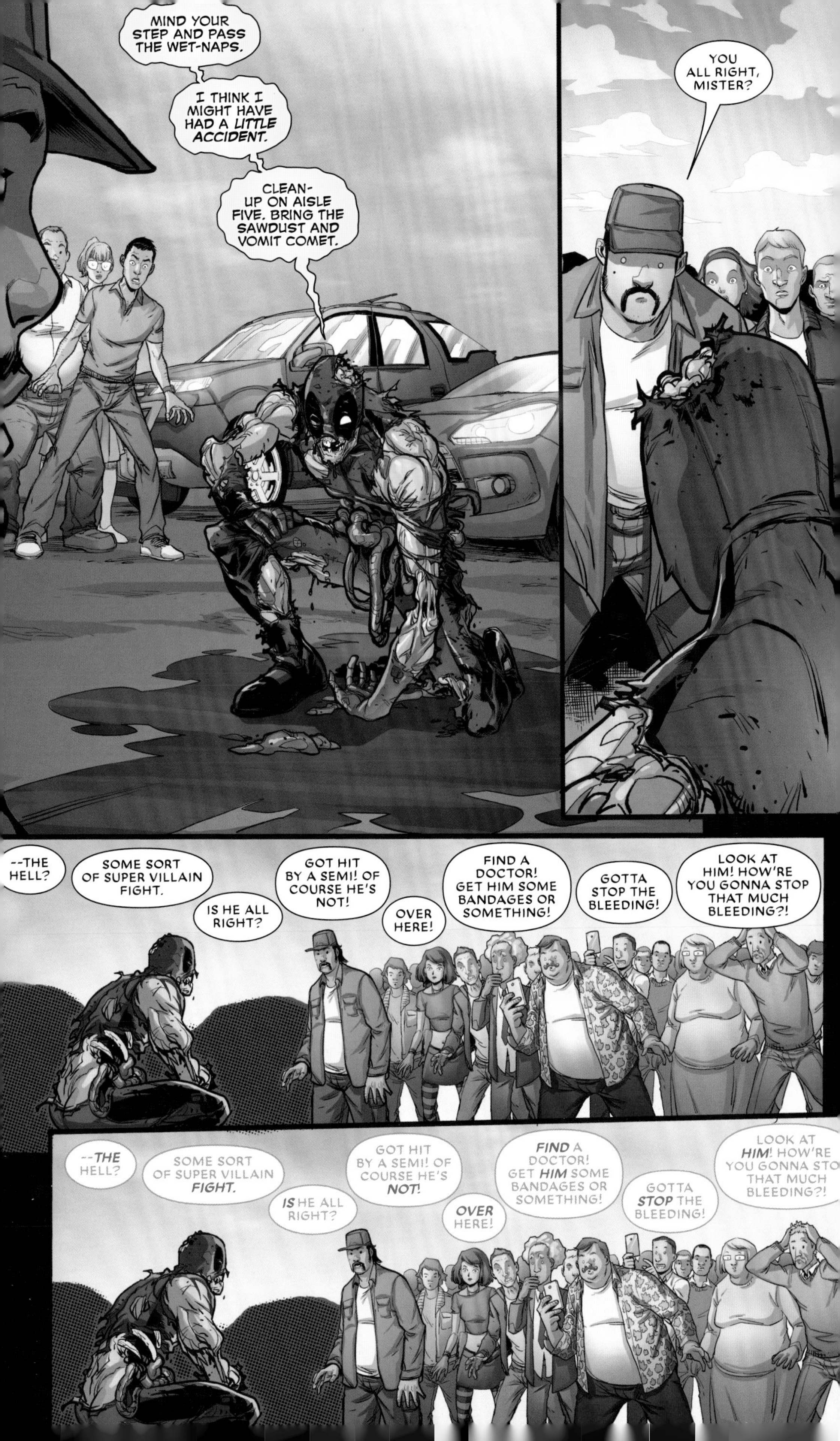
MIND YOUR STEP AND PASS THE WET-NAPS.
I THINK I MIGHT HAVE HAD A *LITTLE ACCIDENT.*
CLEAN-UP ON AISLE FIVE. BRING THE SAWDUST AND VOMIT COMET.
YOU ALL RIGHT, MISTER?
--THE HELL?
SOME SORT OF SUPER VILLAIN FIGHT.
IS HE ALL RIGHT?
GOT HIT BY A SEMI! OF COURSE HE'S NOT!
OVER HERE!
FIND A DOCTOR! GET HIM SOME BANDAGES OR SOMETHING!
GOTTA STOP THE BLEEDING!
LOOK AT HIM! HOW'RE YOU GONNA STOP THAT MUCH BLEEDING?!
--*THE* HELL?
SOME SORT OF SUPER VILLAIN *FIGHT.*
IS HE ALL RIGHT?
GOT HIT BY A SEMI! OF COURSE HE'S *NOT!*
OVER HERE!
FIND A DOCTOR! GET *HIM* SOME BANDAGES OR SOMETHING!
GOTTA *STOP* THE BLEEDING!
LOOK AT *HIM*! HOW'RE YOU GONNA STO THAT MUCH BLEEDING?!

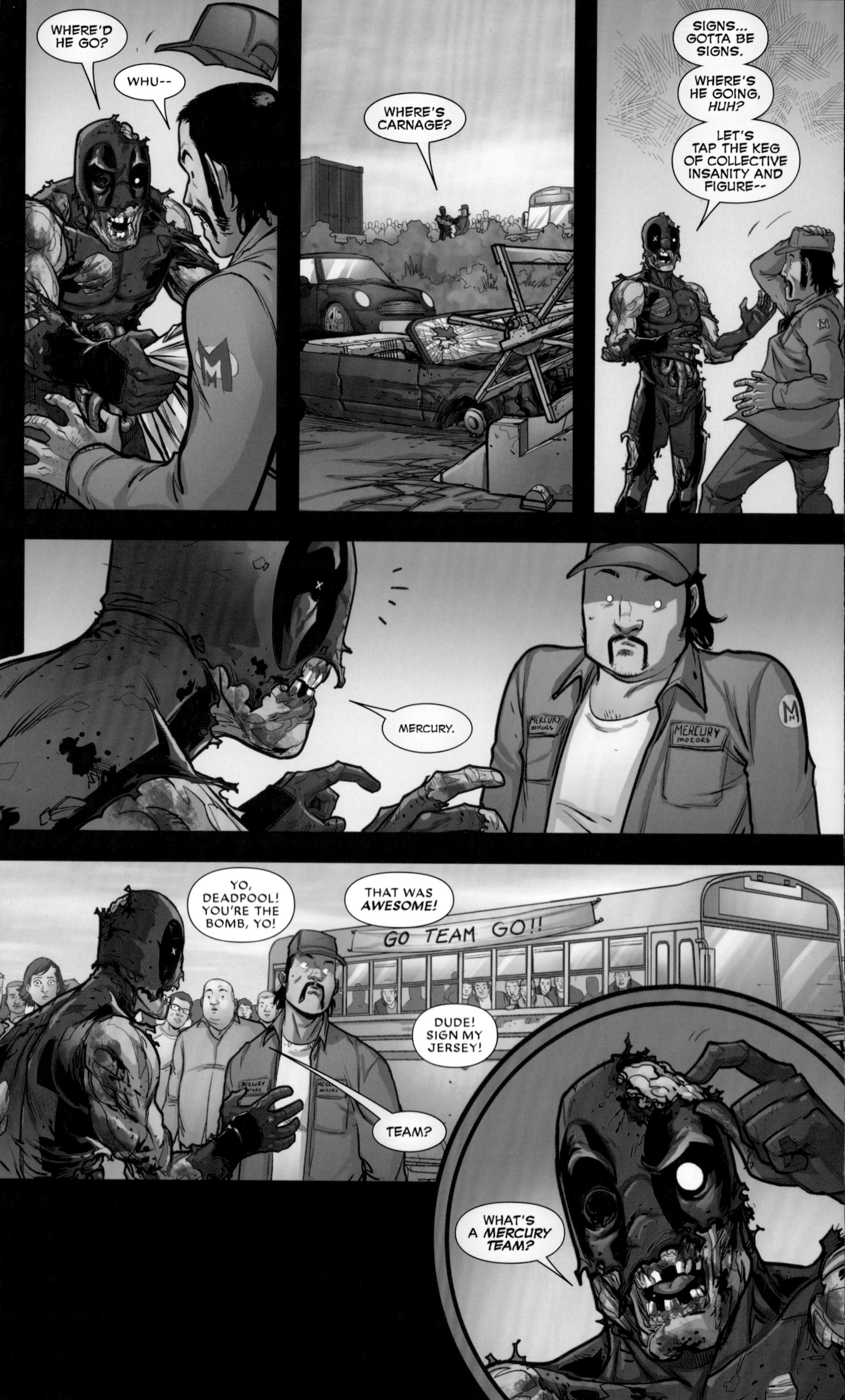

WHERE'D HE GO?
WHU--
WHERE'S CARNAGE?
SIGNS... GOTTA BE SIGNS.
WHERE'S HE GOING, *HUH?*
LET'S TAP THE KEG OF COLLECTIVE INSANITY AND FIGURE--
MERCURY.
MERCURY MOTORS
YO, DEADPOOL! YOU'RE THE BOMB, YO!
THAT WAS ***AWESOME!***
GO TEAM GO!!
DUDE! SIGN MY JERSEY!
TEAM?
WHAT'S A *MERCURY TEAM?*

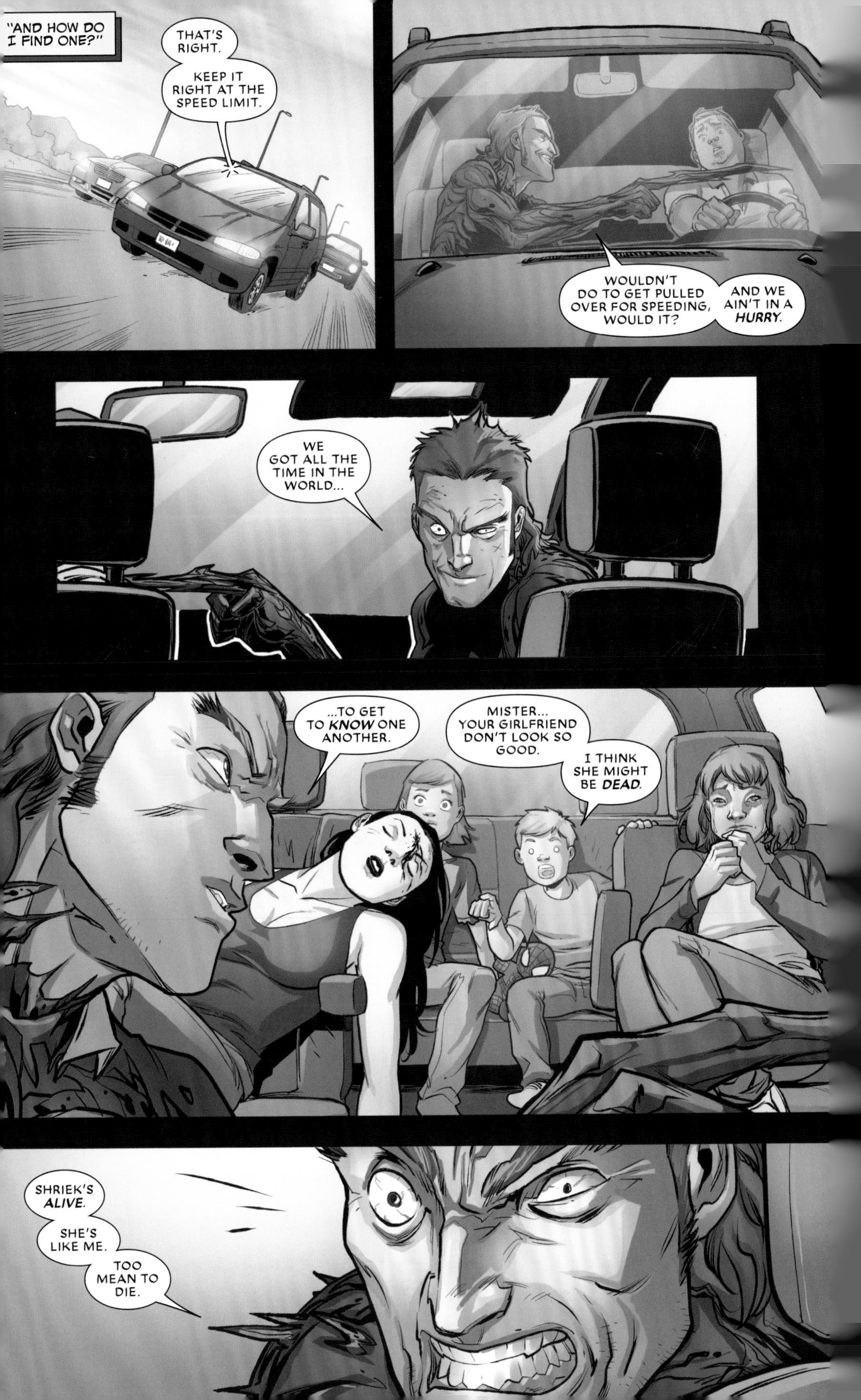
"AND HOW DO I FIND ONE?"
THAT'S RIGHT.
KEEP IT RIGHT AT THE SPEED LIMIT.
WOULDN'T DO TO GET PULLED OVER FOR SPEEDING, WOULD IT?
AND WE AIN'T IN A HURRY.
WE GOT ALL THE TIME IN THE WORLD...
...TO GET TO KNOW ONE ANOTHER.
MISTER... YOUR GIRLFRIEND DON'T LOOK SO GOOD.
I THINK SHE MIGHT BE DEAD.
SHRIEK'S ALIVE.
SHE'S LIKE ME.
TOO MEAN TO DIE.

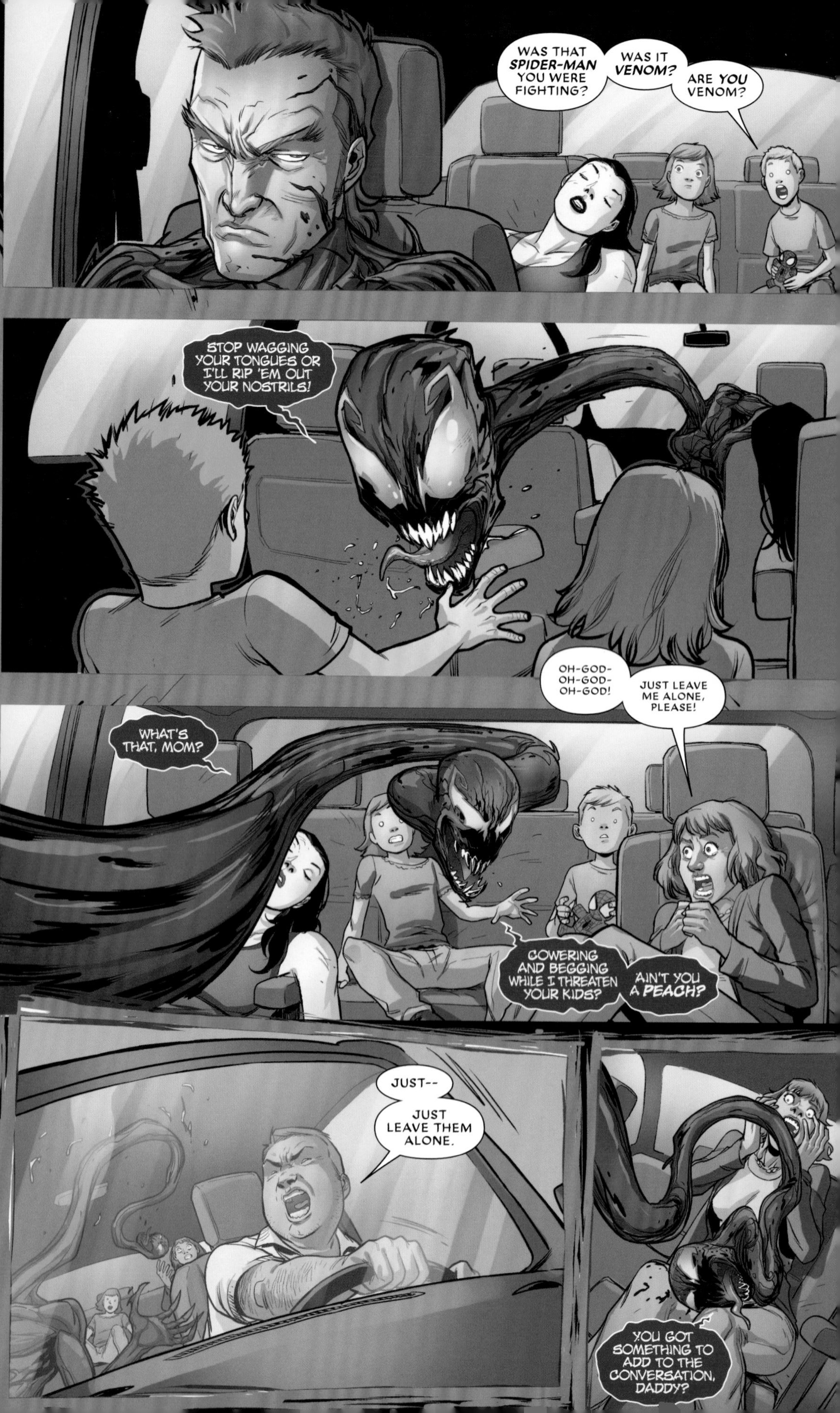
WAS THAT SPIDER-MAN YOU WERE FIGHTING?
WAS IT VENOM?
ARE YOU VENOM?
STOP WAGGING YOUR TONGUES OR I'LL RIP 'EM OUT YOUR NOSTRILS!
OH-GOD-OH-GOD-OH-GOD!
JUST LEAVE ME ALONE, PLEASE!
WHAT'S THAT, MOM?
COWERING AND BEGGING WHILE I THREATEN YOUR KIDS?
AIN'T YOU A PEACH?
JUST--
JUST LEAVE THEM ALONE.
YOU GOT SOMETHING TO ADD TO THE CONVERSATION, DADDY?

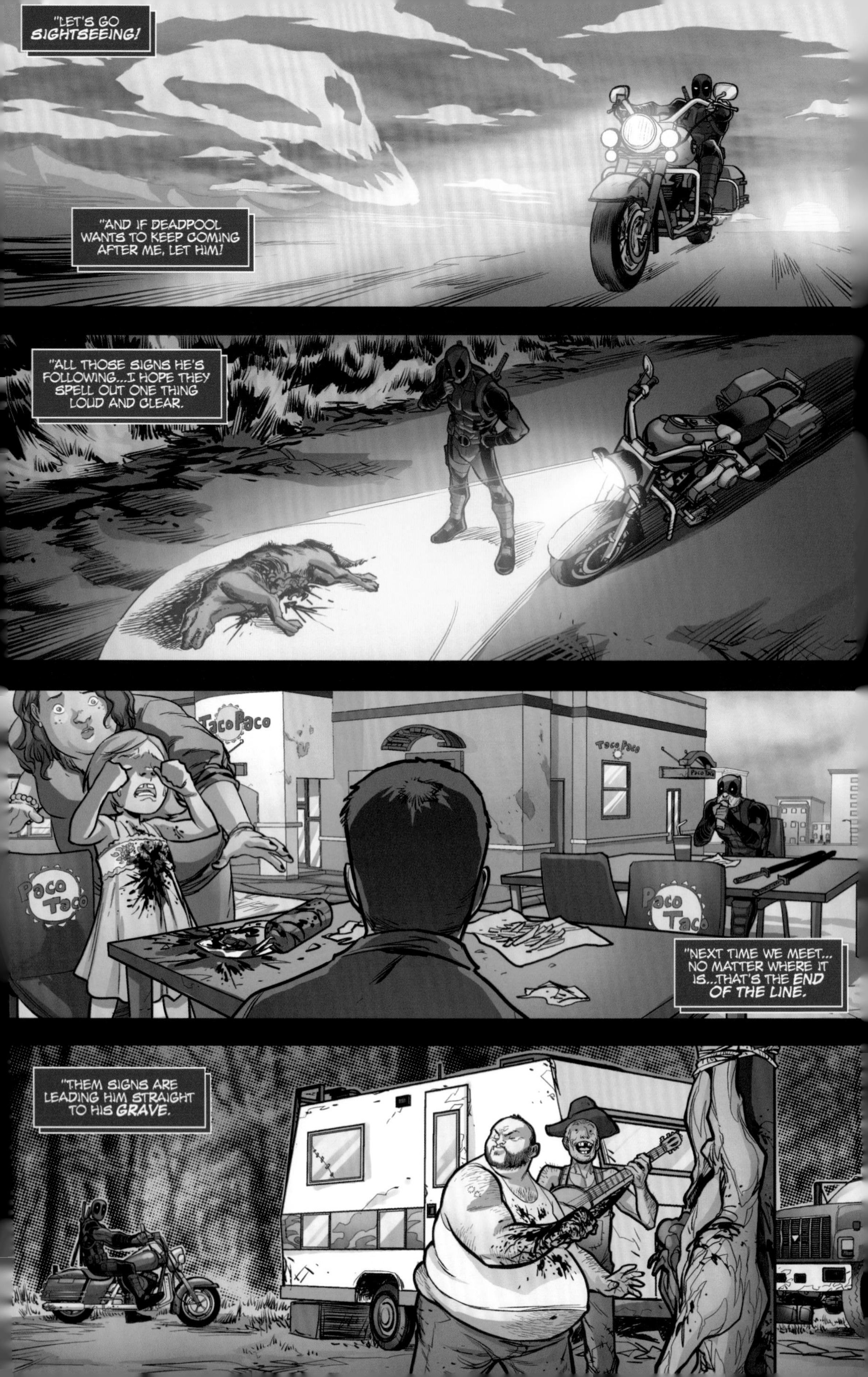
"LET'S GO SIGHTSEEING!
"AND IF DEADPOOL WANTS TO KEEP COMING AFTER ME, LET HIM!
"ALL THOSE SIGNS HE'S FOLLOWING...I HOPE THEY SPELL OUT ONE THING LOUD AND CLEAR.
Taco Paco
Taco Paco
Paco Taco
Paco Taco
Paco Taco
"NEXT TIME WE MEET... NO MATTER WHERE IT IS...THAT'S THE END OF THE LINE.
"THEM SIGNS ARE LEADING HIM STRAIGHT TO HIS GRAVE.

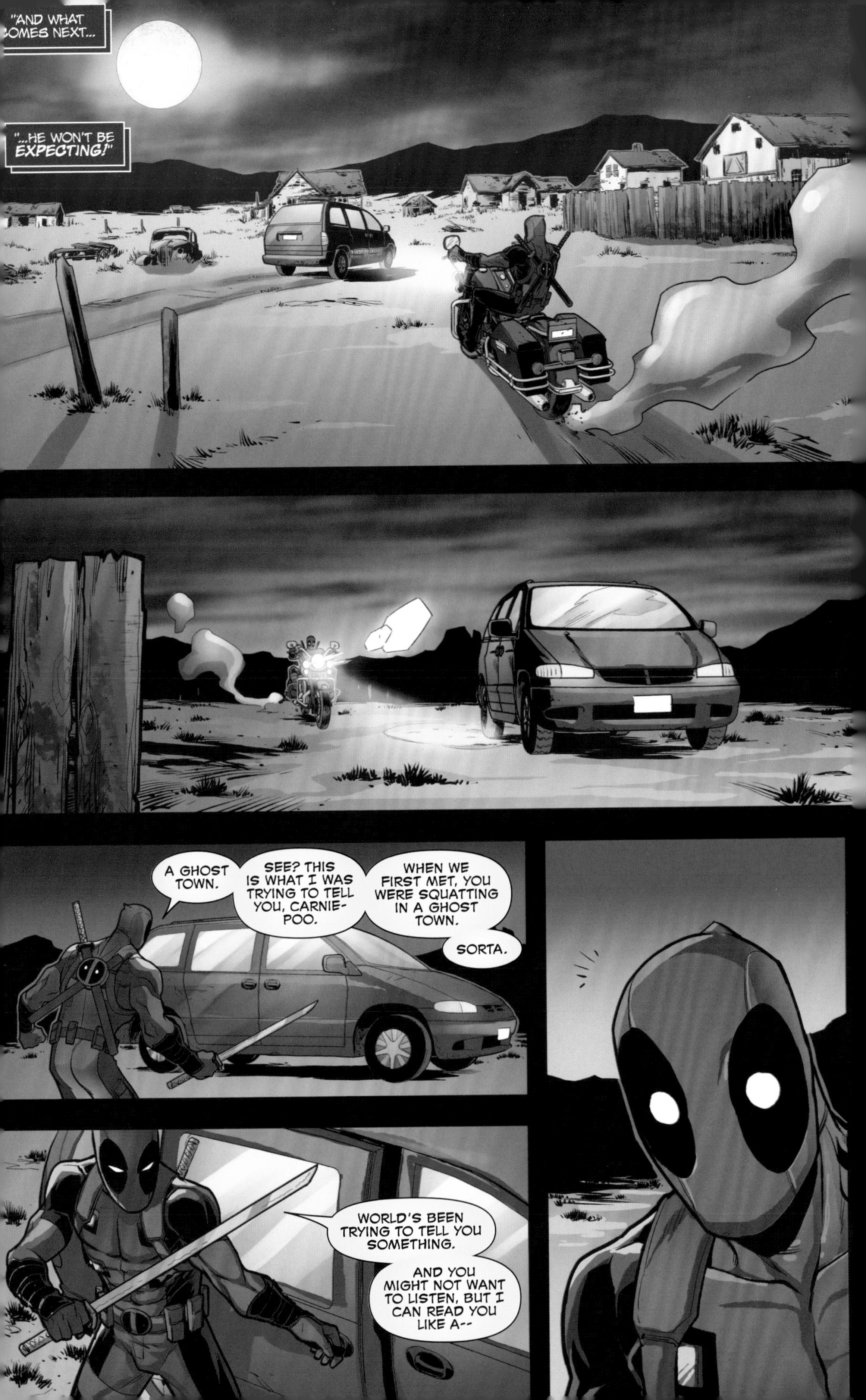
"AND WHAT
COMES NEXT...
"...HE WON'T BE EXPECTING!"
A GHOST TOWN.
SEE? THIS IS WHAT I WAS TRYING TO TELL YOU, CARNIE-POO.
WHEN WE FIRST MET, YOU WERE SQUATTING IN A GHOST TOWN.
SORTA.
WORLD'S BEEN TRYING TO TELL YOU SOMETHING.
AND YOU MIGHT NOT WANT TO LISTEN, BUT I CAN READ YOU LIKE A--

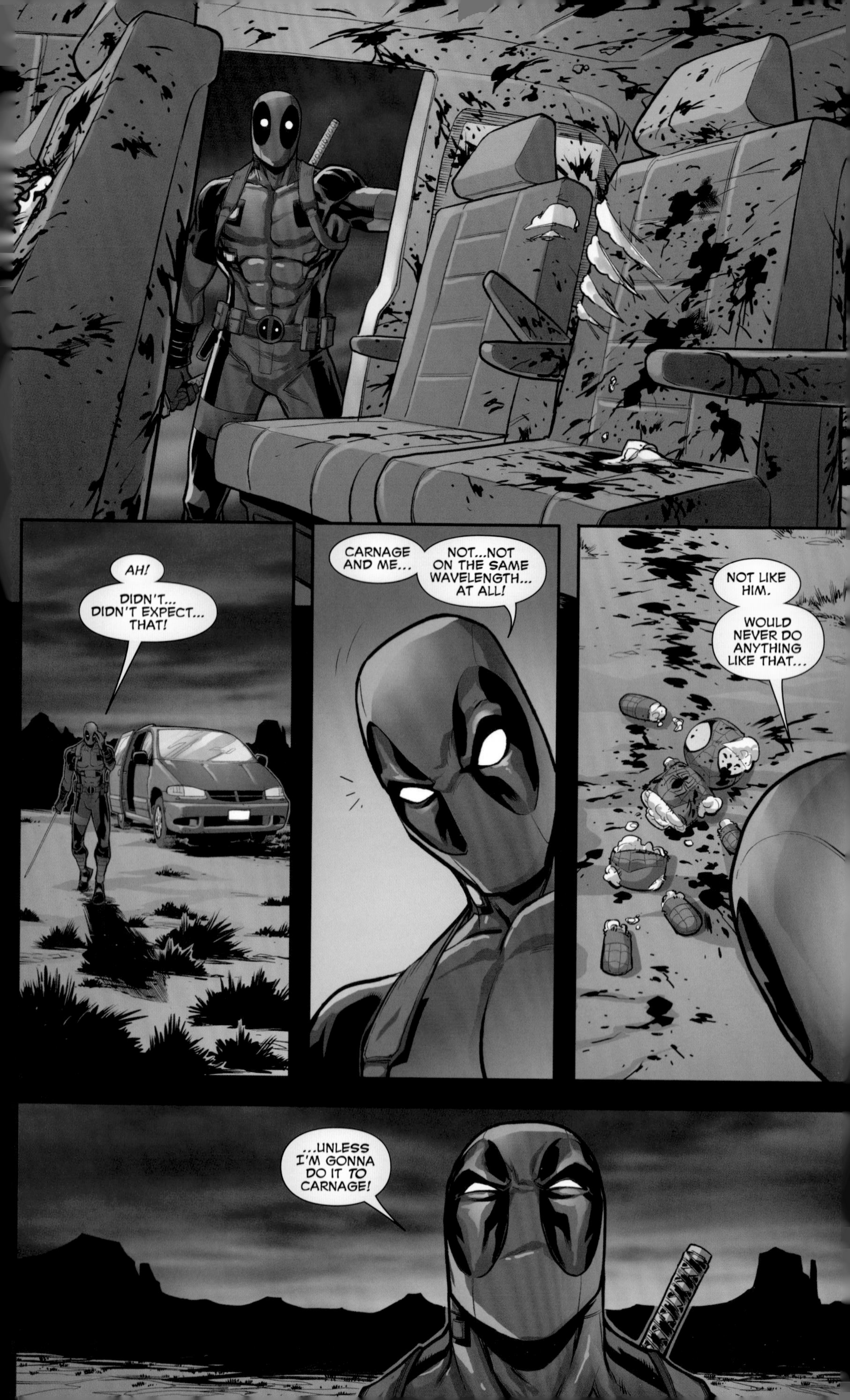
AH!
DIDN'T... DIDN'T EXPECT... THAT!
CARNAGE AND ME...
NOT...NOT ON THE SAME WAVELENGTH... AT ALL!
NOT LIKE HIM.
WOULD NEVER DO ANYTHING LIKE THAT...
...UNLESS I'M GONNA DO IT TO CARNAGE!

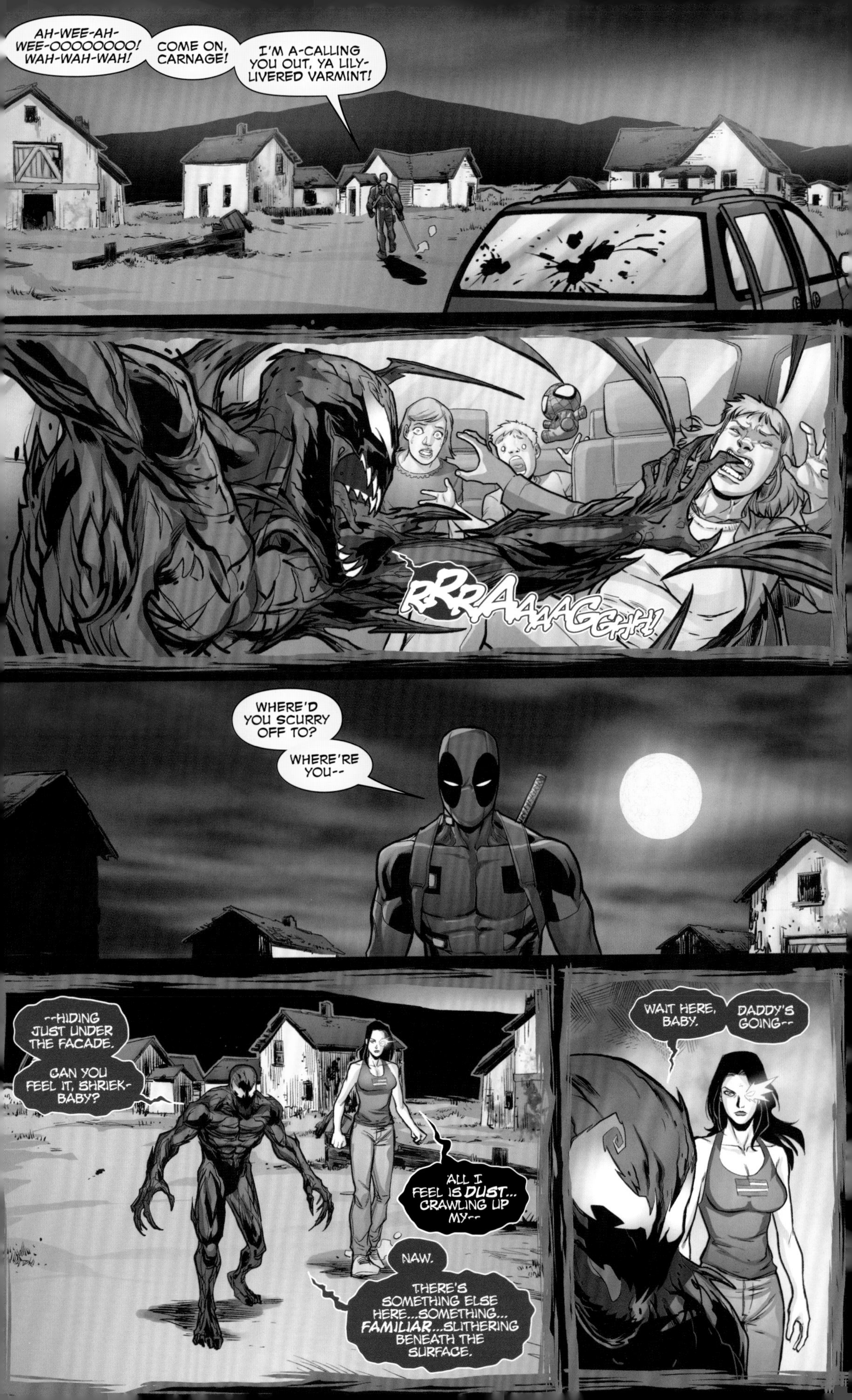
AH-WEE-AH-WEE-OOOOOOOO! WAH-WAH-WAH!
COME ON, CARNAGE!
I'M A-CALLING YOU OUT, YA LILY-LIVERED VARMINT!
RRRAAAAGGHH!
WHERE'D YOU SCURRY OFF TO?
WHERE'RE YOU--
--HIDING JUST UNDER THE FACADE.
CAN YOU FEEL IT, SHRIEK-BABY?
ALL I FEEL IS DUST... CRAWLING UP MY--
NAW.
THERE'S SOMETHING ELSE HERE...SOMETHING... FAMILIAR...SLITHERING BENEATH THE SURFACE.
WAIT HERE, BABY.
DADDY'S GOING--

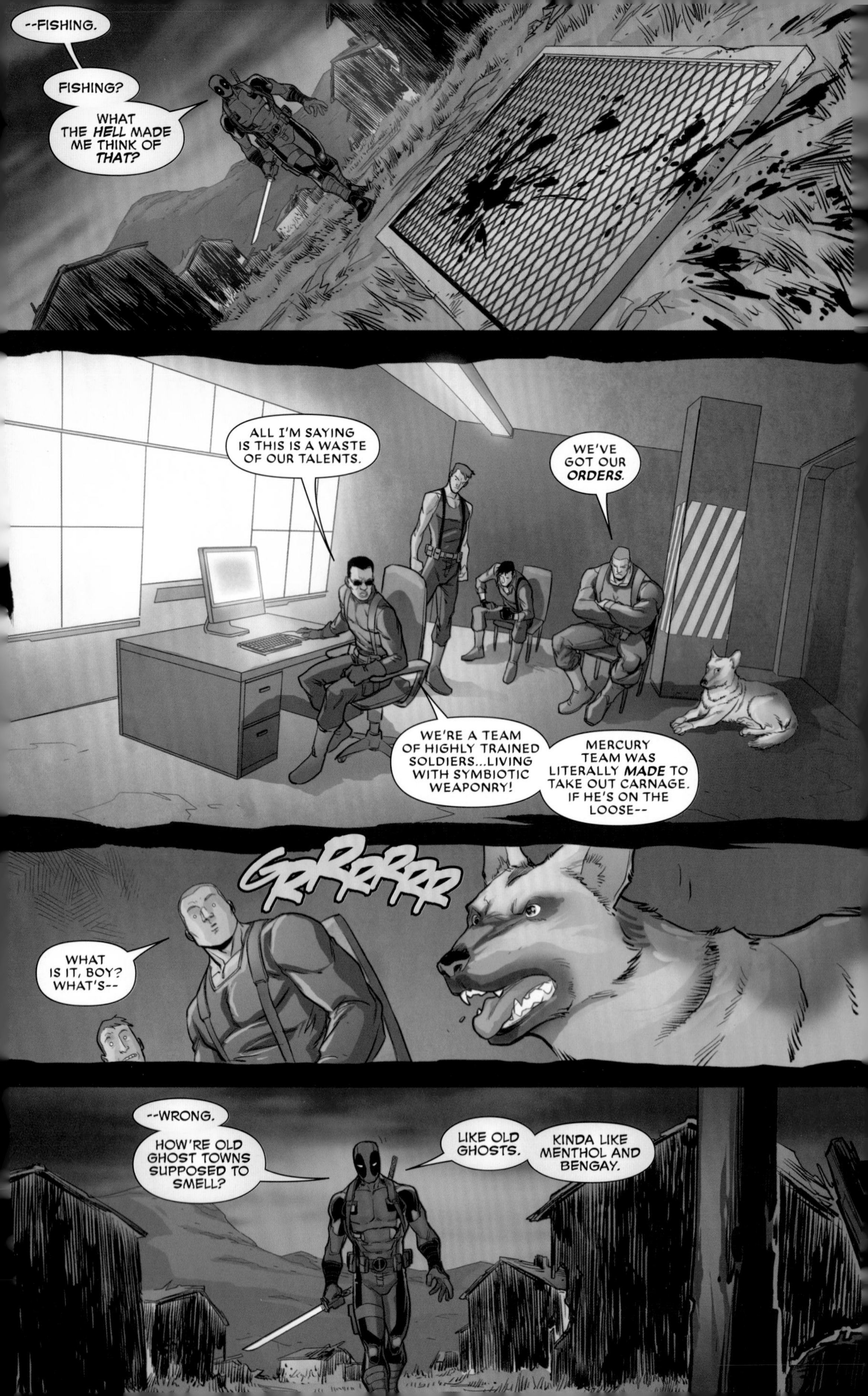
--FISHING.
FISHING?
WHAT THE HELL MADE ME THINK OF THAT?
ALL I'M SAYING IS THIS IS A WASTE OF OUR TALENTS.
WE'VE GOT OUR ORDERS.
WE'RE A TEAM OF HIGHLY TRAINED SOLDIERS...LIVING WITH SYMBIOTIC WEAPONRY!
MERCURY TEAM WAS LITERALLY MADE TO TAKE OUT CARNAGE. IF HE'S ON THE LOOSE--
GRRRRRR
WHAT IS IT, BOY? WHAT'S--
--WRONG.
HOW'RE OLD GHOST TOWNS SUPPOSED TO SMELL?
LIKE OLD GHOSTS.
KINDA LIKE MENTHOL AND BENGAY.

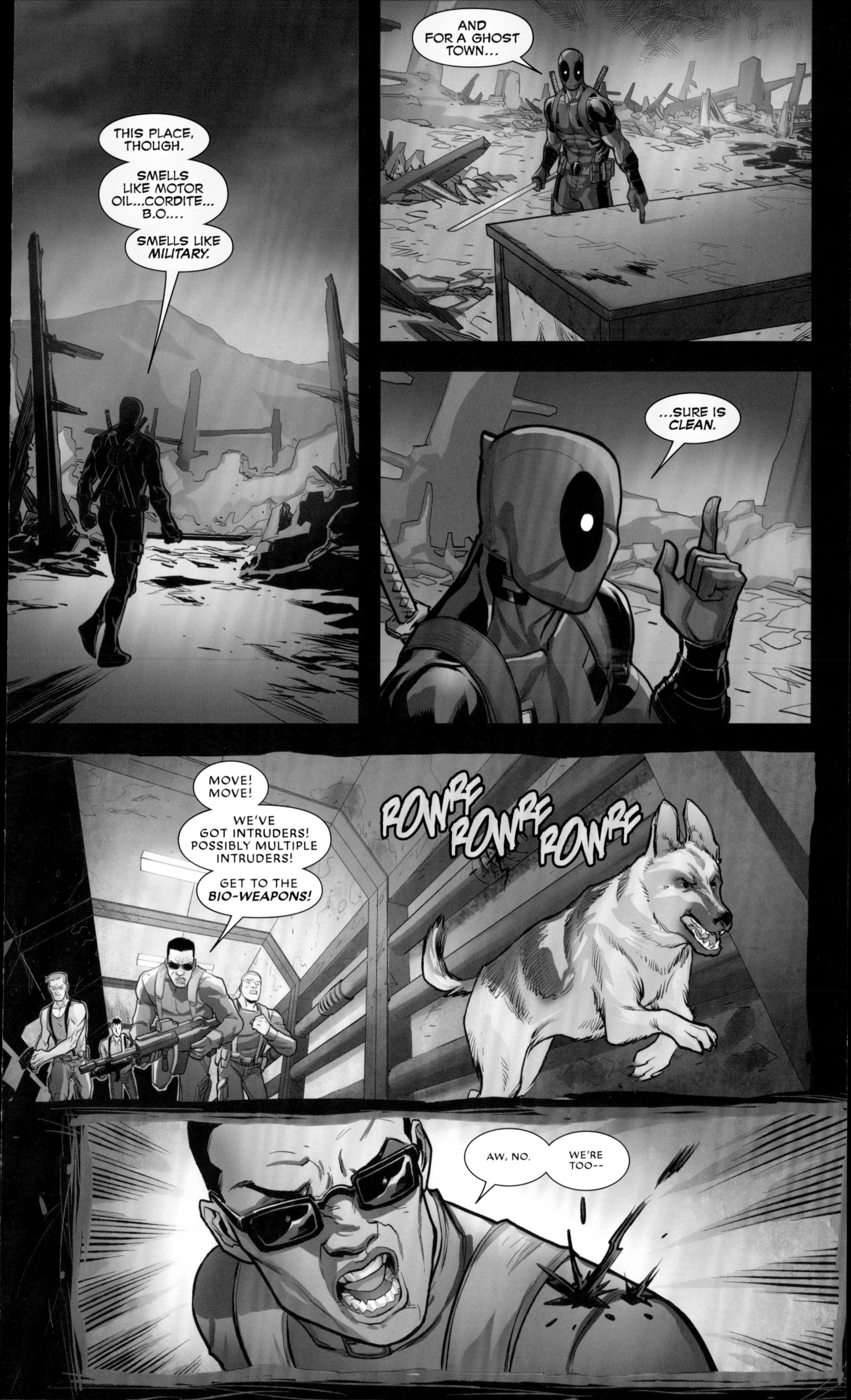
THIS PLACE, THOUGH.
SMELLS LIKE MOTOR OIL...CORDITE... B.O....
SMELLS LIKE *MILITARY.*
AND FOR A GHOST TOWN...
...SURE IS *CLEAN.*
MOVE! MOVE!
WE'VE GOT INTRUDERS! POSSIBLY MULTIPLE INTRUDERS!
GET TO THE *BIO-WEAPONS!*
ROWRF ROWRF ROWRF
AW, NO.
WE'RE TOO--

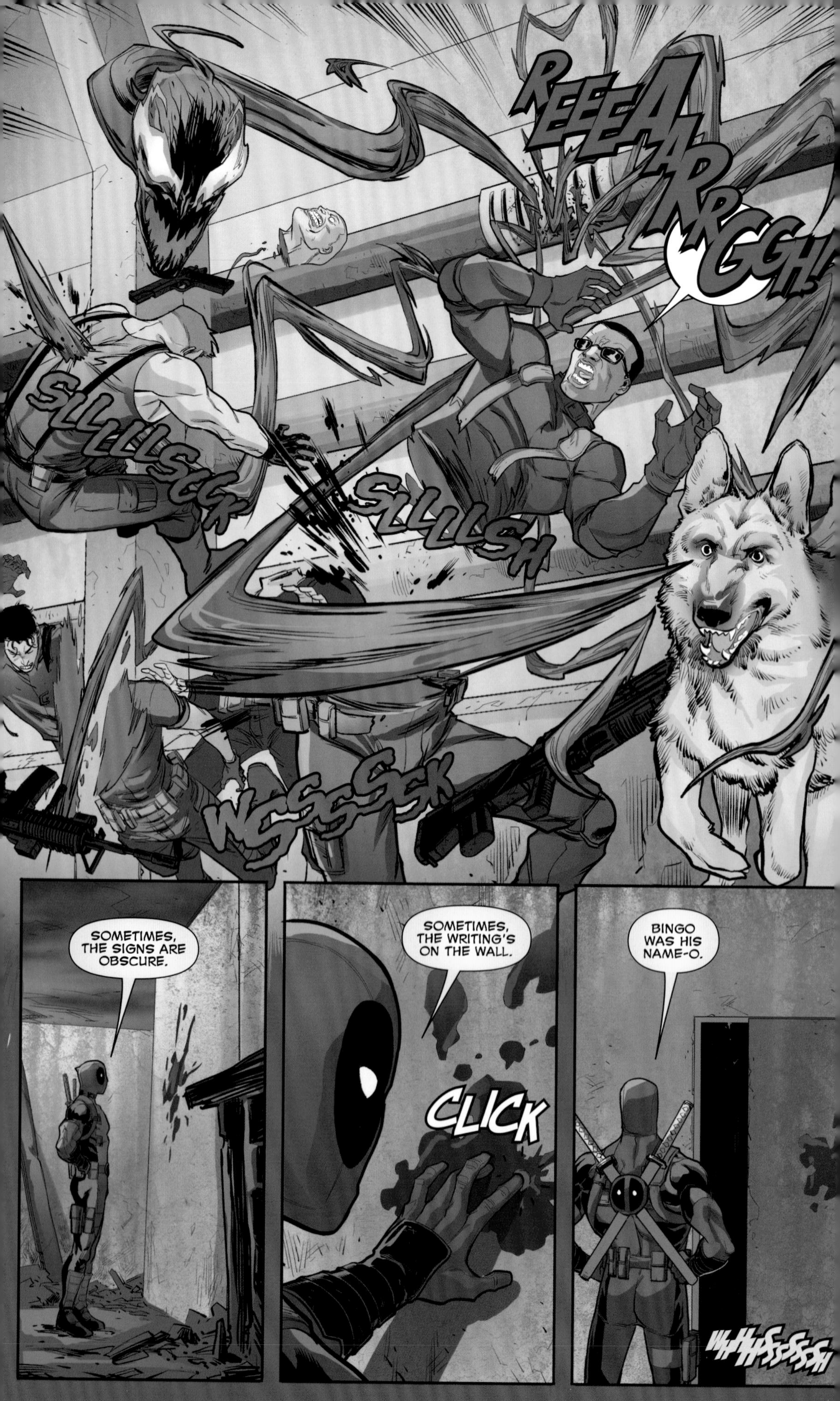
REEEAARRGGH!
SLLLLSCCK
SLLLLSH
SOMETIMES, THE SIGNS ARE OBSCURE.
SOMETIMES, THE WRITING'S ON THE WALL.
CLICK
BINGO WAS HIS NAME-O.

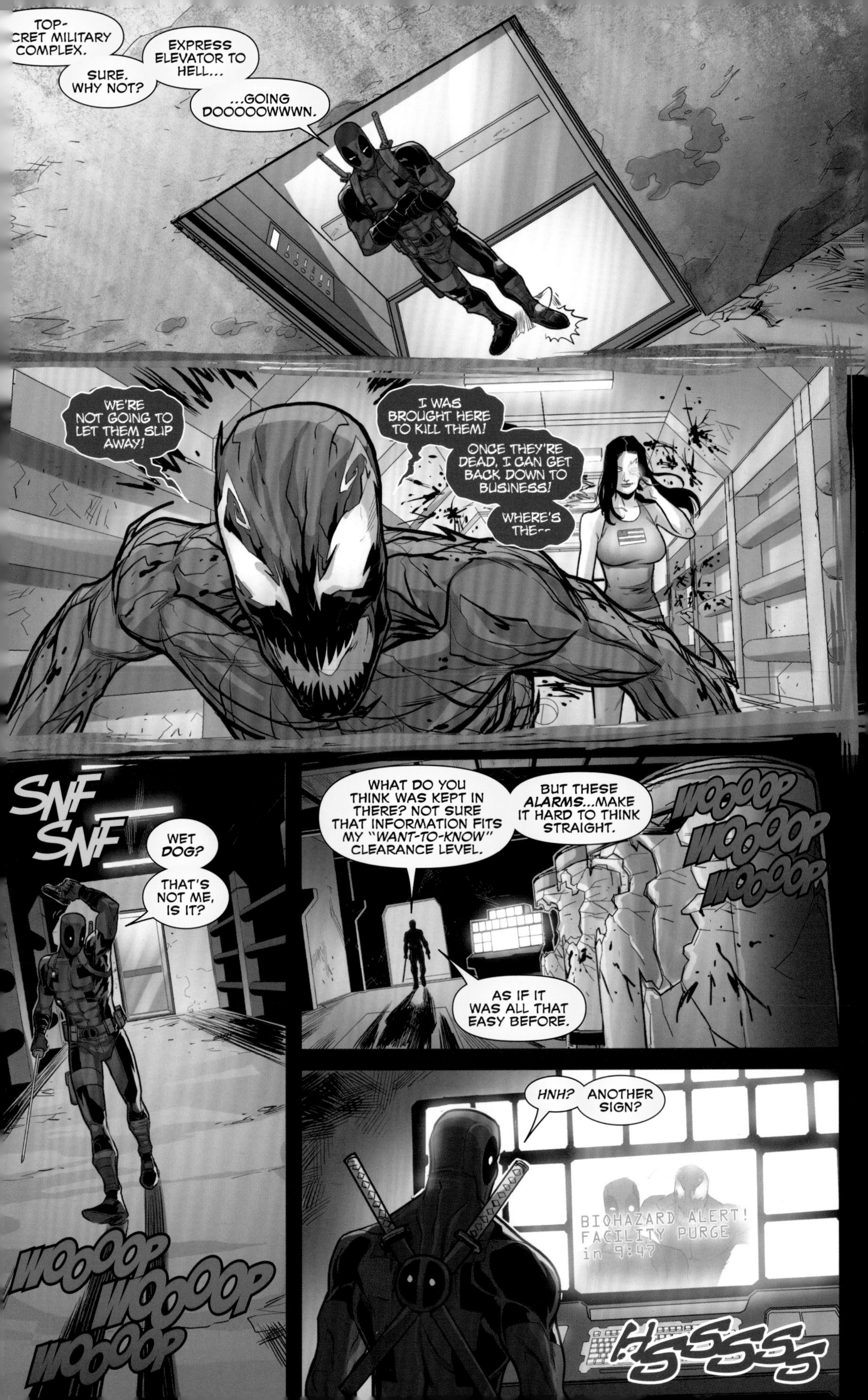
TOP-
CRET MILITARY COMPLEX.
SURE. WHY NOT?
EXPRESS ELEVATOR TO HELL...
...GOING DOOOOOWWWN.
WE'RE NOT GOING TO LET THEM SLIP AWAY!
I WAS BROUGHT HERE TO KILL THEM!
ONCE THEY'RE DEAD, I CAN GET BACK DOWN TO BUSINESS!
WHERE'S THE--
SNF SNF
WET DOG?
THAT'S NOT ME, IS IT?
WOOOOP WOOOOP WOOOOP
WHAT DO YOU THINK WAS KEPT IN THERE? NOT SURE THAT INFORMATION FITS MY "WANT-TO-KNOW" CLEARANCE LEVEL.
BUT THESE ALARMS...MAKE IT HARD TO THINK STRAIGHT.
WOOOOP WOOOOP WOOOOP
AS IF IT WAS ALL THAT EASY BEFORE.
HNH? ANOTHER SIGN?
BIOHAZARD ALERT!
FACILITY PURGE
in 9:47
HSSSSS

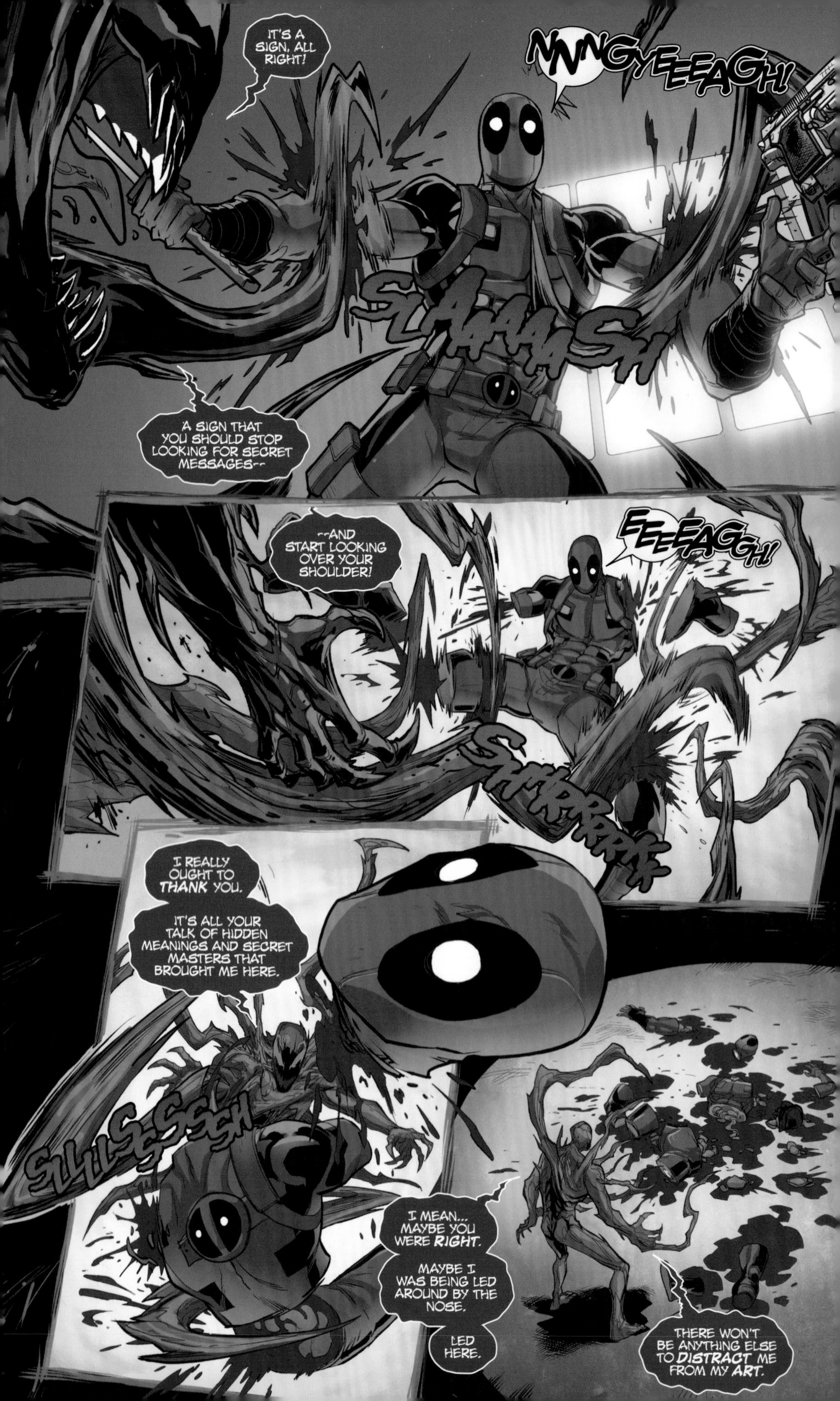

IT'S A SIGN, ALL RIGHT!
NNNGYEEEEAGH!
SLAAAAASH
A SIGN THAT YOU SHOULD STOP LOOKING FOR SECRET MESSAGES--
--AND START LOOKING OVER YOUR SHOULDER!
EEEEAGGH!
SHHRRRRK
I REALLY OUGHT TO THANK YOU.
IT'S ALL YOUR TALK OF HIDDEN MEANINGS AND SECRET MASTERS THAT BROUGHT ME HERE.
SLLLSSSSH
I MEAN... MAYBE YOU WERE RIGHT.
MAYBE I WAS BEING LED AROUND BY THE NOSE.
LED HERE.
THERE WON'T BE ANYTHING ELSE TO DISTRACT ME FROM MY ART.

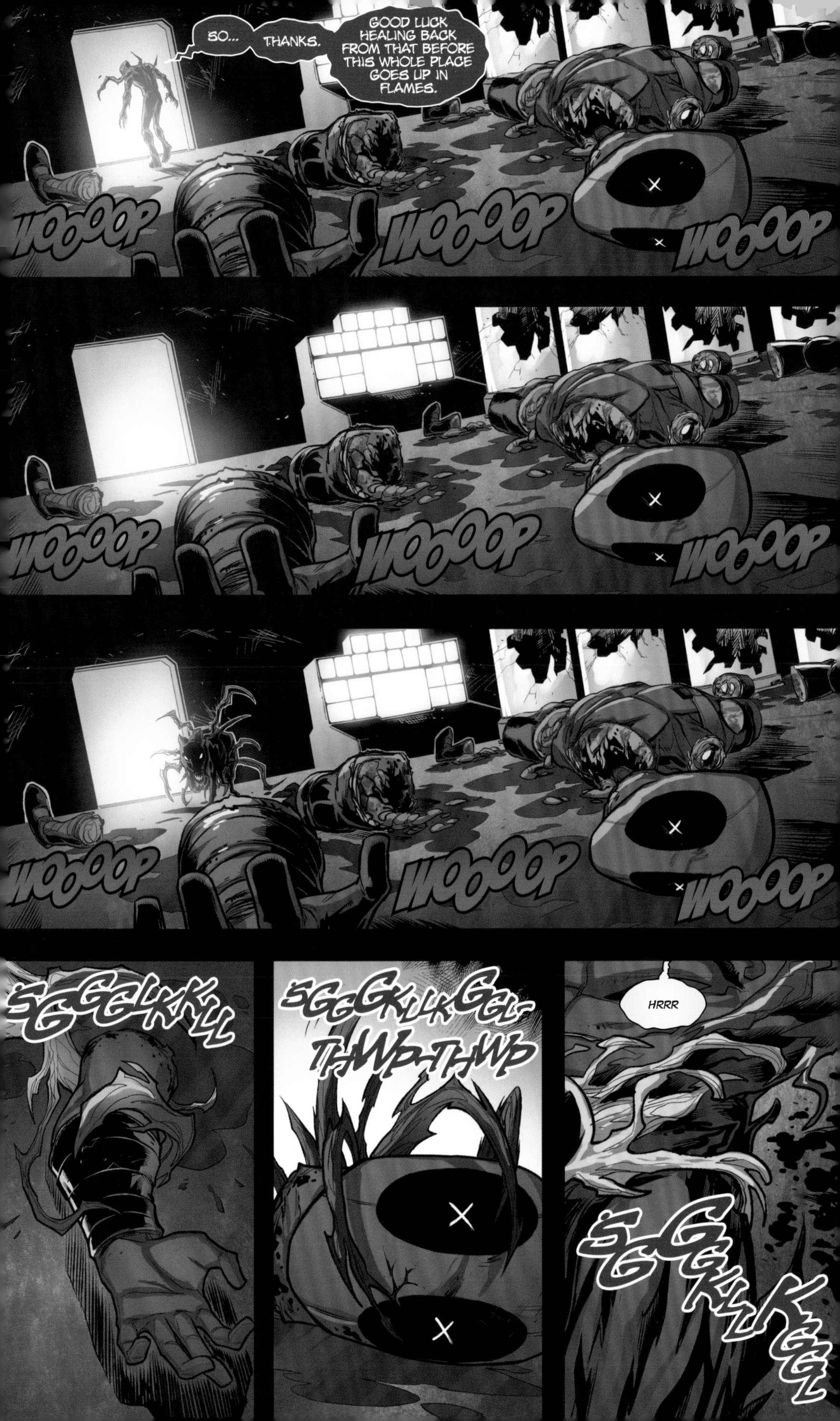
SO...
THANKS.
GOOD LUCK HEALING BACK FROM THAT BEFORE THIS WHOLE PLACE GOES UP IN FLAMES.
WOOOOP
WOOOOP
WOOOOP
WOOOOP
WOOOOP
WOOOOP
WOOOOP
WOOOOP
WOOOOP
SGGGLKKLL
SGGGKLLKGGL-
THWP-THWP
HRRR
SGGGKLLKGGL

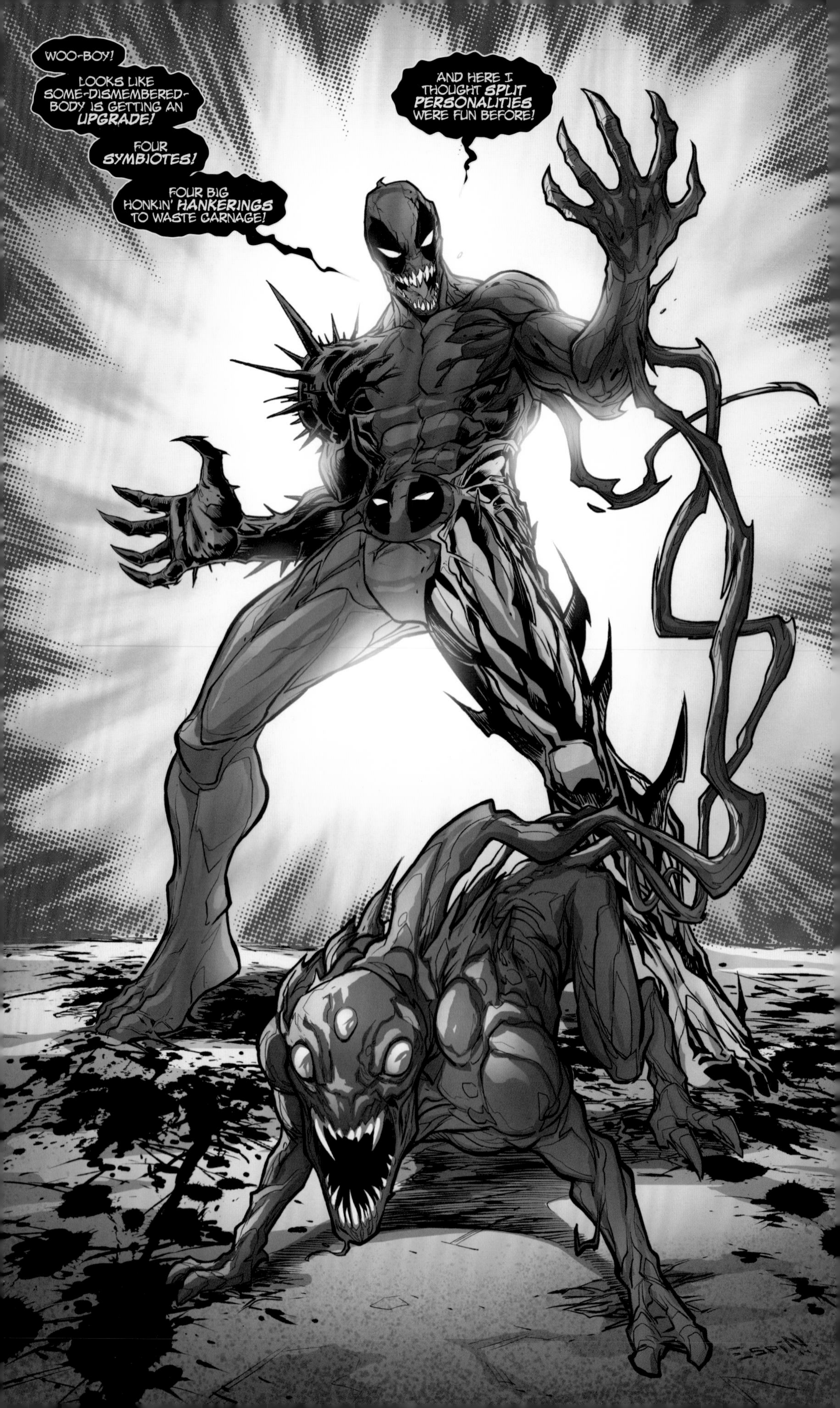
WOO-BOY!
LOOKS LIKE SOME-DISMEMBERED-BODY IS GETTING AN UPGRADE!
FOUR SYMBIOTES!
FOUR BIG HONKIN' HANKERINGS TO WASTE CARNAGE!
AND HERE I THOUGHT SPLIT PERSONALITIES WERE FUN BEFORE!

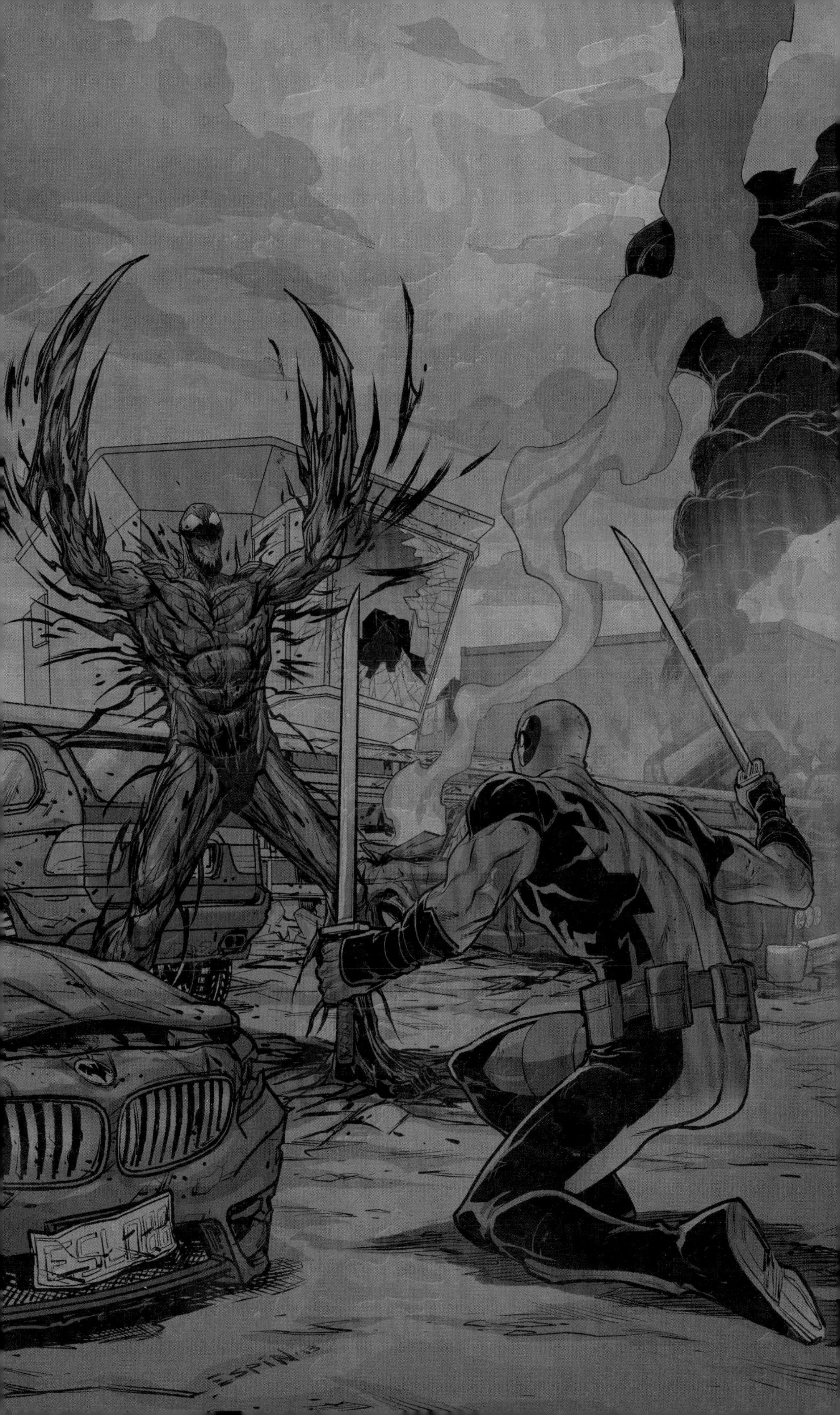

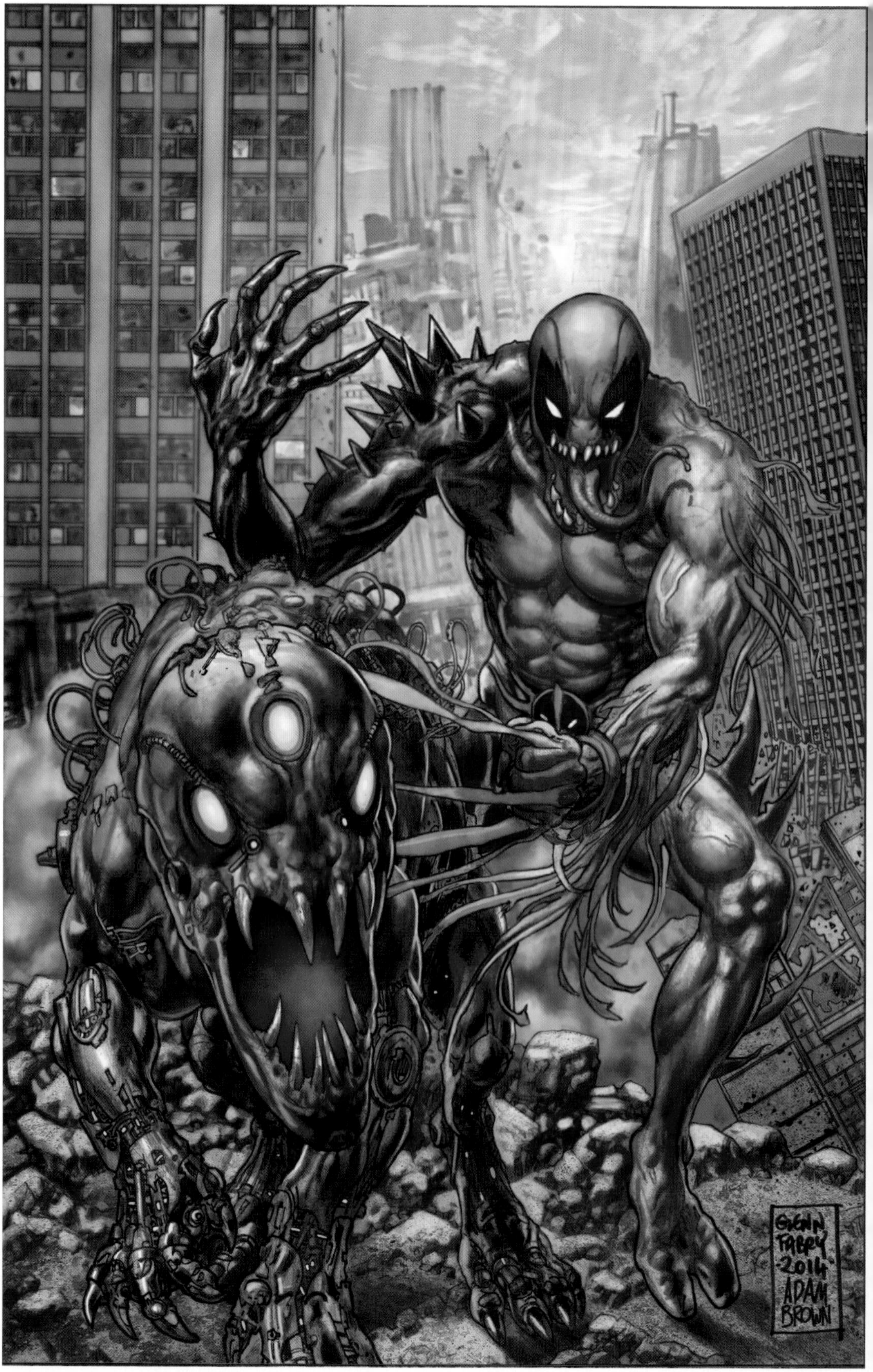
GLENN FABRY 2014 ADAM BROWN

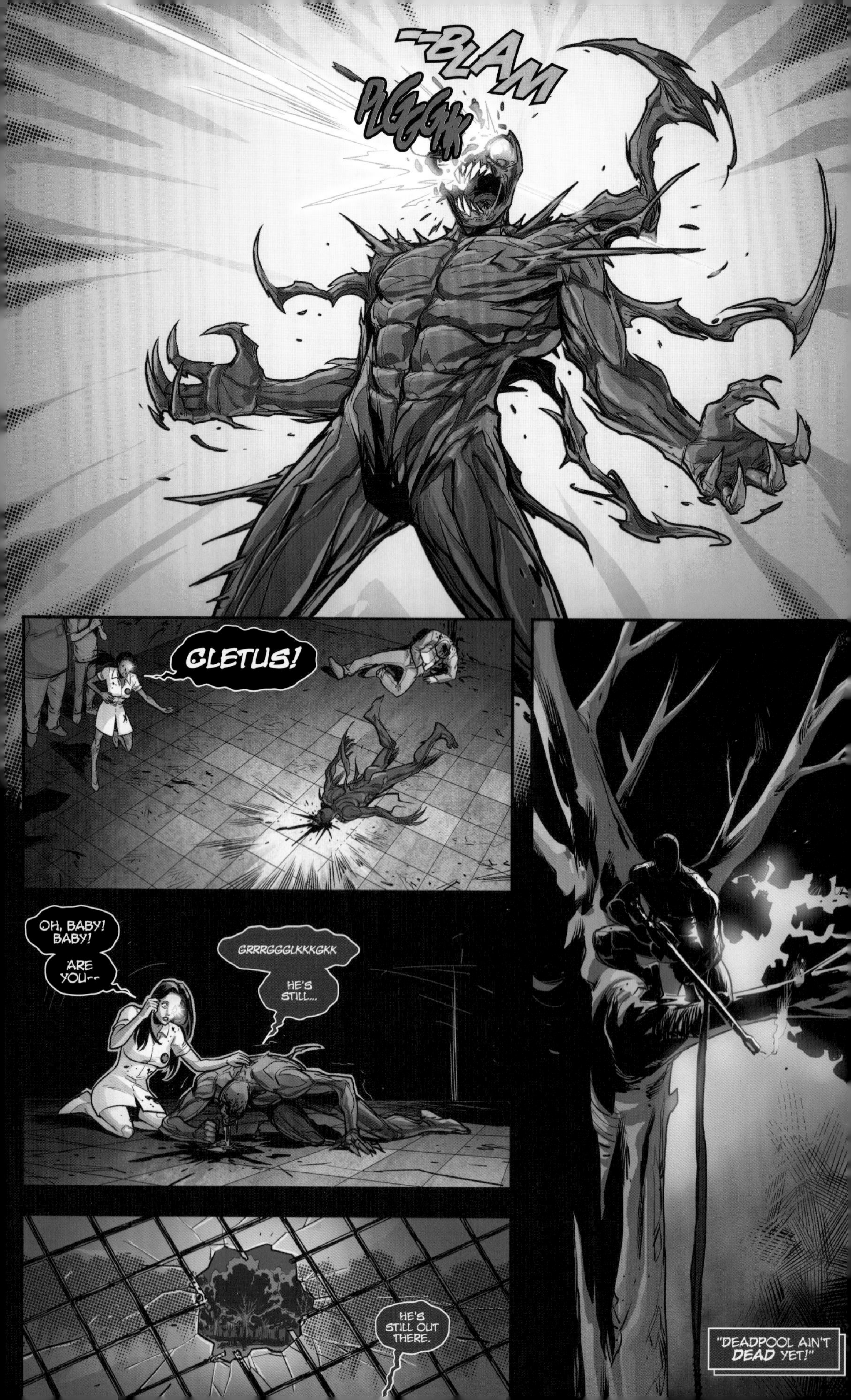
--BLAM
PLGGGHK
CLETUS!
OH, BABY! BABY!
ARE YOU--
GRRRGGGLKKKGKK
HE'S STILL...
HE'S STILL OUT THERE.
"DEADPOOL AIN'T DEAD YET!"

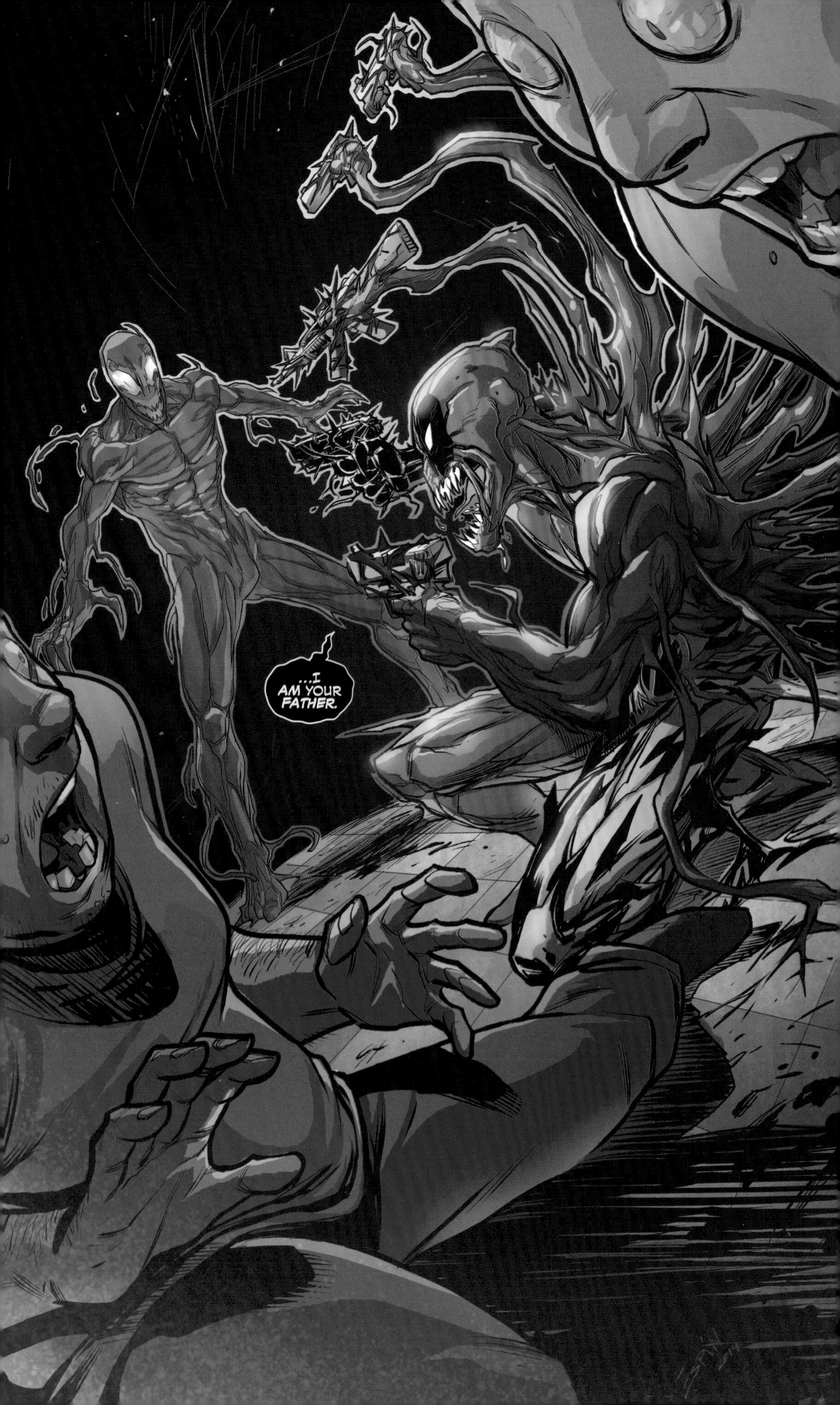
...I AM YOUR FATHER.

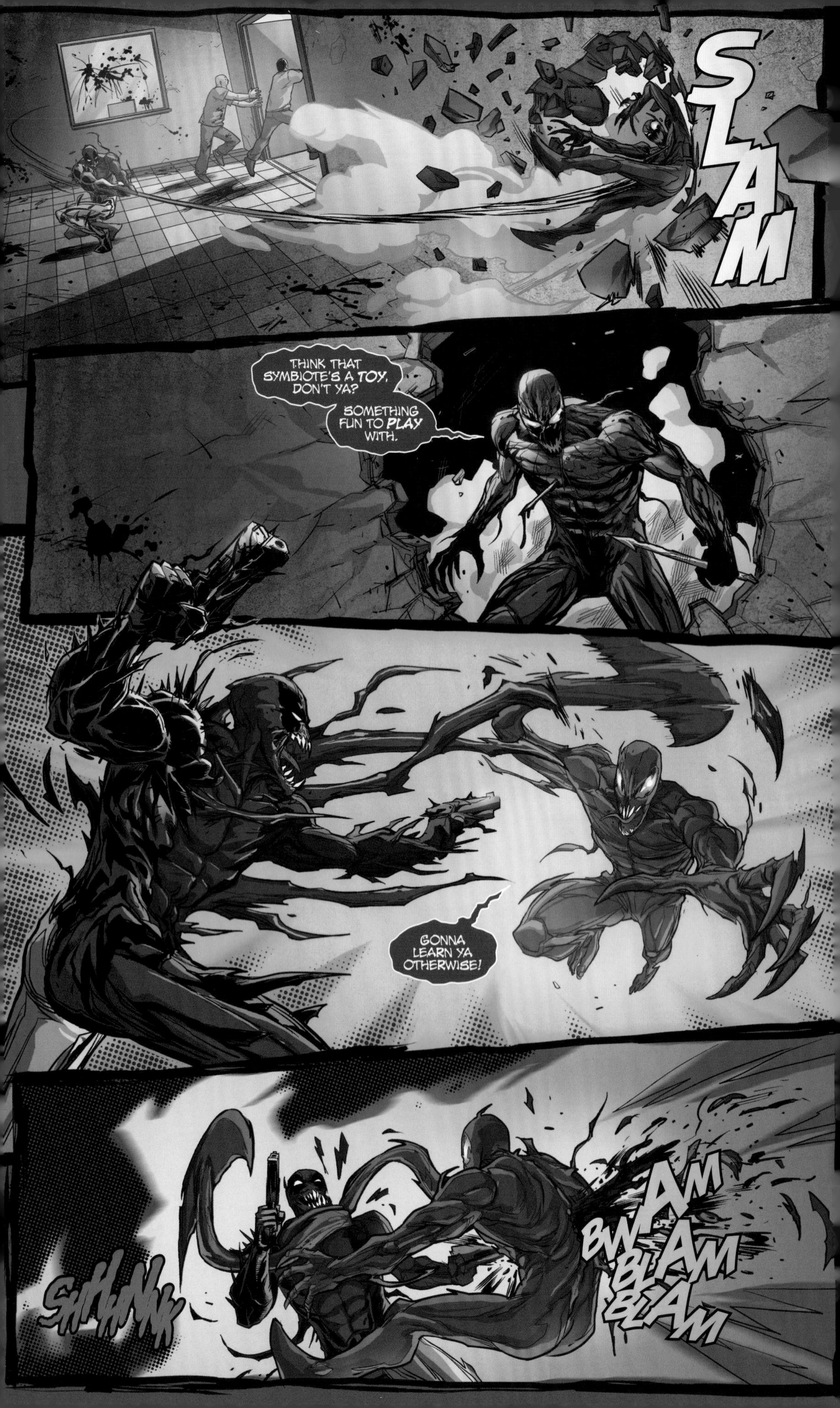
SLAM
THINK THAT SYMBIOTE'S A TOY, DON'T YA?
SOMETHING FUN TO PLAY WITH.
GONNA LEARN YA OTHERWISE!
SHHUNK
BLAM
BLAM
BLAM
BLAM

#1 VARIANT COVER

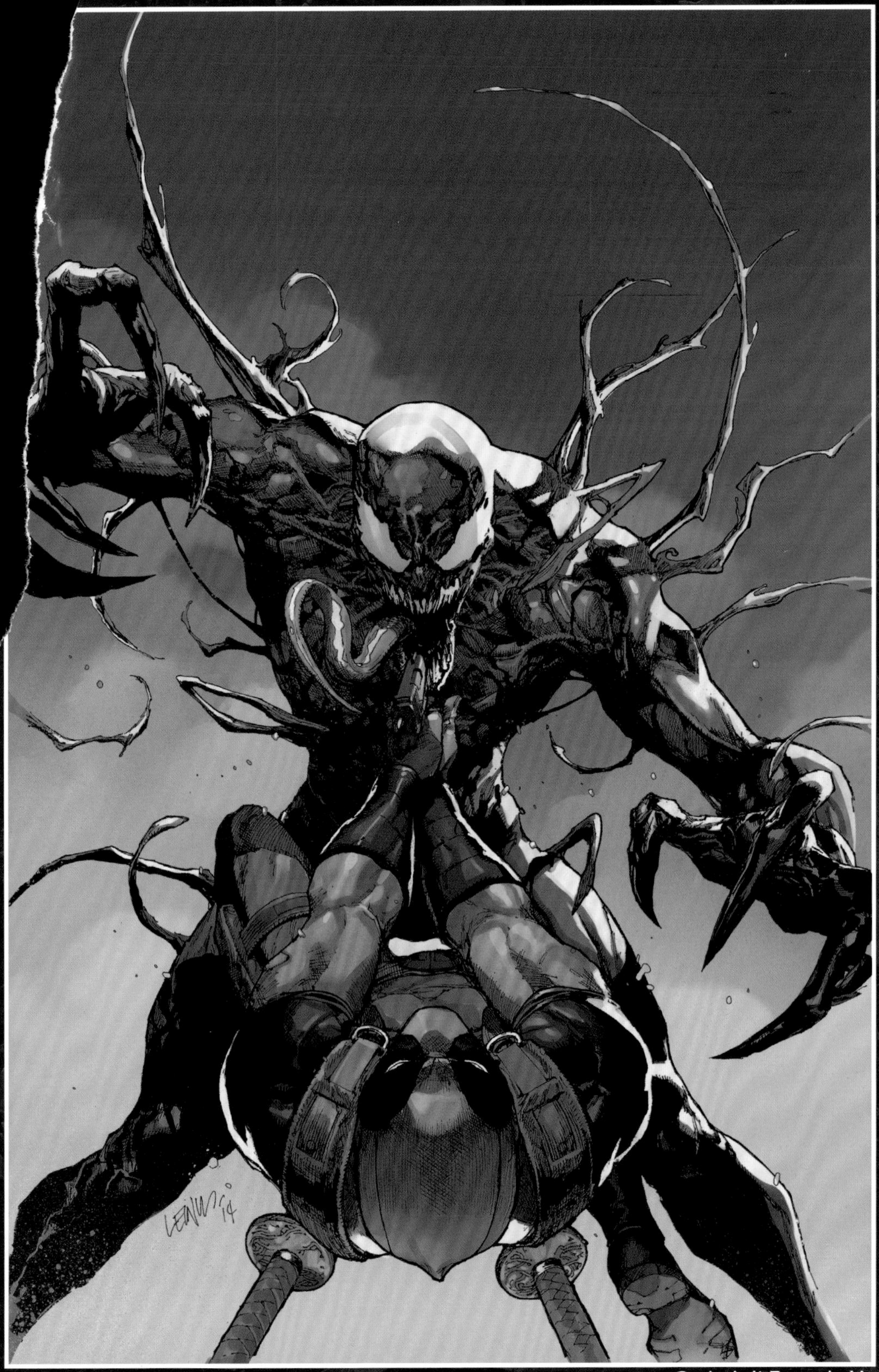

By Leinil Francis Yu

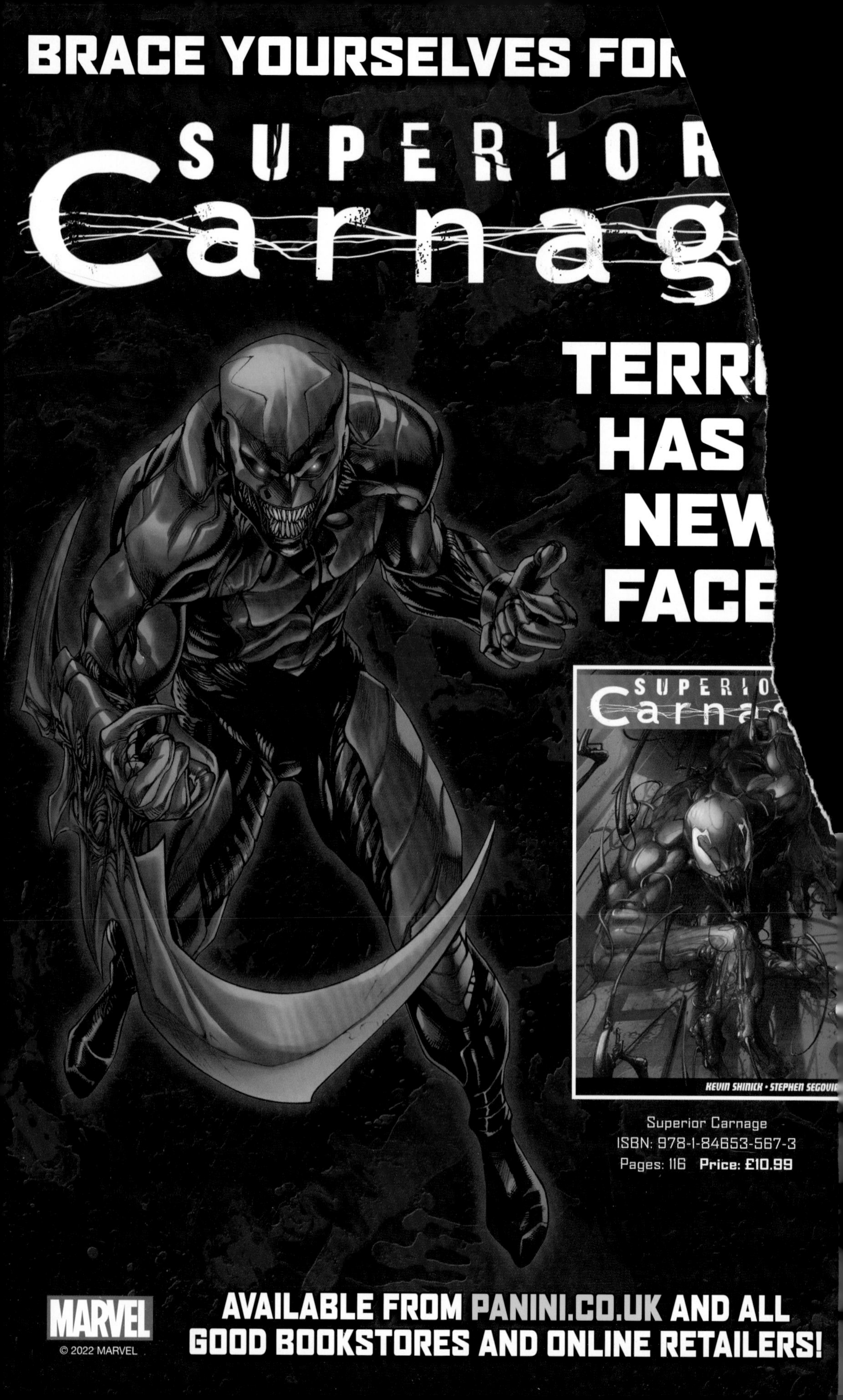
BRACE YOURSELVES FO
SUPERIOR
Carnag
TERR
HAS
NEW
FACE
SUPERIO
Carna
KEVIN SHINICK • STEPHEN SEGOVI
Superior Carnage
ISBN: 978-1-84653-567-3
Pages: 116 Price: £10.99
MARVEL
© 2022 MARVEL
AVAILABLE FROM PANINI.CO.UK AND ALL
GOOD BOOKSTORES AND ONLINE RETAILERS!